2K

WITHDRAWN

D0163450

THE RULES OF THE COMMUNIST PARTY
OF THE SOVIET UNION

The Rules of the Communist Party of the Soviet Union

Graeme Gill

Senior Lecturer in Government
University of Sydney

M. E. Sharpe, Inc.
Armonk, New York

First published in 1988

Published in the United States by M. E. Sharpe, Inc.
80 Business Park Drive, Armonk, New York 10504

Published in Great Britain by the Macmillan Press Ltd.

Printed in Hong Kong

Library of Congress Cataloging-in-Publication Data
Gill, Graeme J.
The rules of the Communist Party of the Soviet
Union.
1. Kommunisticheskaia partiia Sovetskogo Soiuza—
Rules and practice—History.   2. Kommunisticheskaia
partiia Sovetskogo Soiuza—Congresses—History.
I. Title.
JN6598.K7G524 1987 324.247′075   87–4815
ISBN 0–87332–434–X

To my mother, Gwyn, and my late father, Joe

Contents

Preface

This book makes no attempt to be either a general history of the party or a study of the changes in its organizational structure and functioning. Its focus is purely upon the texts of the Rules and the way these have changed over time. Prior to 1917, only those Rules adopted at meetings attended by the Bolsheviks have been included; the Rules adopted by the Mensheviks alone have not been included.

The texts of the Rules and the amendments have been taken from *KPSS v rezoliutsiiakh i resheniiakh s'ezdov, konferentsii i plenumov ts.k.* and checked against relevant congress and conference proceedings. The text of the 1986 Rules has been taken from *Pravda* 7/3/86. The translations are my own.

I would like to thank Heather for her assistance with proof-reading and, along with Fiona and Lachlan, for general forbearance and support.

GRAEME GILL

List of Abbreviations and Glossary

AUCP(b)	All-Union Communist Party (Bolsheviks); name of the party 1925–52
CAC	Central Auditing Commission
CC	Central Committee
CCC	Central Control Commission
CO	Central Organ
CPSU	Communist Party of the Soviet Union; name of the party since 1952
kolkhoz	collective farm
Komsomol	Communist Youth League; synonymous with VLKSM (formerly RKSM)
MTS	Machine Tractor Station
NEP	New Economic Policy
PPO	primary party organization
PUR	Political Administration of Workers' and Peasants' Red Army
RKI	People's Commissariat of Workers' and Peasants' Inspection
RKKA	Workers' and Peasants' Red Army
RKP(b)	Russian Communist Party (Bolsheviks); name of the party 1918–25
RKSM	Russian Communist Youth Movement
RSDRP	Russian Social Democratic Workers' Party; name of the party 1898–1918
RSFSR	Russian Socialist Federated Soviet Republic; name of Soviet state until December 1922; henceforth name of constituent republic of USSR, in form Russian Soviet Federated Socialist Republic
SNK	Council of People's Commissars
sovkhoz	state farm
sovnarkhoz	council of national economy
TsIK	Central Executive Committee of Soviets
USSR	Union of Soviet Socialist Republics
VLKSM	All-Union Leninist Communist Youth League

Key to Rules

Italics   new to this edition of the Rules.
*   part omitted from following edition of the Rules.
**   all omitted from following edition of the Rules.
When either * or ** is found at the beginning of an article, it relates to the whole of the article unless that article is divided into parts, when it relates purely to that part.

Introduction

Throughout the communist party's life, new statutes designed to structure its internal activity have been introduced on fourteen occasions: 1898, 1903, 1905, 1906, 1907, 1917, 1919, 1922, 1925, 1934, 1939, 1952, 1961 and 1986 and formal amendments were made in 1912, 1927, 1956, 1966 and 1971. Many of the changes made at different times were of minor consequence, but the Rules have also been subject to very many changes of major significance in the eighty-eight years between the adoption of the first and the most recent statutes. The magnitude and the frequency of the changes that the party constitution has undergone has few parallels among formal documents either in the Soviet system or in any other. This suggests two basic questions: how significant are the Rules in the Soviet political process, and what are the major changes that the Rules have experienced since 1898? These questions will be discussed in turn.

THE SIGNIFICANCE OF THE RULES

One of the most resilient strands of Western scholarship on the Soviet political system has been the rejection of formal constitutional provisions as having anything more than purely symbolic or even propagandistic value. Studies have emphasized the way in which the party wields power regardless of legal provisions and the way in which constitutional forms are continually violated in practice. Of course, such a view does have some merit; power remains centralized despite provisions making for democratization in formal documents and much life goes on with little concern for formal provisions in legal or constitutional documents. But it would nevertheless be wrong to dismiss the formal statements as nothing more than window dressing, a democratic façade designed to hide an authoritarian political structure. But to understand the role such formal documents as the communist party Rules play, we need to be more discerning about rules and their nature.

Four basic types of rules are present in all political systems:

(1) Formal rules or principles which have as their sole function the provision of a sense of legitimacy. The role of such rules is overwhelmingly symbolic rather than a means of directly structuring

political action. At times of crisis such rules could, because of their legitimizing function, attain normative significance and thereby move from the purely symbolic sphere into the arena of practical politics.

(2) Formal rules or principles which on some occasions will be important in directly structuring political action and on other occasions not. The direct political significance of such rules is thus dependent upon the political circumstances of the time. The possession of normative authority by these rules is therefore determined temporally and circumstantially. When such rules are not observed for an extended period of time, they may simply be left to lie dormant or they may revert to the status of the first type of rule, the legitimizing rule.

(3) Formal rules or principles which possess normative authority and are always obeyed. This is the type of rule with which the term 'law' is most commonly associated. Acceptance of its mandatory nature is, in practice, well nigh universal among relevant political actors, and violation makes one subject to official sanction.

(4) Conventions, informal principles or assumptions which are not formalized by direct statement in the official documents of a political system but are carried in the collective consciousness of the political actors. They consist of assumptions or understandings about appropriate forms of political behaviour, and although their transgression will not result in formal sanctions, they do possess a normative quality; there is a sense that they *should* be obeyed. Such conventions may be procedural, in the sense that they help structure the way in which certain formal institutions of the system operate, or they may be of a more *realpolitik* nature, relating to the actual disposition and exercise of power irrespective of formal institutional provisions.

These four types of rules coexist and interact in a political system, combining to produce a broad regulative firmament within which politics are played out. The relationship between different rules and the importance of different types of rules will vary over time and with circumstances, but it is unlikely that, in a modern state at least, there would be a period when all four types of rules were not present in the ongoing flow of political life, at least while that state was characterized by stability and order.

The importance of conventions in structuring a regulative milieu should not be overlooked. It has long been recognized that organizational structures cannot function purely on the basis of the formal organizational rules and principles which are to be found enshrined in the charters of those organizations themselves or of the constituent units of which they consist. The same is true of a political system and the institutions which are constituent parts of it. Situations which were not foreseen in the charter, administrative developments resulting from new sorts of demands, deficiencies in the projected administrative arrangements, and the propensity of individuals to act in idiosyncratic ways all contribute to the emergence of patterns of action which are not covered in the formal charter. Such patterns of action, on becoming stable and recurring, come to be accepted as the 'normal' way of doing things. As such, they may become codified and attain the status of formal, normative rules. However, many will remain uncodified, retaining their status purely as conventions, but nonetheless central to the functioning of the institution of which they have become a part. Such conventions may facilitate the fulfilment of the tasks at which the formal rules are directed. In such a situation, the conventions may be considered consistent with the formal rules, perhaps being the means of making those formal rules relevant to current conditions. Alternatively, the conventions may structure political activity in a way which directly contradicts a literal reading of the formal rules. In such cases, conventions and formal rules will be characterized by an element of tension and the formal rules will have the status of either the first or second type of rule discussed above.[1]

The importance that conventions have for structuring political activity and for the practical significance of formal rules means that our understanding and study of formal documents must continually be sensitive to the role conventions play in them. The formal principles enunciated in any constitution, charter or set of rules cannot be taken at face value as an accurate description or explanation of either the location of power or the way in which institutions operate. In principle, this is as much the case with regard to the Rules of the Communist Party of the Sovet Union as it is to the rules of a political party in a liberal democratic state. The question that arises is the degree to which the conventions which structure behaviour are at variance with the formal provisions, whether the former are consistent with the latter or contradict them. Paradoxically in the light of much Western opinion, in the case of the Rules of the CPSU, many of the conventions central to the functioning of the party can be seen reflected in many of the formal provisions of the Rules, with the result that the picture presented in the Rules may not be as far from reality as many think, provided one reads those Rules in a way that is sensitive to the typology of rules sketched above and to the role played by conventions in party life.

The best place to start is with the communist party's 'guiding principle': democratic centralism. In principle, this formula establishes two lines of responsibility depending upon the type of interpretation placed upon the elements of the formula and the involvement of other parts of the Rules in the interpretation. The first possible line of responsibility is democratic, vesting sovereignty in the rank-and-file through the party organizations. This interpretation emphasizes the election of leading organs, the responsibility of party organs to report to the organizations which elected them, the subordination of the minority to the majority, and the principle of collectivism in all work. The reference in the formula to the periodic reporting of party organs to higher organs would in this view refer only to informational reports or would be consistent with a convention of automatic acceptance of those reports by the higher body. The mandatory nature of decisions of higher organs for lower would be consistent with such an interpretation if those higher organs were elected from below and, in the intervals between elections, were entitled to exercise such authority. This is the principle which applies in regard to elected governments in Western democracies, albeit with some constitutional limitations imposed on the government during its term of office, and is usually discussed in terms of electoral mandates. The formal organizational structure of the party outlined in the Rules is consistent with such a framework of responsibility. This sort of interpretation emphasizing the democratic aspects of the formula is consistent with various other provisions of the Rules: provisions for convening special congresses and conferences, for party-wide discussion and for freedom of discussion and criticism all imply an active rank-and-file playing a positive part in the consideration of issues.

The second interpretation is much more centralist in nature and vests power in the leading organs rather than the rank-and-file. This interpretation emphasizes those elements of the formula relating to the need for party organs to report to higher organs, strict party discipline, the mandatory nature of decisions of higher organs for lower, and personal responsibility for the implementation of decisions. The question of the election of party bodies and of periodic reporting to the organizations which elected them would be accommodated in this interpretation by reference to other provisions in the Rules and party conventions. Of particular importance here is the power directly accorded to the CC to guide the activities of the party, to select and assign leading cadres, and to supervise the use of party funds. The CC is thus accorded sweeping powers in party life at all levels. Its role in the personnel sphere is significant in this regard.[2] Formally, conduct of cadre policy is disaggregated to lower levels of the party: republican, regional, territory, area, city and district levels of the party all have responsibilities in this field (see 1986 #42e and compare this with the more explicit statement in 1961 #42d). But the power that could be exercised at each of these levels is subject to confirmation at higher level, culminating at the national level in the CC; this is the practical effect of #20. This means that the whole structure of elections provided for in the Rules must be seen within the context of party personnel practices which are codified in the regulations and conventions of the *nomenklatura* system[3] which, in practice, involves the election to office of individuals nominated by higher party organs. Such a practice is clearly echoed in the Rules. If major personnel decisions are made at the higher levels of the structure, ascendant notions of responsibility involving accountability to superiors are clearly more apposite than descendant notions involving the accountability of higher organs to lower.

The party's organizational structure as outlined in the Rules is much closer to reality if we accept that it was built principally upon a notion of ascendant responsibility. The elaboration of various organizational layers of party structure, each virtually identical in both form and powers, accurately reflects the formal organizational divisions of which the party consists. Responsibility for action is largely divided geographically rather than functionally (with the major exception of the primary party organizations), reflecting the responsibility of higher levels to supervise the activities of lower bodies in each of the areas of party work listed in the Rules. Even the provisions fostering the right of widespread criticism from below are consistent with this when seen in conjunction with the convention that, normally, criticism of superiors must be stimulated from higher levels. So too the limitations on discussion and the prohibition on factions are consistent with the notion of ascendant responsibility. Thus the essential power relationship between different levels of the party is reflected in the Rules. Far from that document presenting a picture of a party in which sovereignty is located at the lower levels, it clearly projects the image of a party in which power and authority are highly centralized. Those provisions in the Rules which seem to reflect a principle of descendant responsibility have tended, through the operation of convention, to accommodate the notion of ascendant responsibility and to become rules of either the first or second type in the typology of rules sketched above.

The Rules are less accurate in their description of the locus of power at the national level. The supreme organ of the party, formally, is the congress, which has the power to lay down the party line and to which the CC and the CAC are responsible. This statement was much closer to reality in the early years of Soviet power than it is now. The development of the relationship between congress and CC on the one hand and the CC's executive organs on the other, shaped both by administrative constraints and by the power struggle which culminated in the supremacy of Joseph Stalin, have created a situation whereby the statement about the supremacy of the congress has been transformed into one of those formal rules which has a purely symbolic function. The convention of party life is clear: the congress invariably approves the report presented to it by the General Secretary in the name of the CC, it exercises no stringent supervision over CC action, and it merely ratifies the list of candidates for election to the CC presented to it.[4] The same judgement applies broadly to the relationship between the CC and its executive organs; the principle of the accountability of the latter to the former is symbolic in effect rather than having immediate practical significance. In the post-Stalin period, only in the unsuccessful attempt to remove Nikita Khrushchev in 1957 has the CC played an active role in resolving an issue in its executive organ and in determining its membership, and then it was not exerting a principle of institutional independence but responding to a call from within that executive.[5] The Politburo and Secretariat have, in practice, been largely exempt from serious scrutiny by the CC, and yet it has been in these executive organs that day-to-day power has rested.

The Rules clearly suggest the Politburo as the locus of power on a day-to-day basis. The Rules openly state that the Politburo leads the work of the party between CC plena. Given the formal powers of the CC and the infrequency of its regular meetings, the position which the Politburo occupies in practice is certainly not hidden by the Rules. Similarly, the importance of the Secretariat is reflected in its being bracketed with the party bureau at each level, the explicit attribution to it of responsibility for personnel matters, and the requirements at lower levels for minimum party membership periods for party secretaries but not for other members of party committees. But although the power and importance of these bodies is suggested by the

Rules, no attention is given to the way these bodies operate or the type of relationship that should exist between them. The clearest example of this is the post of General Secretary, initially established in 1922 but not mentioned in the Rules until 1966, and even then no indication was given of the powers or responsibilities an incumbent of this office should wield. Even the minimal information the Rules give in regard to the congress and CC, such as frequency of meeting, is not prescribed in the Rules for these executive organs. Perhaps it should come as no surprise that formal requirements for these organs are not outlined in the Rules. The Soviet Union remains in many respects a secretive society and an absence of specific details about its supreme decision-making centre is consistent with such an approach. But even if one looks at formal constitutional documents in the West, discussion of central decision-making bodies is frequently not to be found.[6] The contours that such bodies adopt usually develop much more as a result of the growth of convention rather than by formal statute.

In discussing the party Rules and possible gaps or deficiencies in that document, it is also important to distinguish between the general organizational principles and broad structural framework found in formal statutes and those administrative regulations which structure the internal operations of individual political institutions. For legislative bodies the latter may take the form of standing orders which govern the conduct of business in the chamber. For administrative organs they are more likely to be in the form of organizational flow charts, procedural regulations and administrative rules. In this way each institution is likely to have a set of domestic housekeeping arrangements, codified in official documents which are separate from but in theory consistent with the more general constitutional provisions. In the case of the CPSU, one source of these domestic administrative arrangements is the plethora of instructions, memos and circulars issued by the executive organs of the CC in the latter's name. These may be published in party periodical publications, and in particular the journal of the central party apparatus,[7] and they may be collected and reprinted in handbooks for party officials at various levels.[8] Many such decisions may also remain unpublished. The domestic workings of the party will thus be structured in part by formal regulations which do not appear in the party Rules. Indeed, the ambiguities and gaps in the latter will often be filled in this way.[9]

As well as such domestic housekeeping regulations, the party's operation is structured by another sort of formal rule, some instances of which may find their way into the party Rules but many of which do not. These are the formal resolutions and decisions of party meetings, most importantly the congress, CC and the Politburo. At the conclusion of a party congress or CC plenum, and sometimes meetings of the Politburo, a series of resolutions or decisions will be issued which, under the Rules, are formally binding on the party. Most of these decisions concern questions of policy but, particularly during the earlier years of Soviet power, they have also dealt with matters of party organization. In such cases many decisions effectively represent amendments to the party Rules, although they are not presented in this way. Sometimes, as at the VIII Congress, such decisions will constitute a blueprint for changes in the party Rules. On other occasions, decisions on specific issues will find their way into the Rules; the X Congress decision barring factions and providing for the expulsion of CC members and the XIII Congress decision on control commissions are examples of this.[10] Other decisions may elaborate in greater detail points which are made in abbreviated fashion in the Rules; an example of this is the XII Congress decision on the organization of central bodies.[11] Finally, some issues may be dealt with through formal party decisions which are not reflected in changes in the Rules even though they directly affect party structure, such as the November 1962 decision restructuring the party along production lines and the November 1964 decision that the General Secretary should not simultaneously be Chairman of the Council of Ministers.[12] In this way the party Rules constitutes only one of the sources of formal regulation of the party's operation, but it is the central one because, at least in principle, all other rules and regulations must be consistent with it. As the party's constitution, it is the standard against which all other rules must be measured, even if in itself it does not always reflect specific organizational changes.

Like all constitutions, the effectiveness of the party Rules in structuring political behaviour depends upon the normative authority political actors attribute to this document. Where such authority is perceived to be of a high order, the likelihood of rules playing an important part in structuring political life will be substantially enhanced; where such authority is perceived to be weak or lacking, rules will be much more important in their symbolic aspects and as weapons to be mobilized in political conflict.

In the initial phase of the party's life, prior to coming to power, the conditions in which party political life was conducted were not conducive to the development of a high level of normative authority on the part of the party Rules. Although the frequent changing of the

Rules during this period reflected a desire to keep the document relevant to the party's needs, it may also have engendered an image of those Rules as temporary and certainly not as a body of law, the authority of which was such as to compel complete obedience. The bitter factional strife added to the bifurcated nature of the party, with the leadership abroad and the rank-and-file in Russia, and meant that the sort of regularized procedures which the Rules required if they were to generate normative authority were not possible. During the initial, Leninist, period of the party's rule, the circumstances the party found itself in and the reaction of the Bolsheviks to those circumstances weakened any potential for normative development on the part of the Rules. The attempt to build a new political system in a hostile and threatening environment, the need to establish political institutions quickly and to make them work effectively under pressure led to a high level of fluidity and improvisation which weakened the pressures for regularity of procedure which began to emerge in the new system. The large role played by Vladimir Lenin personally was another important factor limiting the development of that institutional regularity upon which the successful generation of normative authority on the part of the Rules relied.

The period following Lenin's death was no more satisfactory in this regard. The factional disputes of the 1920s were followed by the emergence of Stalin as the ultimate source of power and authority in the system. The political tensions of the 1920s were so sharp and personalized that formal institutional boundaries and procedures were insufficiently crystallized and consolidated to be able to contain them within the bounds of formalized procedure, with the result that party institutions were unable to develop any independent integrity; they became instruments of powerful political actors. The personal dominance Stalin was able to achieve reinforced this process by making all party bodies subordinate to his will.

While it is true that the Rules were unable to develop a high level of normative authority prior to 1953, it would be an exaggeration to suggest that no advances were made in this direction. The institutional integrity of party bodies had been undermined by the development of the convention that the formal powers over personnel distribution could be used to construct a personalized power base,[13] and therefore the organizational chart and power distribution within the Rules was qualified by considerations of a power political nature, but until the late 1920s most major policy initiatives and the defeat of the opposition groups were brought before party congresses for formal ratification.

This may suggest two things. Firstly, that there was a view among leading circles that this body was the appropriate forum for decisions of this type, even if in practice this constituted little more than ratification of a decision taken elsewhere. Secondly, that leading circles of the party believed that the provision of the Rules according formal supremacy to the congress was widely accepted among the lower ranks of the party. The need to maintain at least the outward forms prescribed by the Rules during the 1920s may thus reflect a certain sense in which those forms were deemed to have normative authority by lower level party leaders and rank-and-file members, even if not all the elite. Such considerations were, presumably, substantially weakened during the 1930s and 1940s when the party, at least at the top levels, atrophied.

Steps have been taken to remedy the weakness of party institutions and the associated fragility of the normative authority of the Rules in the post-Stalin era, and particularly after 1964. The thrust of the de-Stalinization campaign fostered by Khrushchev was a move away from personalized authority and towards the restoration of the party as the principal institution in Soviet society. Efforts were made to revive the party structure at all levels and to place its operations on a more regularized footing. The effect of such efforts was, in the short term, substantially weakened by the idiosyncratic way in which Khrushchev performed his role as First Secretary and by some of the policies he introduced, in particular the regular turn-over of personnel, the establishment of the sovnarkhozy and the bifurcation of the party apparatus.[14] His overthrow in October 1964 brought to power a collective leadership which espoused a policy which, in effect, involved a strengthening of the normative authority of the Rules. The emphasis upon 'Leninist principles of party life', collective leadership and 'stability of cadres' involved a commitment to institutional regularity and intra-party 'legality'. Henceforth greater efforts were made to abide by the formal provisions in the conduct of party life, to shift the emphasis from rules as a rationalization to rules as a means of structuring political activity. This attitude, plus the greater regularity of procedure observed in the party, has created a more favourable environment for the development of normative authority on the part of the Rules than has existed before.

In a practical sense, the question remains, what is meant by conformity to the Rules? In essence, the Rules provide little more than an organizational chart of the party with suggestions about the effective source and means of power, and a set of principles governing the conditions of party membership. If one keeps in mind the conventions about the essentially ratificatory nature of larger party gatherings and the meaning of the 'confirmation' of party bodies, the Rules do outline the broad conditions under which power is exercised and decisions formalized. Within this context, adherence to the Rules would require not a significant democratization of power within the party (which would be essential only if the conventions embedded in party practice and Rules were ignored) but general adherence to the principles governing party membership and the timetables and lines of ascendant responsibility contained in that document. In this sense, it is probably true that the Rules have constituted a much closer reflection of reality since 1964 than at any time prior to that date.

Finally, something must be said about the relationship between party Rules and party policy. In one sense, all provisions of the Rules express policy on a particular issue of party structure and functioning. However when it comes to substantive policy areas outside the question of party organization and intra-party life, the Rules are like their constitutional counterparts elsewhere: while they may reflect the sorts of social, economic and political structures which may have developed as a result of official policy,[15] they will not normally embody specific policy provisions. The area where policy is most clearly reflected is the concern in the Rules with party membership. The provisions introduced at various times changing entry criteria (such as in 1939, 1966 and 1986) reflect changes in official recruitment policy, though even in this field the link is less than perfect; the fluctuations in recruitment policy between 1939 and 1986 are not reflected in corresponding changes in the Rules.

The Rules are more important as a generalized reflection of mood within the party than they are of party policy. For example, the increased emphasis upon discipline and vigilance in the 1930s echoed the mood inside the party which made possible and contributed to the purges, while the ethos of the post-Stalin Rules signifies in both cases (1961 and 1986) clear changes in mood. In this way the Rules may be seen as a thermometer of the quality of party life, of the sort of general environment within which party members operate at any one time, though clearly changes in Rules may lag significantly behind shifts in mood. Nevertheless, changes in the Rules may be seen as embodying a message from leadership to rank-and-file about the way party membership is perceived and how its responsibilities are to be carried out. The focus in the 1961 Rules upon active participation by party members, and upon the importance of individual responsibility in the

Rules of 1986 are instances of such messages to the rank-and-file. This means that the Rules may help to structure political life not merely in a formal, institutional sense, but by helping to shape the expectations and assumptions of party members about the appropriate ways of acting in the political sphere.

The Rules are thus more important than many have previously acknowledged. They do not offer an accurate, literal description of the way the party works, but when taken in conjunction with conventions, they give a basic framework for an understanding of the party's structure and organization that is no more misleading than are the state constitutions of many sovereign states. Certainly Soviet leaders have believed the Rules to be important for structuring some aspects of political life, as reflected in the frequent changes of the Rules throughout the life of the party. While propagandistic considerations may have had some part in these changes, they are an inadequate explanation for the range and type of changes made at different times. Thus while the Rules may, in their literal form, have purely symbolic elements, within a broader, conventional, context, they do have some descriptive power and some prescriptive significance.

The discussion will now turn to the major changes occurring in successive editions of the Rules.

PRE-OCTOBER REVOLUTION PERIOD

The inaugural congress of the party convened under conspiratorial conditions in Minsk in March 1898. It was very much a transitory affair, lasting only three days and ending with the arrest of most of the delegates and the seizure of the party press. Its only achievement was the formal establishment of the party, a fact signified both by the convocation of the congress itself and by its adoption of a set of principles which, although not formally labelled as such, constituted the first set of organizational rules the party had.

The party reflected in this document was to be a much more decentralized structure than was to be envisaged in later editions of the Rules. A federal structure was envisaged through the admission of the Bund as an autonomous organization, independent in questions concerning the Jewish proletariat (#1). Local committees were granted significant independence from the CC; in exceptional cases they could refuse to implement CC decisions and, when they did implement such decisions, this was to be in the form which they considered to be most suited to local conditions. In other matters they were completely independent within the constraints imposed by the party programme (#7). The CC, as the executive organ of the party (#2), was responsible for the day-to-day operation of the party (#3 and 8), for which it was accountable to the congress as the party's supreme organ. In its work, the CC was to be guided by decisions of the congress and, when possible, was to delay decision on contentious questions until a congress could be convened (#3 and 4). Party funds were placed at the disposal of the CC. The Rules also established an official foreign representative organization and a party newspaper.

The organizational structure presented in 1898 was very sketchy in outline. Neither the regularity of meeting of major party organs nor the relationship that should exist between higher organs and lower was specified, but in practice this was of little consequence because the organizational structure found in the Rules adopted in 1903 was almost completely changed from that of 1898. The principle that the congress was the supreme organ of the party was retained, as it has been in all subsequent editions of the Rules. But the congress was envisaged as a different type of organization: in 1898 this was to consist of representatives of local committees (#9), but by 1903 these were to be joined by representatives of the Party Council, CC, Central Organ and organizations considered the equivalent of committees. Such a composition clearly accorded a much higher profile to the central organs than the party founders had envisaged.[16] The only other provision carried forward was the attribution to the CC of responsibility for distributing the manpower and funds of the party and for directing enterprises of general significance. This provision has appeared in all subsequent editions of the Rules, albeit with changes in terminology.

The II Congress of the Russian Social Democratic Workers' Party was crucial for the course of the party's future development. It was here that the split between Bolsheviks and Mensheviks which was to have such a debilitating effect on Russian social democracy was formalized, and it was over #1 of the Rules that the dispute burst onto the public scene.[17] The Rules were debated and adopted by the congress during the period between the outbreak of the dispute and the withdrawal of the delegates from the Bund and the League of Russian Social Democrats Abroad, and therefore when Lenin and his 'hard' supporters were in a minority. As a result, the draft Rules which

Lenin had proposed were significantly amended,[18] while the Rules which were adopted reflect a composite of the Bolshevik and Menshevik positions.

The 1903 Rules, which were declared to be 'binding for all sections of the party',[19] for the first time broached the question of party membership, defining it in terms of the proposal presented by Iulii Martov (#1). However, the Rules went no further than a definition: there was no consideration of the duties, obligations or responsibilities of party members[20] and no provision was made regularizing party entry procedures. Such matters were not raised until 1917, when the mass influx into the party made consideration of such questions imperative. This vagueness on matters of party membership was matched by a similar lack of attention to local party organs. The 1903 Rules gave them a part in the convocation of extraordinary party congresses and provided for their representation at congresses (#2 and 3), granted them autonomy within their own areas of responsibility (#8), imposed an obligation on them to report to the CC and the editorial board of the party newspaper (#11), accorded to them rights of co-optation and expulsion of members[21] and declared that all issues were to be resolved in all party bodies by majority vote (#12). The Rules remained silent about the formation and registration of new committees and about the structure and activities that should characterize such bodies. Reflecting the underground existence of these organs, no elaborate structure of accountability was established apart from the obligation of regular reporting to the centre, nor were serious constraints imposed on the freedom of action of local organizations. *Ad hoc* action based on local conditions was not to be restricted by the imposition of formal regulations which, in any case, were impossible to enforce.

Reflecting the fact that most of those participating in the congress were *emigrés* whose day-to-day lives were spent abroad, the Rules showed far greater concern for the construction of an elaborate network of central party organizations than it did for those bodies which had to work in the underground in Russia. The Rules established an interlocking network of three bodies beneath the party congress, which remained the supreme organ: the Party Council, the CC and the Central Organ (the party newspaper) (#2, 4, 5 and 12). Despite the Council's formal supremacy and the allocation of responsibility over ideological matters to the editorial board of the Central Organ (#7), day-to-day power lay with the CC. The description of the powers of this body in essentials, with terminological changes and substantial additions, has remained in force to the present day. The CC was given the power to organize party institutions and to direct their activities, to direct enterprises of general significance, to distribute party personnel and funds, to resolve disputes between party bodies and generally to co-ordinate all the practical activity of the party (#6). Furthermore, the membership of all party organizations except those confirmed by the congress (#4) was to be confirmed by the CC, thereby vesting ultimate authority over the composition of local party organs in the CC. The autonomy of local committees contained in the 1898 Rules was modified by the provisions that decisions of the CC were mandatory for all party organizations (#8) and that all party organizations had to supply the CC and the editorial board with complete details about their personnel[22] and activities (#11). In addition, the autonomy of the Bund was revoked.

The strength of centralist sentiment was reflected in the erosion of local autonomy in the Rules. But the effect of this centralization of authority was undermined by the practical difficulties of ensuring that central decisions were carried out in the localities and by the structure of central authority presented in the Rules. The interlocking nature of the leading organs contained significant potential for dispute, disagreement and deadlock, particularly given the proposed physical location of the CC in Russia and the other two bodies abroad. While the factional conflict translated this danger into reality, it is nevertheless true that the Rules themselves created a structure in which the possibility of deadlock at the centre was high. In addition, the vagueness of the provision regarding party finances (#9) left the centre with little formal means of gaining adequate finance from lower party bodies. In a real sense, the result was little diminution in the practical autonomy of local party bodies.

The Rules adopted at the II Congress were superseded by a new edition approved at the III Congress in April 1905.[23] This was an entirely Bolshevik gathering,[24] a fact reflected in the substitution of Martov's definition of a party member by that proposed by Lenin in 1903 (#1). Although this set of Rules remained valid for just 12 months, it introduced some interesting changes.

At the central level, the most striking change was the abolition of the interlocking network of leading organs, reflected most graphically in the elimination of the Party Council. The congress remained the supreme organ, and for the first time mandatory regularity of convocation was established by the provision that it was to meet annually (#2); in 1903 it was, 'if possible', to meet every two years. The conditions for convening an extraordinary congress remained unchanged, although provision was now made for the establishment of an Organizational Committee which could call such a congress should the CC refuse to do so (#2).[25] Representation rights at the congress shifted in favour of non-central organs[26] and the period of fully-fledged party existence necessary for the representation of organizations was halved (#3), thereby making it easier for newer groups entering the party to participate in delegate selection and, through this, in party congresses.

The position of the CC was strengthened in the 1905 Rules, emerging unambiguously as the focus of power between congresses. Henceforth the CC was to be elected by the congress rather than appointed as previously (#4), with new members being co-opted between congresses by unanimous vote of the committee, as in 1903 (#12). To the basic tasks outlined in 1903 were added direct responsibility for relations with other parties (as in 1898; in 1903 this responsibility had rested with the Party Council) and the appointment of the responsible editor of the party newspaper (#5). The latter task had previously been allotted to the congress. In principle, the change made the central newspaper directly responsible to the CC.[27] Under certain circumstances (see below), the CC was given the right to dissolve a local committee (#9), while the reporting of local organizations to the CC was placed on a regular fortnightly basis (#11). Furthermore, local party organizations now had an obligation to publish CC declarations if so requested by the CC (#7) and an attempt was made to regularize party finances by specifying the proportion of their income that local committees had to despatch to the CC (#8).

The 1905 Rules introduced a new form of party organization at the local level, the 'periphery organization' (#6, 8 and 12). The nature of these bodies is not clear from the Rules, and the debate at the congress shows some ambiguity in the minds of the delegates.[28] However, the term seems to refer to party groups operating under the leadership of a party committee, usually with much more narrowly conceived functions (being restricted to agitation and propaganda) than the committee as a whole. According to one delegate at the congress, often they adopted the character of the (executive) organ of the committee.[29] There was also some ambiguity at the congress about the relationship between periphery organization and local committee. This is reflected in the argument of some delegates that local committees should be dissolved by the CC upon the agreement of two-thirds of CC members and two-thirds of the members of the periphery organization.[30] The vaguer formulation finally adopted (#9) reflects the compromise reached on this issue. Generally the Rules were clearer about the supremacy of the committee over the periphery organization; while all party organizations were autonomous in their own particular areas of responsibility, the range of autonomy of periphery organizations was to be defined by the committee under the aegis of which they worked (#6); the membership of local periphery organizations was to be confirmed by the local committees (#8), albeit under the general authority possessed by the CC over the distribution of party forces (#5); and local committees were given an unambiguous right to appoint their members to places in the periphery organizations (#12).[31] Besides this right of appointment, all local party bodies had the right to co-opt and expel members by a two-thirds majority vote, except for candidates proposed by the CC or periphery organizations for membership in 'committees and similar organizations', which only required a simple majority vote for co-optation (#12). Provision was thus made for easy overlap between party bodies, with, in theory, committees more easily able to establish a presence in periphery organizations than vice versa.

The Rules adopted at the III Congress lasted only until the IV (Unified) Congress brought about a formal reunification of the two wings of the party in April 1906. The new statute introduced at this time was shorter than that of 1905. The periphery organizations were no longer formally acknowledged and provisions regarding party publications, the dissolution of committees, rights of appeal and address, the presentation of regular reports by local bodies to the CC and the general principles on co-optation and expulsion were omitted. In addition, the mandatory nature of CC decisions for the remainder of the party was no longer included in the Rules, and the level of financial obligations owed by lower party bodies to the CC was reduced. The effect of these omissions is to give an impression of the erosion of the centralist principle which had been considered so important at the all-Bolshevik III Congress.[32]

The 1906 Rules were the first to refer to democratic centralism as the guiding principle of the party (#2). Although no attempt was made to spell out what this meant,[33] it may be instructive that the provision immediately following this restored the right of autonomy of party organizations omitted from the Rules in 1905. A number of changes introduced at the apex of the party suggest an erosion in the position of the CC: resolution of questions of a political character by the CC must involve the editorial board (#7), the editorial board was to be elected by the congress rather than the CC (although vacancies were to be filled by the CC acting jointly with the remainder of the board), its rights of confirmation over party committees seemed to have been weakened (#4 (cf. 1905 #8)), and casual vacancies on the CC were no longer to be filled by co-optation but by the entry of candidates who had been appointed by the congress (#7).[34] This final change foreshadowed the position of candidate member of the CC. The expansion in the powers of the congress was accompanied by a partial regularization of its proceedings. For the first time a ratio of representation was established for party organizations in order to take account of the differing sizes and importance of different party organizations, elections for delegates had henceforth to take place on democratic principles, and a minimum time period between the announcement of a congress and its agenda and the date of meeting was established (#8). The validity of a congress and the support necessary for calling an extraordinary congress were now expressed in terms of party members rather than party organizations as in preceding editions of the Rules (#8). This change and that establishing a ratio of representation for party organizations clearly reflects a shifting of emphasis in favour of the large party organizations at the expense of the small.

The Rules also provided for the establishment of a new level of party organization, that of the region. Regional committees were to be formed by party organizations in individual districts at regional congresses or conferences (#5). New party organizations were to be confirmed by regional conferences or by two neighbouring party organizations, subject to CC supervision (#4). A slightly modified version of the Leninist position on membership was adopted (#1).

The debate on the Rules at the IV Congress[35] was short and reflected little real difference between Bolsheviks and Mensheviks. Four articles of the Rules were adopted without debate (#2, 3, 5 and 6) and on only two were serious differences aired: in the commission which drew up the draft Rules,[36] a Menshevik proposal to make the calling of an extraordinary congress incumbent on support by two-thirds of all party members was rejected in favour of the weaker Bolshevik proposal outlined in #8,[37] and on the method of appointment of the editorial board, the Bolshevik preference for this to be done by the CC was defeated.[38] Virtually all accepted the need for the emphasis in the party's activities to remain on clandestine revolutionary work, hence the acceptance of strictly centralized organization and the refusal to readmit on an autonomous basis the social democratic parties of Poland and Lithuania and Latvia.

A number of changes to the Rules were introduced at the V (London) Congress in May 1907. The most important of these was the restoration of CC control over the editorial board of the party newspaper (#7). The CC was also called upon to convene three to four-monthly meetings (a regularity which was changed to 'as often as possible' in 1912) of party organizations to discuss major questions of party life, although decisions of these meetings would enter into force only upon CC confirmation (#8). Norms of representation at congresses were changed in 1907, while an amendment of 1912 removed the determination of such norms from the Rules and accorded it to the CC (#9). The qualifying period before a party body could send delegates to a congress was reduced from the six months of 1905 to three months in 1907 (no mention was made of this in 1906) (#9). A third amendment in 1912[39] reintroduced co-optation as a right of party bodies. The 1907 Rules, even in their slightly amended form of 1912, differed less from the statute of 1906 than any other two sets of Rules in the pre-revolutionary period. Furthermore this set of Rules remained in force for far longer than any of its predecessors, although this may be less a result of general satisfaction with it than of the inability of party leaders to convene another congress before August 1917.[40]

The VI Congress was held in August 1917 when there were more pressing issues to discuss than a new party statute. Discussion of the Rules was brief,[41] and although various amendments were moved and voted upon, there were no serious conflicts over any of the provisions of the draft presented to the congress; the most extensive debate concerned an unsuccessful proposal to add a supplement to the Rules providing for the establishment of autonomous national sections in the party.[42]

Reflecting the mass influx into the party during 1917, the Rules devoted much more attention to the question of party membership than at any time in the past. To the qualities demanded of members in earlier Rules, acceptance of the party programme, membership of one of its organizations and financial support (regularized for the first time in the form of membership dues (#3)), was added a new requirement: party members were to submit to all party decisions (#1). No longer were party members simply subsumed under the general provision that decisions of the CC were mandatory for all party organizations;

obedience to all party decisions was now a condition of membership. The increased emphasis upon unity and discipline that this seems to suggest was reinforced by the attention devoted to the question of expulsion of a party member (#4). Provision for expulsion of members had been made in the Rules adopted in 1903 and 1905, but it had been omitted in 1906. It was reintroduced in 1917 along broadly similar lines to that adopted earlier except that it was not part of a more general provision about the working of party bodies; it now became a provision in its own right and was therefore much more prominent than it had been before. The 1917 Rules also introduced a principle that was to remain until 1961: the automatic departure from the party of those who had not paid membership dues for three months. In the absence of any other formal provisions, this was the only means the Rules provided for resigning from the party. Some attention was also devoted to the mechanism of party entry. Henceforth, new members were to be recommended by two existing members, admitted by local party organizations, and confirmed by the following general meeting of members (#2).

While the 1917 Rules offered only a slightly more expanded explanation of the party structure at lower levels,[43] a greater regularization of party life at the centre was evident. This was most marked with regard to the party congress. For the first time the Rules referred explicitly to the tasks the congress was to carry out: it was to hear and approve the reports of central party institutions, review and change the party programme, establish the tactical line of the party on issues of the day, and elect the CC and the newly-established auditing commission (#12). Regular congresses were to be convened annually, while the convocation of an extraordinary congress was, in principle, made easier: instead of such a congress requiring the support of at least half of all party members as in 1907, from 1917 what was required was the support of one-third of all members represented at the last congress.[44] The CC obtained the right to call a congress on its own initiative (#10) and retained the power to establish the norms of representation.

A number of other changes were made concerning the CC. Although the Rules no longer accorded it responsibility for resolving conflicts between party institutions or for co-ordinating the activities of the party, it gained the power to confirm new party organizations in the absence of a regional party committee (#8).[45] The tenure of the CC was formally set at one year, thereby making explicit what had been implied in the annual regularity of the party congress; vacancies in the CC were to be filled in the order in which candidates were elected by the congress (thereby eliminating the anomaly created in 1906 and established the candidate status in the form it was to retain until 1939); and provision was made for an executive body for the CC (#13).[46] Plenary sessions of the CC now had to be held at two-monthly intervals, a provision that may have been introduced to compensate for the elimination of the requirement that the CC convoke conferences of representatives of all party organizations as often as possible. Despite a congress resolution that the CC should include members from both the regions and the major centres,[47] no mention of this body's composition appears in the Rules.

The 1917 Rules also introduced a new executive body, the auditing commission. This body, to be elected annually at the congress, was to exercise financial supervision over the central party treasury and all enterprises of the CC. It was to be responsible to the congress.

The period prior to the seizure of power was characterized by a party that was weak organizationally and, for much of the time, fractured internally by ongoing factional conflict. While factional disagreement was clearly of some importance in the formulation of the Rules in 1903, by 1906 cross-factional agreement on the need for a centralized revolutionary organization reduced the scope for major disagreement on issues with which the Rules were concerned,[48] with the result that factional conflict was not a major continuing influence upon the shape of the party Rules.

The party's weak organizational structure was reflected in the vagueness and ambiguity of many sections of the Rules. Party membership remained a matter of nothing more than a simple definition until the mass influx of 1917 forced some regularization of both entrance procedures and the financial obligations members owed to the party. Similarly, the organizational structure at the lower levels of the party remained very loosely articulated; the powers of the various party bodies and the lines of accountability were not spelled out. Nevertheless, general principles providing for centralized leadership were instituted from an early date, although once again the form was not clearly enunciated. From the earliest Rules the congress was established as the supreme organ of the party with the CC as its executive body exercising power between congresses. In the CC was vested the power over the distribution of the forces and funds of the party. This meant that, in principle, the CC exercised control over personnel and financial aspects of the party's operation. While the latter was qualified from 1905 by the stipulation in the Rules of a set proportion of a party organization's income which was to remain in its own hands (80 per cent in 1905, 90 per cent thereafter), and therefore not subject to the direct control of the CC, the former remained as a general principle untrammelled throughout this period. Even when the membership of party bodies was to be confirmed by other organizations, such confirmation always was subject to CC supervision. The responsibility for personnel and finance vested in the CC clearly signalled a centripetal flow of power.

The much greater attention paid to the central organs of the party than to those at lower levels reflects the importance in the party leaders' eyes of the ideologically-based conviction of the importance of correct leadership for a revolutionary movement. It probably also reflects a preoccupation with the conditions of their own political life at the expense of the larger enterprise. But it may also signify a realistic assessment of the practical situation: committees in the underground were, by virtue of the conditions of their existence, outside the control of central party organs. Under such circumstances, the adoption of elaborate regulations structuring the party hierarchy and its mode of operation were, in practice, bound to be fruitless. It is likely that the only section of the party for which such rules appeared relevant were those central organs upon which the Rules principally focused. But it also meant that there was a significant imbalance in the treatment accorded the party as a whole by the Rules.

THE PARTY IN POWER: THE FIRST STAGE

The party's assumption of power confronted it with tasks and problems which were completely new to it. Instead of seeking to build up a clandestine network and avoid the blows of the tsarist authorities, it had now to concern itself with the administration of a vast area and all the problems that involved. The new tasks demanded a new, more regularized party structure, and therefore a new party statute. One of the most prominent themes of party life during the initial years of Bolshevik rule concerned the most appropriate organizational structure and principles of operation for the party's needs. This debate dominated the first regular party congress after the seizure of power, the VIII Congress in March 1919.[49] The formal outcome of the debate on the organizational question was a resolution[50] which, along with submissions from local party bodies, formed the basis of the Rules formally adopted at the VIII Conference of the party in December

1919.[51] In many respects these Rules reflect the concerns and views expressed by participants in the debate at the VIII Congress and the decisions adopted there about the form the party should take. The changes to the Rules involved in the adoption of new party statutes at the XII Conference in August 1922.[52] and following the XIV Congress in December 1925[53] and the amendments to the latter at the XV Congress in December 1927 reflect both the adjustment of the party apparatus in the light of experience and the general shift in party opinion. The introduction of state constitutions in 1918 and 1924 also necessitated some adjustments in the party's administrative structure.

The Rules adopted in the pre-October period were all simple in structure: none had internal divisions into sections, reflecting both the internal simplicity of the party itself and the lack of concern for lower-level bodies as noted above. However, with the enormous growth of the party once in power, both in terms of membership and organizational complexity, the Rules became a much more complex document. In terms of sheer size, the Rules adopted after 1917 dramatically overshadowed those adopted some three months before the Bolshevik victory: the fourteen articles of 1917 expanded to sixty-six in 1919 and 1922, and 100 in 1925. Furthermore, from that time the document was divided into sections dealing with different aspects of party life. The Rules adopted in 1919 contained twelve sections: on party members, candidate members, organizational structure, central institutions, regional organizations, provincial organizations, county organizations, parish organizations, party cells, party discipline, finances, and party fractions in non-party institutions and organizations. In the 1922 Rules, a thirteenth section on control commissions was added. Two more sections were added in 1925, concerning area organizations and party organizations in the Red Army.

Throughout this period there was a high level of concern in the party about the possible consequences of building socialism in a predominantly peasant country. This was reflected graphically in the fear that the proletarian element in the party would be swamped by the petty bourgeoisie, a fear stemming both from the massive influx into the party after October and from the conditions of NEP.[54] This concern was expressed in the Rules by increasingly elaborate provisions concerning party membership.

Concern about petty bourgeois infection is most clearly reflected in the institution of the candidate stage of membership in 1919. This was envisaged both as an educative and a testing period; during this time candidates were to become thoroughly acquainted with the programme and tactics of the party, while their personal qualities were assessed to judge their suitability or otherwise for full membership (1919, #5; 1922, #5; 1925, #7). All prospective members had to pass through the candidate stage, although in the 1919 Rules provision was made for this stage to be by-passed in exceptional cases or during a party week (#2).[55] Such a provision was eliminated in 1922, thereby rendering the candidate stage mandatory for all.[56] Concern about the class nature of party recruits is also reflected in developments with regard to membership criteria and the length of the candidate stage. Admission to candidature in 1919 was subject to the recommendation of two party members of six months' standing (compared with no mandatory party membership period for referees in 1917), verified by the local party committee (#6); the minimum period of candidacy for workers and peasants was one-third that of other categories (#7).[57] In 1922, following the introduction of NEP, this became much more complex, with the division of applications into three categories with different membership criteria and lengths of candidacy.[58] The categories were workers and Red Armymen from worker and peasant backgrounds, peasant and handicraft workers who did not exploit the labour of others, and others. Applicants from the first two categories needed recommendations from three party members of three years' standing and were to serve a candidacy period of at least six months for the first category and one year for the second. Those from the third category needed the recommendations of five members of five years' standing and served a candidacy period of at least two years (#2 and 7). Recommendations were subject to confirmation by the local committee, and inaccurate recommendations rendered the referee subject to penalization. The 1925 Rules modified this tripartite division[59] through the introduction of a sub-category in the first category and the easing of membership criteria for those in the first two categories (#2). Category one was divided into full-time industrial workers (including transport workers) on the one hand and non-industrial workers, Red Armymen from worker and peasant backgrounds, and farm labourers on the other. Applicants from the first sub-division needed two recommendations from members of one year's standing and those from the second sub-division two recommendations from members of two years' standing. Those from category two required three recommendations from members of two years' standing, and for those from category three the requirement remained as it had been in 1922: five recommendations from persons of five years' standing. Periods of candidacy were respectively six months, six months, one year and two years. The Rules therefore clearly reflect an attempt to expand the party's recruitment among workers, peasants and Red Armymen, and in particular to facilitate the entry of industrial workers into party ranks, an aim which also had factional implications during the 1920s. In 1922 and 1925 special provision was also made for those who were former members of other parties, who could join only through a production cell,[60] and youth, who were to join only through the Russian Communist Youth Movement (#2).

Concern over the quality of membership and the early development of a more centralized personnel system is evident in the changing procedures for admission. The 1919 Rules simply repeated the provisions introduced in 1917: new members were admitted by local committees and confirmed by the next general meeting of the organization (#2). In 1922 supervision from above was introduced: applications were first examined by the cell, decided by the general meeting of the party organization, and confirmed by the county committee for category one and the provincial committee for categories two and three (#2). The same provision applied in 1925, with the addition of the district committee in towns and industrial centres for the first category and the area committee for the other two categories (#2).[61] The more suspect the social category from which an applicant came, the higher the level at which his admission was to be confirmed.

Having met all the conditions for acceptance as a candidate member of the party, from 1922 individuals had to go through the same procedure of recommendation, verification, decision and confirmation in order to transfer to full membership (1922, #6; 1925, #8). They also had to have achieved a level of political literacy (#2). The candidate stage, during which an individual possessed speaking but not voting rights in open party meetings,[62] was clearly envisaged as a screening process. Its success in fulfilling this role was substantially weakened in practice by the recruiting practices adopted in the mid-1920s.[63]

The introduction of the candidate stage was the major innovation with regard to party membership during this period, but three other changes made at this time should also be mentioned. The first related to the definition of a party member, and in particular that aspect of the definition which had been considered so important in 1903: membership of a party organization. In a change which, for Politburo member Grigorii Zinoviev, had 'major organizational, party and political significance',[64] from 1919 members had not only to belong to a party organization, but also to work in it. This change suggested that the sort of passivity which could have been consistent with the previous definition and with the purely careerist motives for joining the party about which the leadership was so concerned in the early years of power, was no longer acceptable. Active party work was now required. This principle remains an element of the definition of a party member in the current edition of the Rules.

The second change related to the transferral of membership from one party organization to another and reflects the effort to tighten central control over personnel. In 1919 a provision was introduced which enabled an individual's membership of one party organization to be transferred to another organization if that individual was moved into the area of work of the latter, subject only to the agreement of his former organization (#3). In 1922 this was supplemented by a provision which seemed to make transfers within a province incumbent upon the agreement of the provincial committee while transfers between provinces were subject to rules established by the CC (#3). By 1925, all transfers between organizations were to be in accordance with the rules established by the CC (#5). This formal control over transfers supplemented the general provision according power over the distribution of personnel to the CC and the more specific rights of confirmation of committee membership, both of which are discussed below.

The final significant change in the sphere of membership related to the issue of expulsion. The 1919 Rules confirmed the provision introduced in 1917 that a decision on expulsion from the party had to be taken by the local organization of which the person was a member,[65] and added that that decision took effect only upon confirmation by the relevant provincial committee. Moreover, the expulsion was to be reported in the party press, along with the reasons for it, while suspension of party membership was applied from the time the decision was made until its confirmation (#4). In the 1922 Rules, decisions on expulsion could still be made by the organization to which the person belonged, but they could now also be made by the provincial control commission. While such decisions remained formally subject to confirmation by the provincial committee (#4), as a later article of the Rules demonstrated (#50), this was not as simple as it appeared. In 1925 the provincial (or area) control commission was given the power to make decisions on expulsion and, along with the provincial (or area) committee, to confirm such decisions if made by local organizations (#6). The uneasy insertion of the control commission into this process and the subsequent expansion of its role reflects the institutional rivalry that developed between party committees and control commissions at this time.[66]

Reflecting the increased complexity of the party's structure in power, henceforth the party Rules focused principally upon that organizational structure. Section III contained general principles relating to the party structure, and it remained largely unchanged throughout this period. The principle of democratic centralism, introduced in 1906, was reaffirmed as the guiding principle of the party's organizational structure, and it was now declared to operate along territorial lines: all party organizations within a particular geographical area were considered to be subordinate to an organization serving the area as a whole (1919 and 1922, #11; 1925, #13). This principle operated all the way up the hierarchy from individual cells to national organs and applied in all aspects of party life (1919 and 1922, #15 and 16; 1925, #17 and 18). In effect, this established the right of the national organs to make decisions for the country as a whole and thereby to overrule decisions made at lower levels, despite the provision that party organizations remained autonomous in local questions (1919 and 1922, #12; 1925, #14).[67] A pyramidal organizational structure was thereby established. The highest leading organ of each organization[68] was to be the general meeting, congress or conference which was to elect an executive organ to conduct the work of the organization between meetings of the larger body (1919 and 1922, #13 and 14; 1925, #15 and 16). The committees thus established were empowered to form departments to work under them in areas of special concern (1919 and 1922, #17; 1925, #19). This section also accorded to every confirmed party organization the right to acquire its own press, but now only with the sanction of the appropriate higher body (1919 and 1922, #19; 1925, #20 (compare with 1917, #6)). The only major change which appeared in this section during this period[69] related to the confirmation of the membership of party organizations. The 1919 and 1922 Rules both included a section setting out a more complex structure of confirmation than had existed in 1917: below the county, all organizations were confirmed by the county committee with the sanction of the provincial committee, and organizations at the county level and above were confirmed by the committee at the next higher level with verification by the level above that up to the CC (#18). This provision although included in the draft, was omitted from the 1925 Rules. For some party bodies this omission made little difference because the source of confirmation was explicitly mentioned in the more extended organizational provisions for each level of the party structure later in the Rules. But no clear responsibility for confirmation was established for the national communist parties and for the regional, territory, provincial and area party organizations. Presumably this was to be inferred from the general organizational scheme of the party offered in #17 and the powers over personnel distribution accorded to the CC in #25.[70]

The general provisions outlined in Section III were applied more specifically to the various levels of party organization in the subsequent sections. The first to be discussed were the party's central institutions, and here the changing provisions of the Rules clearly reflect the centralization of power that was taking place at this time. But while the Rules reflect this process, they neither adequately describe nor explain it. The supreme organ of the party remained the party congress. Until a 1927 amendment changed the frequency to every two years, this organ was to continue to meet on an annual basis. The powers of the congress remained broadly as they had been spelled out in 1917, with the addition in 1922 of the power to determine the size of the CC (#23) and in 1925 to elect and supervise the Central Control Commission and the Central Auditing Commission (#23).[71] The same provision in the 1925 Rules gave the congress the power to amend the Rules,[72] the first time responsibility for this had formally been established. The criteria for the validity of a congress were eased in 1919 (#20), while the involvement of the regional committees in establishing the norms of representation at a congress was eliminated through the attribution of this responsibility to the CC in conjunction with a regular pre-congress conference (1919 and 1922, #20). The centralization this seemed to imply was taken further in 1925 when the right to establish those norms was vested solely in the CC (#21).[73] The provision for convening an extraordinary congress remained throughout this period in the form first specified in 1917.[74]

More significant changes occurred with regard to the CC. Changes introduced at the VIII Conference in December 1919 reflect the heavy criticism the party leaders had come under nine months earlier at the VIII Congress where the Democratic Centralist opposition charged, *inter alia*, that the CC provided little leadership, failed to act as a collegial organ, and rarely kept local committees informed about its activities.[75] These points were partly addressed in the resolution of the VIII Congress[76] and in the provisions of the 1919 Rules. Henceforth the CC was to meet in plenary session at least twice per month on dates set beforehand (#24), it was to convene three-monthly conferences of committees from Moscow, Petrograd and the provinces (#26), and it was to send monthly reports on its activities to those committees (#27). The size of the CC also was fixed by the Rules (#23), but the failure to establish a quorum meant that the charge that individuals were supplanting the collegial organ was not adequately met. The powers of the CC were expanded at this time by giving it the authority to direct the central soviet and public organizations through the party fractions inside them (#24). This provision made formal what had previously been only implicit in the Rules.

Most of these changes were short-lived, being overturned in 1922 and 1925. In 1922 the congress was given the power to determine the size of the CC (#23), the regularity of CC meetings was reduced to once every two months, and candidate members were accorded the right formally to participate in meetings with a consultative vote (#24). Furthermore, the three-monthly conference was abolished and replaced by a new type of body, an annual conference of representatives of party committees above the territory level,[77] regional bureaus and political sections of the armed forces (#26). In 1925 this provision was reworded in terms of one conference of representatives of local party organizations between each party congress, a timetable which in practice mirrored that of 1922 until the 1927 amendment altering the regularity of congresses changed the regularity of conferences to once every two years. No consideration was given to the powers or responsibilities such a conference might have. Finally, the monthly reports the CC was to despatch became two-monthly in 1922 (#27) and in 1925 were transformed into an exhortation to 'regularly inform' party organizations about its work (#28).[78]

The changes that were made in the operating profile of the CC during this period suggest a decline in the level of its responsiveness to lower-level party bodies. This took place beside an even more emphatic assertion of its powers than ever before. The list of enumerated powers to be exercised by the CC carried forward from 1903 already gave the CC extensive power over party activity, personnel and finances. In 1925 the Rules for the first time stated what had been implicit earlier: the CC was the supreme organ between party congresses (#25). The 1925 Rules also accorded the CC the power to confirm the membership of the presidia or bureaus of committees at the territory, region and republican levels (#33) and the editors of the party newspapers of the major local organizations (#25). The latter reflects both the increased emphasis upon the need for strengthening the party's educational and propaganda efforts at this time and the recent experience of the Leningrad opposition.[79]

The most important change to this section of the Rules, particularly in the light of the decline in frequency of the formally-required meetings of the CC and the congress, was the provision for the establishment of executive organs of the CC (1919, #25). A precursor to these was to be found in the 1917 Rules and in the practices which had emerged since October, but the immediate stimulus was the increased workload at the summit of the party added to the untimely death of the party's secretary, Yakov Sverdlov, in March 1919. The result was the formal establishment of the Politburo, Orgburo and Secretariat at the VIII Congress. The congress resolution establishing these bodies was far more detailed than the new provision in the party Rules. The latter simply stated that the CC was to form a Political bureau for political work, an Organizational bureau for organizational work and a Secretariat headed by a member of the Orgburo. In contrast, the VIII Congress resolution[80] set out the membership sizes of these bodies and the rights of attendance by non-members at Politburo meetings, declared that the Politburo had the power to adopt decisions on pressing issues between CC plena, and that the Orgburo was to direct all the party's organizational work and was to meet at least three times per week, made some brief remarks about the internal structure of the Orgburo and Secretariat, and established the principle that these bodies had to report to the regular session of the CC. The 1922 Rules were slightly more expansive than the Rules of 1919, setting out a membership size for the Orgburo, establishing that three CC members were to work full-time in the Secretariat, and defining the responsibilities of the Orgburo in terms of 'general leadership of organizational work' and 'current work of an organizational and executive character' (#25). No attempt was made in the Rules to determine the relationship between these bodies until 1925 when the responsibilities accorded to the Orgburo in 1922 were split up: the Orgburo was to exercise 'general leadership of organizational work' while the Secretariat concentrated on 'current work of an organizational and executive character' (#26).[81] While this formulation clearly signalled the formal supremacy of the Orgburo over the Secretariat, the precise relationship that was to apply between these bodies was left vague. Nor was any clear indication of the power that was to reside in these organs conveyed by the Rules.

The establishment of a Central Auditing Commission was signalled in the 1922 Rules, at which time a minimum period of ten years' party standing was set for its members. Its size, initially set by the Rules, was from 1925 to be established by the congress, while its responsibilities were expanded in 1922 from inspection of the treasury and enterprises of the CC to embrace broad supervision of the handling of business by the central organs of the party and the proper functioning of the apparatus of the Secretariat (#28).[82] This body seemed to have very broad powers of checking and supervision over the party apparatus. In practice, its brief was much more restricted.

The final major innovation with regard to the central institutions during this period[83] was introduced by way of amendment in 1927. This established the conditions under which an All-Union discussion could be carried out in the party. These were recognition of the need for it as an exceptional measure by several provincial or regional level party organizations, the absence of a firm majority in the CC on an important question of party policy, or if such a discussion was considered necessary by the CC to verify the correctness of its policy. The amendment was clear in its statement that such a discussion could take place only upon decision of the CC, thereby placing ultimate authority over the mounting of such discussions in the hands of the CC.

The centralization of power that was occurring in the party at this time was thus reflected in various provisions of the Rules adopted during this period. The declining frequency of meetings of leading organs, the accretion of power by the CC and the establishment of executive organs at the apex of the party structure all reflect the process of centralization which was taking place. Echoes of it are also evident in the way in which the Rules handle the lower level party organs.

The highest level of the party below the national organs remained that of the region, joined in 1922 by the national republics[84] and in 1925 by the territory level of organization.[85] Regional and territory organs within the RSFSR were considered the equivalent of leading party organs in the national republics which made up the federal state, being directly responsible to the central organs in the same way as those at the republican level. The introduction of national communist parties therefore did not represent an embracing of the federal principle and a concomitant decentralization of power within the party. The party remained unitary in form, the principle of democratic centralism continued to bind it tightly together, and the national communist parties were no more independent from the centre than were party organizations at other levels of the party. No separate structure was created for the RSFSR, which was to be administered by the central organs.

The structure of the party at the regional/republican/territory level reflected the general principles enunciated earlier in the Rules: the supreme organ was the conference or congress, which elected a committee, which in turn elected a presidium or bureau.[86] The powers of the conference/congress and committee were essentially scaled-down versions of the powers wielded by the equivalent organs at the national level, and they experienced the same sort of expansion as those at that level in 1925.[87] The same trend of centralization witnessed at the national level was also evident here: the period between regular conferences/congresses changed from six months in 1919 and 1922 (#31 and 33) to twelve months in 1925 (#35)[88] and between committee meetings from two weeks in 1919 (#32) to one month in 1922 (#33) and two months in 1925 (#35),[89] the reports that had to be sent to the CC at three-monthly intervals in 1919 (#32)[90] became monthly in 1922 (#33) and at whatever intervals the CC established in 1925 (#36),[91] and by 1925 the role of provincial committees in establishing the norms of representation at party conferences had been ceded to the regional committees.[92]

Notwithstanding this, the provincial level of organization appears to have been considered a more important level of organization than the region. The powers and responsibilities to be exercised by party organs at both levels were broadly the same,[93] but the provincial conference was accorded one right not specifically granted to the regional, territory and republican bodies – the election of delegates to the national party congress.[94] But what suggests the greater importance of provincial level organizations than those at the higher sub-national levels is the attention devoted to the secretaries of the provincial committees. From 1922 the Rules declared that these people had to be confirmed by a higher party instance and established minimum periods of party membership for people taking on these positions – pre-October 1917 in 1922 (#35) and seven years in 1925 (#38).[95] From 1922 the Rules also provided for no less than three members of the provincial committee bureau to be occupied full-time in party work, a provision which was clearly meant to refer to the secretaries and reflects recognition of the need for a permanent apparatus at this level. The greater practical role that this seems to imply for the provincial committees is confirmed when it comes to frequencies of meetings: although the frequency of meetings of provincial conferences[96] and committees (and the reports the latter had to make to other bodies[97]) exhibited the same trends as at the regional level, by 1925 the frequency of provincial committee meetings was twice that of the regional committees.[98]

The next level of organization was the county, although in 1925 an area level of organization was introduced[99] to provide a party form for the area administrative division established in 1924 to cater for minority nationality groups in the RSFSR.[100] What is noteworthy about this level of organization is that in 1919, for the first time below the national level, it was felt necessary to declare that some members of the executive organ should be occupied full-time in party work.[101] In 1919 it was the secretary of the presidium of the county committee (#39), in 1922 two members (#40) and in 1925 three members of the bureau (#49);[102] at least three members of the area bureau were also to be thus employed (#43). Minimum party membership periods of three years were to apply for county committee secretaries (1922 and 1925) and five years for the area committee secretary. The provision of 1919 regarding full-time party workers marks the emergence in the Rules of that segment of the party that was to become of central importance, the full-time party apparatus. The remaining provisions on the county and area level organs were similar to those for the provincial level,[103] although they did not specify any frequency for meetings of the county committee.

The following level was that of the parish, the formal structure and responsibilities of which were similar to those of higher levels. The highest organ was the monthly general meeting of all party members in the parish, with provision made for this to be replaced by a conference in large parishes. No provision was made for how the latter might be constituted. Reflecting the closer links of these bodies with the rank-and-file, as well as many of the more general tasks allotted to higher bodies, parish level organizations had certain specific personnel responsibilities: the general meeting had power to decide questions of admission and expulsion from the party (see Note 65), after 1922 with confirmation from above, while the parish committee registered party members, organized new party cells and presented them to the county committee for confirmation, and handled agitational and propaganda activities. From 1925 the secretary of the parish committee (this post was not classed as a full-time position) had to be of one year's party standing (#54) and the committee was instructed to meet at least once a fortnight (#55); no frequency had previously been set.[104] Three other organizational innovations were introduced at this level in the

1925 Rules: provision was made for the district organization which was to be found in the urban areas and was equivalent to the parish,[105] for the organization of party matters in those parishes where there were less than three cells and no parish committee was therefore formed, and for the parish general meeting to send delegates to the county and other conferences.[106] In 1919 provision had been made for a parish auditing commission, but this was abolished in 1922 (1919, #45; 1922, #46).

The basic level of organization was the party cell. This was to have no less than three members, to be organized by the parish committee, and to be confirmed by the county, district, city (only in 1919) or area (1925) committee. Provision was made in 1919 for the division of large cells into smaller cells (#47), a provision dropped in 1922 but revived specifically on an enterprise basis in 1925 (#58).[107] The cell's task, as the link between worker and peasant masses on the one hand and leading party organs on the other, is reflected in its responsibilities: implementation of party policy, attraction and education of new members,[108] assistance in the committees' organizational and agitational work, and general participation in the economic and political life of the country. Provision was also made for an executive officer for the cell, the secretary who from 1922 had to be of at least one year's party standing, and an executive organ called the bureau which was to be elected on a monthly (1919, #49), three-monthly (1922, #49) and finally six-monthly (1925, #60) basis.[109] No specific provision was made for the cell to elect delegates to a parish level assembly, even in those cases when the parish was sufficiently large to warrant the general meeting being replaced by a conference.

The next section in the 1919 Rules concerned party discipline; in 1922 and 1925 this was preceded by sections dealing with the control commissions. Both sections can be handled together. Previous editions of the Rules had not approached the issue of discipline in a systematic fashion. This was initially subsumed by the general provisions relating to the mandatory nature of central decisions (a provision omitted in 1917) and to the expulsion of party members. The introduction of a section on discipline in 1919 reflects the continuing presence of opposition in party ranks throughout this period. The party commission charged with drawing up the draft Rules for the VIII Conference rejected the view that those Rules should include recognition of the right of every party member to his own judgement because it was deemed that this 'did not accord with the history of our party'.[110] Instead, reflecting the call for military-style discipline in the party,[111] the Rules affirmed that the maintenance of the strictest party discipline was the primary duty of all party members and organizations and declared that the decisions of party centres had to be implemented quickly and exactly (1919, #50; 1922, #51; 1925, #83). The same article also introduced a principle that was to be important in future party life: freedom of discussion of contentious issues was to exist only until a decision was reached, after which that decision was to be implemented without demur. This was a significant departure from the position espoused in the VIII Congress resolution which was generally so important as a basis for the Rules and which provided for the right of appeal against a party resolution once that resolution had been carried out.[112] That right of appeal now ceased to exist.

The Rules also made provision for the punishment of both individual party members and organizations committing 'criminal misdemeanours'. A range of punishments was listed (and amended in 1925), with the explicit rejection from 1922 of transfer to candidate status as a measure of party punishment (#52). Punishment thus became more flexible, and able to be fitted to the crime much more satisfactorily than had been the case when expulsion was the only recourse to errant action provided for in the Rules. But while punishment may have become more formalized, the same did not apply to party crimes. The 1919 Rules acknowledged the failure to implement the decisions of higher organizations as a misdemeanour (#51) and an amendment of 1927 made a member's failure to answer the questions of control commissions truthfully the subject of immediate expulsion, but no list of misdemeanours and appropriate punishments appeared in the Rules. The definition of a 'criminal misdemeanour' was left to the determination of 'public opinion in the party'. Misdemeanours were to be examined by party committees, general meetings and, after 1922, control commissions, with the decisions subject to the same general principles of confirmation which applied to other matters of importance in the party (1919, #52 and 53; 1922, #53; 1925, #83).

Control commissions were established formally at the IX Conference in September 1920[113] and first appeared in the 1922 Rules. The 1922 provisions were based directly on the X Congress resolution dealing with control commissions.[114] The commissions were established to 'strengthen the unity and authority of the party' (#50), but by 1925, when the section on these bodies had greatly expanded,[115] the commissions were also meant to attract the best part of the working class into the party, to struggle with infringements of the programme and Rules, to ensure the maintenance of the party line in the work of the soviet organs and to help improve and strengthen the soviet and economic apparatus (#61). Such formal statements do not convey the spirit in which the control commissions were created, as a response to the widespread criticisms of bureaucratism emanating from the opposition at this time.[116] The regulations governing the control commissions reflect the perceived need to have these bodies as independent tribunals to which complaints against bureaucratic excesses could be taken by individual party members. Independence from the party apparatus was to be ensured through the stipulation that these bodies should be elected by the national congress and the conferences at the regional, provincial and, after 1925, territory and area levels (1922, #50; 1925, #61). Party committees could not countermand the decisions of corresponding control commissions, but the decisions of the latter came into force only with the agreement of the former. If disagreements could not be resolved by a joint meeting, the issue was placed before the party congress/conference or a higher control commission (1922, #50; 1925, #62). Members of control commissions were forbidden to be members simultaneously of corresponding party committees (some exceptions were allowed in 1925, #64 and 69), although certain members of the commissions were empowered to attend meetings of committees, congresses and conferences in a consultative capacity. At the centre this included the formal right of designated members to attend sessions of the CC, Politburo, Orgburo and Secretariat (1925, #66 and 71).[117] Provision was also made for joint plena of the CC and the Central Control Commission at which members of both bodies enjoyed a decisive vote. This was a party forum which was to be very important in the 1920s.[118]

Membership of the commissions was to come from among workers and peasants[119] who had been party members for ten years for the national level, seven years for regional and territory levels, and five years for lower levels (1925, #63 and 68). The structure of commissions envisaged for all levels was first outlined in the 1925 Rules and was broadly uniform[120] with a Central Control Commission heading a structure of republican, regional, territory, provincial and area commissions. This structure had only bare hints of the type of co-ordination within the control commission apparatus envisaged at the XI Congress.[121] Formally, control commissions were given some directive power over members and organizations within their spheres of responsibility (#67 and 73), but the regulations for control commissions, which largely reflected the discussions at the XII

Congress,[122] were seriously deficient if they were meant to create organs independent of the party apparatus. By failing to establish an independent apparatus for them, the Rules left the commissions reliant upon the committees, from which they were meant to be independent, for their resources and for the performance of their basic administrative tasks. Furthermore, to take effect, the decisions of control commissions required the assent of the corresponding party committee. Thus if in practice the independence of these bodies was swiftly undermined,[123] the Rules provided them with no weapons to prevent this process.

Party finances were dealt with in a special section of the Rules. The source of funds for party organizations remained vague; the Rules mentioned only membership dues, subsidies from higher party organizations and other receipts (1919, #54; 1922, #54; 1925, #86). It is likely that the reference to 'other receipts' referred in part to funds transferred from the state. For the first time membership dues were pegged, being set at fixed proportions of an individual's earnings. Four grades of dues were established, but no indication was given in the Rules of the monetary boundaries of each of the grades (1919 and 1922, #55; 1925, #87).[124] Entry dues were also established, initially in rouble terms, but from 1922 in terms of proportion of earnings (1919, #56; 1922, #58; 1925, #90). Non-payment of dues for three months without a valid reason constituted automatic withdrawal from the party (1919, #58; 1922, #59; 1925, #91). A provision of the 1919 Rules establishing the financial obligations of lower party organizations to organizations at higher levels of the party structure (#59) was omitted from later versions of the Rules. This eliminated a principle which dated back to 1906 and left a gap in the Rules regarding the levels of financial support that party bodies could expect from their subordinates.

The final common section in the Rules concerned party fractions in non-party bodies. Fractions were to be formed in all bodies where there were at least three party members.[125] These were meant to liaise between the party and the body in which the members worked, ensuring that the latter followed the party line. Members of the fraction had to caucus on important issues[126] before they came up for discussion in the non-party body and to vote unanimously in that body the way the fraction as a whole had decided (1919, #65 and 66; 1922, #65 and 66; 1925, #98 and 99). The fraction was subject to normal party discipline[127] and was to work under the direct supervision of the appropriate party committee, a supervision ensured by the structural relationship envisaged between both bodies (1919, #61–64; 1922, #61–64; 1925, #94–97).[128] By 1925 fractions even had to route their contacts with fractions in lower-level bodies through the appropriate party committee (#100).[129] The fractions were clearly central to the party's aim of guiding the activities of that vast range of organizations outside the party structure.

The 1925 Rules introduced a new section that was neither in the earlier editions of the Rules nor in the draft Rules of 1925. This concerned party organization in the armed forces.[130] The hierarchy envisaged here was different from that in other sections of the party. Overall leadership of party work lay with the Political Administration of the Army (PUR) which had the status of a military department of the CC.[131] It was to exercise its leadership through appointed political departments at various levels of the armed forces, through appointed military commissars, and through party commissions elected at army conferences. Below these were cells and party collectives (#78). The precise relationship between these different bodies was not made clear in the Rules, although the role of the party commissions as the functional equivalent of the control commissions in the armed forces was evident.[132] The relationship between these organs inside the armed forces and those elected party bodies outside was clearly uneasy. Questions of personnel and discipline in the armed forces were to be led by the local party committees and control commissions, consistent with the earlier provisions of the Rules on such matters (#2 and 6), while local committees were to be kept abreast of all aspects of political life in the military (#82). However, at the same time, political departments and commissars were responsible only to the PUR, which was itself responsible to the CC, with the result that the party structure in the armed forces had a formal semi-independence from the party structure as a whole, except at the top.

Thus during the initial decade of Bolshevik rule, three editions of the Rules were introduced, each of which sought to bring a higher level of systematization to the party structure and to bring it more into line with the needs of the party in power. A hierarchical system of congresses/conferences and committees was established. General principles of responsibility were laid down and a division of power and responsibility was created, almost purely on the basis of territorial jurisdictions. Questions of membership and discipline were given more extended treatment over this time. But although the Rules contained a good deal more detail about the formal structures than they had prior to 1917, several important gaps remained. The paucity of detail about the operating procedures of executive bodies at all levels and about the nature of misdemeanours were two significant areas in which the treatment accorded by the Rules seems clearly deficient. Another area of party concern not even mentioned in the Rules was the network of party schools that was expanding during this period. But despite such gaps, the Rules do reflect two important aspects of party life: the centralization of power that came about with the construction of a more coherent political machine; and the emphasis upon discipline that was such a significant aspect of the political disputes of the period leading ultimately to Stalin's victory.

THE STALINIST PERIOD

The Rules adopted in 1925 remained in force, with the amendments of 1927, until the XVII Congress in February 1934, when they were superseded by a new party statute. The new statute ushered in a period of stability in the party's formal regulative milieu which contrasts sharply with the political upheavals of that time. New editions of the Rules were introduced in 1934, 1939 and 1952, with no amendments being made in the interim periods. The thirteen-year gap between the 1939 and 1952 Rules was the longest of any period up to that point in Soviet history. Some significant changes were made to the party structure in the Rules of this period, but with one addition the structure of the Rules remained the same as those adopted in the early part of the 1920s. The Rules were divided into sections, twelve in 1934 and 1952, thirteen in 1939. In 1934 the sections dealt with party members and their responsibilities, candidate members, groups of sympathizers, organizational structure, central organizations, territory/regional/republican organizations, city and district organizations, primary organizations, party organizations in the Red Army, party groups in non-party organizations, intra-party democracy and party discipline, and finances. In 1939 the section on groups of sympathizers was omitted, sections on area organization and the Komsomol were added, and the scope of a number of sections changed, while remaining basically concerned with the same areas as in 1934. In 1952 the separate section on party discipline was omitted; also omitted in 1952 was a major structural innovation in the 1934 Rules, the preamble.

The preamble consisted of a series of broad statements of principle about the nature of the party and its role. The party's place in the international communist movement was emphasized along with its role as the 'leading organized detachment' of the Soviet working class. Reflecting the claimed achievement of socialism in 1936, the task of the party changed from 'the struggle for the dictatorship of the proletariat, for the victory of socialism . . . the successful construction of socialist society' in 1934 to 'the struggle for the strengthening of the dictatorship of the working class, for the strengthening and development of the socialist structure, for the victory of communism . . . the successful construction of the communist society' in 1939. Furthermore, the party's leadership over 'the proletariat, the working peasantry and all the working masses' in 1934 had become by 1939 'the working class, peasantry, intelligentisia, of all the Soviet people'. The preambles in both Rules also placed significant emphasis upon the need for unity and discipline in the party with the first reference to the inadmissibility of fractional groupings and, in 1939, to the purge as a general principle of party operation. The latter Rules also established the theory of Marxism–Leninism as the guide for the party and, in a phrase which foreshadowed the 1977 state constitution, referred to the party as 'the leading nucleus of all the organizations of the workers'. Both preambles finished with a short statement about the responsibilities of party membership, couched in broad terms of general principle. A separate preamble was omitted from the 1952 Rules, although elements of those from 1934 and 1939 were included in #1 of the 1952 statute.

The first section of the Rules dealt with party membership. In all three editions of the Rules this section was more extensive than it had been in the 1920s. This was reflected in the changing title of the section to include members' responsibilities in 1934 and, from 1939, their rights also.

The definition of a party member remained unchanged from that of 1925 in the 1934 and 1939 Rules (#1), but had substantial additions in 1952. To the existing elements were added the provisions that a member had to be a working person who did not exploit the labour of another; a Soviet citizen; had to accept and assist in the implementation of the party Rules and programme; and not merely to submit to party decisions but to carry them out (#2). The party member of 1952 was envisaged as a much more active individual than in 1934 or 1939, a fact reflected in the dramatic expansion in the enumerated responsibilities of the party member in 1952. In 1934 three responsibilities were listed (#2), in 1939 four (#2) and in 1952 eleven (#3). In some respects the expansion of 1952 was more apparent than real. A number of the additions could easily have been subsumed under more general statements appearing in the earlier Rules; generally the additions strengthen the emphasis upon discipline and unity and a high level of exactingness in work.[133] Nevertheless, the fact that these points were now listed separately, and thereby given increased prominence, indicates the creation of expectations in the party about higher levels of performance on the part of party members.

As well as the responsibilities of a party member, the Rules of 1939 and 1952 also listed the rights party members were to enjoy. These remained the same in both Rules (1939, #3; 1952, #4) and concerned the right to participate in the discussion of policy and personnel performance up to the level of the CC, and to participate in the party electoral process as both voter and candidate. The rights were presented as broad statements of principle with no indication of the mechanisms about how they might operate.

Admission to the party remained via the candidate stage and, reflecting a rejection of some of the admission practices associated with the 1920s, was to be carried out on an individual basis. In 1934 new members were to have completed the candidate stage and be politically literate, as in 1925, but they were also to have mastered the party programme and Rules. In 1939 and 1952 this final provision was replaced by the injunction that workers, peasants and intelligentsia could be admitted to the party if they were 'conscious, active and devoted to the cause of communism' (1939, #4; 1952, #5). Changing criteria of desirability of different sources of recruitment were also evident during this period: in 1934 the bias in favour of proletarian recruitment had been maintained, but in the middle of that decade the emphasis shifted toward recruiting 'the best and foremost people'.[134] This shift of focus away from social origin to personal quality is reflected in the way in which the Rules dealt with the admission question. The 1934 Rules established four categories from which members would be drawn (#3). The categories differed from the three established in 1925 (#2) principally by a differentiation within the industrial working class between those with five years' experience and those with less. The other categories remained broadly the same, with some adjustments to take account of the effect of agricultural collectivization and the development of industry in the First Five Year Plan period. In line with the emphasis upon proletarian recruitment, entry was easier for the first two (worker) categories than for the others, and easiest of all for the most experienced industrial workers.

This complicated category system was abolished in 1939. Henceforth, all who entered the party required recommendations from three party members of three years' standing who had worked with the candidate for at least one year. These new provisions for all entrants (except former members of other parties who were dealt with separately) were less stringent than the requirements for those of the most privileged first category in the 1934 Rules and are consistent with the desire to regenerate the party after the decimation wrought by the purges. The new policy was also reflected in the devolution of the power of confirmation of membership to the district or city level in 1939 (#4(b)) and 1952 (#4(b)) compared with the regional or territory committe or CC of the national communist party for categories two and three in 1934 (#3(c)). From 1939 prospective members had to be at least eighteen years of age (#4); previously no age criterion had existed.

The 1939 Rules also introduced three changes in the area of recommendations, all of which were carried forward into 1952. Henceforth members and candidates of the CC were forbidden to provide recommendations for prospective members because of fears that recommendations from such a source could unduly influence local authorities,[135] while those who gave recommendations were now given the option of participating in the discussion about the admission of those they recommended (1939, #4(a) & (b); 1952, #5(a) & (b)). In addition, the responsibility of those who provided recommendations was phrased purely in terms of the quality of their recommendations rather than the more open-ended responsibility for those they had recommended of the 1934 Rules (1934, #4; 1939, #5; 1952, #6).

This section of the Rules also dealt with the question of the expulsion of party members. A number of changes were made here. While decisions on expulsion remained the responsibility of the organization of which the person was a member, as in 1925, in 1934 the level at which that decision had to be confirmed was changed: those from the third and fourth categories were to be confirmed at the city or district level while those who were presumed to be more reliable because of their proletarian background (categories one and two) had to be confirmed at higher levels, the region or territory (#8). In 1939 and 1952 decisions on expulsion by the primary party organization were to be confirmed by the city or district committee, which were in turn verified by the regional or territory committee or CC of the communist party of a union republic (1939, #9; 1952, #10). A significant restriction on the power of a PPO to take decisions about expulsions (and also about transfer to candidate status) was introduced in 1952. Such decisions about members of party committees from the district level up could not be taken by the PPO to which that member belonged, but could be taken only by a two-thirds vote in the committee of which that person was a member; CC members were explicitly included in this (see below p. 53) (#11 and 12). In this way the power of expulsion of leading figures at the district level and above was removed from the hands of the primary organizations and vested in the relevant committee. The role of the control commissions in expulsion, introduced in 1922 and expanded in 1925, was omitted in 1934.

The attitude to people facing expulsion also seems to have shifted during this period. The 1934 Rules repeated the provisions of 1925 that members were to be suspended from party work once the local organization had decided on expulsion pending confirmation of that decision at a higher level, and expulsions and the reasons for them were to be reported in the party press (#8). In 1939 and 1952, this position was replaced by the statement that, pending confirmation, the person remained a member of the party and retained the right to attend closed party meetings (1939 and 1952, #10). The provision about publication of expulsions was retained in 1939 but omitted in 1952. The latter two Rules also included injunctions about carefully investigating the charges against members (1939, #11; 1952, #14)[136] and the need for the mobilization of education and influence in response to petty misdemeanours (1939, #11; 1952, #14); provision was also made for appeal against expulsion (1939, #12; 1952, #15). New provisions in 1952 dealt with the treatment of party members who committed crimes punishable in a court of law (#13) and reintroduced the provision omitted in 1922 of transfer to candidate status as a form of punishment (#14). The only other major change to this section during this period was the introduction in 1934 of provision for periodic party purges, including a list of categories of people from whom the party must be cleansed (#9). This was omitted from subsequent party statutes.[137]

The section on party membership thus underwent important changes during this period, particularly in the areas of the duties and responsibilities of members, admission and expulsion. Only two major changes were made in the section devoted to candidate membership. When recruitment categories were abolished in 1939, the candidate stage was set at one year (#15), and in 1952 greater detail was provided about the steps to be taken if, during the course of candidacy, a person was unable to satisfy the PPO that he or she was worthy of admission as a full member of the party (#18). This article clearly established the principle that the candidate stage was no mere formality and, along with the expansion of the discussion of members' responsibilities, reflects a higher level of party demand upon party members.

The only other major innovation in the membership area, and one which was not carried into 1939, was the establishment of groups of sympathizers (1934, #15–17).[138] The groups were envisaged as a preliminary stage to party entry for those desiring such entry but prevented from realizing this by the ban on recruitment that accompanied the purge instituted in January 1933. When recruitment recommenced,[139] these groups became irrelevant and this section was omitted.

The following section of the Rules was concerned with the organizational structure of the party and, from 1939, intra-party democracy. A number of significant developments occurred in this section of the Rules during this period. The most important was the elaboration of the principles of democratic centralism. This formula had been left undefined in earlier party statutes, but in 1934 it was outlined in the form which it substantially retains (with one important addition) to this day (#18). Democratic centralism consisted of four elements:[140] the elective character of all leading organs,[141] periodic reporting by party organs to their organizations, strict party discipline and the subordination of the minority to the majority, and the mandatory character of the decisions of higher organs for lower.[142] This formula sought to combine centralized leadership with popular control. The latter was to be achieved through elections, principles of accountability and the subordination of minority to majority. The former was reflected in strict party discipline and the mandatory character of leading organs' decisions. The centralist and democratic elements, seemingly inconsistent, could be co-ordinated only through the introduction of the notion of a mandate. The Rules established that higher-standing bodies were regularly accountable to and elected by representatives of the party rank-and-file, and between these elections decisions of these bodies were mandatory for all within the area of competence of the body concerned. Implicit in this is the notion of a mandate: the rank-and-file agree to pass their mandate over to the leading bodies and to obey them until the time comes for that mandate to be renewed, a process which confirms the principle of rank-and-file sovereignty. Through this mechanism, the elements of democratic centralism were not inconsistent, at least in principle.

The concern for intra-party democracy reflected in the title of this section in the 1939 and 1952 Rules is evident in a number of provisions which do not appear in this section of the 1934 Rules. A new provision of 1939 forbade the use of voting lists in party elections; voting was to take place by separate candidate and by secret ballot, with an unlimited right to challenge and criticize candidates (1939, #23; 1952, #26).[143] Provision was also made for *aktivs* (the leading or most active members of an organization) to meet to discuss the most important decisions of party and government (1939, #24; 1952, #27). In addition, #57 in the 1934 Rules, originally introduced in a 1927 amendment, was moved into this section of the Rules in 1939 (1939, #25; 1952, #28). This provided for the discussion of party policy by party members, declaring this to be an inalienable right flowing from the principles of intra-party democracy. However, such a right of discussion had to be exercised in such a way that it contributed to self-criticism and party discipline rather than leading to disunity and a weakening of the party. Therefore, it was argued, wide party discussion could take place only on the basis of the conditions laid down by the 1927 amendment discussed above. This section of the Rules therefore combined two matters: the right of the individual party member to discuss and criticize party policy; and the conditions under which party-wide discussion could take place. However, by couching the rights of discussion in terms of the duty not to breach party discipline, the Rules impose conditions which seriously limit the principles of free discussion which are described as the inalienable right of the party member.

This section also included general provisions relating to the organizational structure of the party. A schema of organization based on territorial divisions was outlined in the same manner as the earlier Rules, although some of the specific levels differed reflecting changes in the administrative structure of the country. As well as the territorial principle, that of production was declared to be basic to the party's structure (1934 and 1939, #19; 1952, #22). Democratic centralism was to operate within geographical and production frameworks, subordinating organs within those areas or production units to organs serving those areas/units as a whole, thereby reasserting the dominance of the central organs noted above. This was reinforced by the provision that the autonomy of local organs in local decision-making extended only in so far as those decisions did not contradict decisions of the party, meaning its higher organs (1934 and 1939, #20; 1952, #23). Although in 1939 the provision which explicitly established the order of 'subordination, accountability, the passage and questioning of party decisions' (1925, #18; 1934, #24) was eliminated, the principle was effectively embodied in the discussion of democratic centralism, the right of discussion and the formal organizational structure.

The only other major change to this section related to the right of party committees to establish departments to deal with particular areas of responsibility, first introduced in 1919. The changes in the 1930s reflect the reorganizations of party secretariats at the national, republican, regional and territory levels at the XVII and XVIII Congresses. In 1934, the departments had rested on an 'integral-production branch' basis. This meant that all aspects of, for example, agriculture were handled in the Agriculture Department, whether personnel, verification of the implementation of decisions, supervision of lower organs, or agitation and propaganda. However, by 1939 this was deemed to be inefficient and was replaced by departments established principally along functional lines[144] so that, for example, all aspects of personnel work across all fields of concern were the responsibility of the Cadres Department. In the 1934 and 1939 Rules the names of the departments of each committee were enumerated, thereby presenting an organizational chart of the party bureaucracy which was meant to serve committees at each level. It should be noted, however, that the lists in 1939 are incomplete, excluding the Special Sector and the Administration of Affairs or Chancellery. The importance attached to agitation and propaganda and to personnel matters is reflected in the injunction in the 1939 Rules that leadership of these departments in regional and territory committees and the CCs of the communist parties of the union republics should be entrusted to special secretaries. The provision relating to these departments was omitted from the 1952 Rules.

Turning to the central organizations of the party, or as they were called from 1939, higher organs, several important changes were made during this period. The frequency of party congresses, which had been held every two years following the 1927 amendment, became once every three years in 1934 (#27) and once every four years in 1952 (#29). Similarly, the frequency of CC meetings declined from once every two months in 1925 to once every four months in 1934 and 1939 (#31 and 34) and to once every six months in 1952 (#33). The formal powers of both bodies also underwent some change. In 1934 the congress acquired the power to nominate the membership of the Commission of Soviet Control (#29), but it lost this in 1939 when the CC was accorded the power to form the Party Control Commission, or, as it was called in 1952, the Committee of Party Control (1939, #34;

1952, #35).[145] The structure and powers of the control organs were discussed in a much more abbreviated fashion than they had been in 1925 in all three editions of the Rules during this period. In 1934 the control organs were to supervise the implementation of party and CC decisions and deal with those who violated party discipline or ethics (#36). Verification of the work of local party organizations was added to this list in 1939 while the concern for party ethics was replaced by an emphasis upon the party programme and Rules (#35). In 1952 some indication was given about what constituted an infringement of the restored party ethics, the power to examine appeals against expulsion was given to the Committee of Party Control, and it was granted the right to have its own representatives independent from local party organs (#35). In 1934 and 1939 the independence from the committee structure that this and the earlier Rules had sought to establish does not appear to have been considered important, with the result that no provision was made for this in the Rules of those years.

The CC retained the right under these Rules to form executive organs, but they underwent some change in 1952. The Politburo was now called the Presidium and its task was described as leadership of the work of the CC between plena of that body (#34). This was the first time that the Rules had explicitly accorded this power to the CC's leading executive organ. At the same time the Orgburo disappeared from the Rules[146] while the functions of the Secretariat were described in a slightly expanded form: 'leadership of current work, chiefly the organization of verification of the implementation of decisions of the party and the selection of cadres'. The Secretariat was thus clearly identified as the means through which the CC exercised general guidance of the party and, more specifically, wielded its power over the distribution of party forces.[147]

In 1939 provisions were introduced making for annual All-Union conferences of representatives of local party organizations (#37–39), thereby reviving the type of conference envisaged in 1922 (#26). Its powers were to be restricted to discussion of pressing questions and the renewal of up to 20 per cent of the composition of the CC. The decisions of such conferences were subject to confirmation by the CC, except for those decisions dealing with CC membership. The provisions dealing with the conference were omitted in 1952.

This section of the Rules also made specific provision for the creation of political departments and the assignment of party organizers by the CC (1934, #34; 1939, #40; 1952, #37).[148] Despite the same name, these were not the same type of departments referred to in the earlier discussion. Rather than being bureaucratic departments servicing party committees, these were to be bodies especially created to deal with particular problems of economic construction. They were to be means of by-passing the normal territorial structure of the party and of establishing what virtually amounted to *ad hoc* bodies at the places where the problems occurred. They were to work directly under the CC through the departments of the Secretariat enumerated earlier in the Rules (1934, #25; 1939, #27), and once the particular problem had been overcome, they could be transformed into normal party organs on the production-territorial principle (PPOs). These bodies were clearly envisaged as means for the centre to establish direct control over lagging sectors of the economy without being constrained by the territorially-based party structure.

The drift toward greater centralization evident during the earlier period was also clear in the Rules of this period. The growing infrequency of meetings of the congress and CC reflect the inability of these bodies to exercise ongoing real power even if political considerations had been such as to make such a role possible. The greater attention devoted to the executive organs, principally in the form of the increased detail on the departments of the party secretariat, is consistent with the expanded functions such bodies had to carry out at this time. The central intervention into local levels through the other type of department is also consistent with the trend toward greater centralism. The apparent autonomy of the Committee of Party Control in 1952 does not conflict with this trend because this organ, like all others in the party, was subject to the principles of democratic centralism and therefore to general control by the central party organs.

Party structure below the party centre was significantly streamlined during this period. The 1934 Rules had three basic levels between the central organs and the PPOs, those of the regional/territory/republican organizations and of the city and district organizations. The 1939 and 1952 Rules also made provision for an area level of organization. The provincial, county and parish levels of 1925 disappeared. The highest organ of the regional/territory/republican level remained the conference or congress, which was now to meet every eighteen months rather than annually as in 1925.[149] The powers of the conference/congress remained as before with one addition, discussed below, and it was now explicitly stated that their activities would be guided by the general decisions of the AUCP(b) and its leading organs (1934, #38, 1939, #43; 1952, #60). From 1934, committees were to be convened at three-monthly intervals (1934, #42; 1939, #47), a frequency which reverted to the 1925 regularity of two months in 1952 (#44).[150] The only change to the powers of the committees in 1934 and 1939 was the extension of their guidance over party groups in non-party organizations (1934, #41; 1939, #46). In 1952 their enumerated responsibilities were extended again to include the implementation of party directives, concern for the performance and education of party members, direction of the activities of the soviets and public organizations (basically a reformulation of the addition to these bodies' powers made in 1934 and 1939 noted above) and the systematic presentation of reports on their activities to the CC (#43). The operational effectiveness of the committees was enhanced by the provision that these bodies could *choose* executive organs (changed to *elect* those organs in 1952) for the conduct of current work. In addition, they could install secretaries to serve both the executive organ and the committee itself. In 1934 and 1939 the secretaries were to be elected separately from the executive organ and it is not clear that, formally at least, they were to be members of that body. This was rectified in 1952, when they were to be elected as part of the executive organ (1952, #42; compare 1934, #40 and 1939, #45).[151] In 1934 the number of secretaries was set at two, 1939, four to five and 1952, three.[152] However, it was not until 1952 that formal provision was made for the establishment of secretariats at this level. These bodies were to be formally responsible to the executive organs of the regional/territory/republican committees, and minimum periods of party membership were set for the secretaries; similar minimum periods were not set for ordinary committee members, reflecting the importance of the secretariat in the party structure. Both secretaries and committee members were subject to CC confirmation.

The area level of organization introduced in 1939 was similar to that of the region/territory/republic. The area conference was to meet once every eighteen months (1939, #49; 1952, #46) compared with the annual frequency of 1925. The enumerated responsibilities were narrower than those of the region/territory/republic, being concerned solely with domestic party matters. The committee's responsibilities were wider, mirroring those at the next higher level, including the expansion of 1952 noted above (1939, #51; 1952, #48). The frequency of committee meetings was not set in 1939 but was set at a month and a half in 1952 (#47); this compared with one month in 1925. Provision was made for the committee to elect an executive organ and a number of secretaries. Only in 1952 were these secretaries clearly designated as members of the executive organ (called the bureau), as at the higher level (1939, #50; 1952, #47). The importance of the secretaries is again reflected in the setting of a minimum period of party membership for them and the need for their confirmation at the next level, neither provision being specifically made for the ordinary committee members. Generally, the treatment of the area-level organs is less extensive than it was in 1925.

The city and district levels of the party organization were discussed in very similar terms to the regional/territory/republican organs. The regular conference was to be convened annually. Its powers were much narrower than those of the regional/territory/republican organs, focusing purely on domestic, party housekeeping matters, and seem to have constituted the model for the area level organizations discussed above. The city and district committees were to exercise the standard array of functions accorded to party committees, and therefore had wider enumerated responsibilities than the conference to which they were responsible, but in addition they had specific responsibility for organizing and confirming PPOs and keeping records of all communists. The powers of the committees were expanded in 1952 in the same terms as the committees at the higher levels discussed above (1934, #46; 1939, #54; 1952, #51). A minimum party membership period was specified for secretaries, significantly lower in 1939 and 1952 than 1934, but not for committee members, and from 1952 the secretaries were explicitly declared to be part of the bureau elected by the committees (1934, #45 and 46; 1939, #53; 1952, #50). The frequency of committee meetings was not fixed until 1939, when it was set at one and a half months, a frequency increased to one month in 1952 (1939, #55; 1952, #52). A final article made provision for the establishment of district organizations in large cities subordinate to the city committee.

The 1934 Rules for the first time spelled out the system of indirect elections which still operates in the party. In 1925 those levels immediately below the national level, the regional, territory and republican levels, were not formally empowered to send delegates to the national congress. This was rectified in the 1934 Rules which empowered city and district party conferences to elect delegates to the territory or regional conference or congress of the republican communist party which in turn elected delegates to the national congress. From 1939 the area conference had the same powers as the city and district bodies in this regard. But in one respect this structure of indirect elections as set out in the Rules lacked a base: explicit provision was not made in the Rules for PPOs to send delegates to the city or district conference.

The next section of the Rules was an almost total revision of the discussion of basic level party organizations, now called primary party organizations. These were to be formed in all organizations and institutions where there were at least three party members and confirmed by district or city committees or by an appropriate political department as provided for earlier in the Rules. Provision was also made for the establishment of a party presence in organizations where there were less than three party members (1934, #48; 1939, #57; 1952, #54) and of sub-units in big organizations where there was a large party membership (1934, #49; 1939, #58 and 59; 1952, #55 and 56).[153] As the basic link between leading party organs and the population, the PPOs had responsibility for agitation and propaganda, the attraction of new members into the party and general assistance to higher party organs. From 1952 they were also responsible for the political education of their members and for the development of criticism and self-criticism. The PPOs also had an important role in production. They were to mobilize the workers for the achievement of production plans, the strengthening of labour discipline and shock work (until 1952) and socialist competition (from 1939). They were also to struggle with deficiencies in the management of enterprises and in the living and working conditions of workers and *kolkhozniks* (1934, #50; 1939, #60; 1952, #57). In the 1939 Rules the ability of the PPOs to exercise a supervisory role over the management of work in enterprises was enhanced by extending their rights of supervision over administration in these bodies. Such supervisory functions could not be exercised in people's commissariats (ministries from 1952) where their role was much more advisory in nature (1939, #61; 1952, #58).

It was not until 1952 that the highest organ of the PPO was specified, this being the monthly general meeting of the organization (#54). From the outset provision was made for the creation of executive organs of the PPO (1934, #51; 1939, #62; 1952, #59). In party organizations with no less than fifteen members a committee or, after 1939, a bureau, was elected; those with less than fifteen members chose a party organizer or, after 1939, elected a party secretary. In those party organizations with less than a hundred members, party positions were filled in a part-time capacity; for PPOs over that size, full-time administrative positions were established. Minimum party membership periods of two years in 1934 and one year in 1939 were set for these secretarial positions. Thus from 1934 the full-time party bureaucracy had its roots in the larger PPOs. A signal of the importance with which the party leaders invested the role of the PPOs in the people's commissariats was the provision from 1939 that the secretaries of PPOs in the commissariats were subject to confirmation by the CC.

In 1939 a new section relating to the Komsomol was introduced into the Rules. This body had previously been mentioned only in connection with its role as the mandatory channel for youths wishing to enter the party (1934, #3(f)). While it now retained this role, the Komsomol was also charged with assisting the party in state and economic construction, carrying out party decisions and exercising a watching brief over the performance of primarily economic institutions. The Komsomol had the same organizational structure as the party except for the PPOs and was to work under direct party supervision at all levels. Upon joining the party, a member of the Komsomol left that organization unless he/she filled an executive position, a provision which helped to ensure that all leading positions in the Komsomol were filled by party members. This section was carried virtually without change into the 1952 Rules.

The following section dealt with party organization in the army, expanded in 1939 and 1952 to include the navy and transport. The main difference between the 1934 Rules and those of 1925 was the increased length of party membership required for heads of political departments (1925, #79; 1934, #53) and the omission of provisions relating to the role of party commissions, local committees and control commissions in personnel matters (1925, #80–82). The provisions of 1934 were carried forward into the later Rules with little other than terminological changes reflecting the expansion of the focus of this section noted above. One terminological change should be noted. The reference to 'military commissars' in 1925 and 1939 was replaced in 1934 by 'military commissars (assistants for political affairs)', a change which reflects oscillations in party policy on unity of command in the armed forces.[154] Thus the principles of the structure of party organization in the military remained basically unchanged, with vertical responsibility to the CC and horizontal links to the local committees, although the precise relationship between civilian and military party organs at each level remained unclear in the Rules. In practice, the military organs were largely independent of their civilian counterparts,[155] a power relationship reflected in the move away from military commissars independent of the military commander noted in the textual change above; the emphasis in the commissar's responsibilities lay on political education, organization and military efficiency rather than supervision over military decisions.

The next section concerned party groups (called fractions in 1925) in non-party organizations. This section, which was carried from 1934 into the later Rules with only minor textual amendments, differed from that which preceded it through a number of substantial omissions. Omitted were provisions concerning representation of fractions in party committees when the work of the fraction is being discussed (#94); the rights of the committees with regard to personnel in the fractions; the fraction's autonomy in its internal affairs; the resolution of committee-fraction disputes (#95); the way in which the fraction operates in non-party organizations (#96–99); and fractions' links with other fractions (#100). The major addition in 1934 concerned the party groups' tasks. To the strengthening of the party's influence and the execution of its policy was added a concern for party and Soviet discipline, the struggle with bureaucratism and the verification of the implementation of party and soviet directives (#55). The group was to elect a secretary for current work, was to be subordinate to the appropriate party committee and was to follow strictly the decisions of leading party organs.

The penultimate section in the 1934 Rules was entitled 'On Intra-Party Democracy and Party Discipline', retitled 'Penalties for Violations of Party Discipline' in 1939 and omitted as a separate section in 1952. The initial article of this section in the 1934 Rules was that relating to freedom of discussion in the party, which was transferred to Section III of the 1939 and 1952 Rules, as discussed above. The section went on to affirm that the maintenance of party unity was the principal responsibility of all party members and organizations (1934, #58; 1939, #72). In 1934 a provision was introduced for the punishment of members of the CC and the Party Control Commission who violated party discipline (1934, #58; 1939, #74). Their cases were to be judged in a CC plenum attended by all members of the Party Control Commission.[156] In 1939 the reference to the control commission was eliminated, leaving CC members to be judged solely by their CC colleagues whose decision necessitated a two-thirds vote (presumably of all members because no reference was made which should have restricted it only to those present). In 1952 the congress was accorded the right to judge the cases of CC members, with the CC itself exercising this prerogative between congresses. The Rules repeated the range of punishments for misdemeanours, but again without specifying those misdemeanours (1934, #59; 1939, #73). Most of these provisions were moved in the 1952 Rules into the section dealing with party membership (#12–14). The provision introduced in 1927 about the expulsion of anyone who failed to answer truthfully the questions of the control commissions was not carried forward from the 1934 Rules.

The final section of the Rules dealt with party finances. The sources of party income were almost the same as in 1925, with the exception that subsidies from higher organizations were replaced by income from party enterprises. The bulk of this section was taken up with the issue of membership dues. In 1934 and 1939 there were seven categories of members based upon their monthly earnings. For the five lower categories, dues were expressed in monetary terms; for the upper two categories, in proportion of monthly earnings (1934, #62; 1939, #76). In 1952 the categories were reduced to five and all were expressed in terms of percentage of earnings. Entry dues were reduced in 1934 to 2 per cent earnings.

The three congresses at which these three party statutes were adopted were very different affairs. The XVII 'Congress of Victors' opened in 1934 in the wake of the enormous struggle and mass dislocation resulting from agricultural collectivization and the First Five Year Plan. It was also at a time when there was some high level disquiet over Stalin's power and his policies but when the excitement of building a new society remained at a high level. The XVIII Congress convened in 1939. The war clouds were gathering in Europe, socialism had officially been achieved in the USSR, the party and system had just been subjected to the terror and the purges, Stalin was totally dominant and vigilance was the watchword. The XIX Congress opened in 1952 with post-war reconstruction well advanced, Stalin personally dominant, political structures becoming set in their ways and some uneasiness about the possibility of a further unleashing of the terror. These different contexts are reflected in the way the successive editions of the Rules handled the discipline issue. The tensions created by a high level of popular opposition to the collectivization campaign and the purges are reflected in the much greater emphasis given to the question of discipline in 1934 and 1939 compared with the less tumultuous post-war period. But other aspects of the Rules clearly reflect the longevity of the system: the easing of entrance requirements and the lessening of mandatory periods of party membership for tenure of executive positions are instances of this. The concern for economic production is reflected in the much greater attention devoted to the party's tasks in this area. More generally the party's transition to a more regularized organization (which is not to say that in practice it functioned in a regularized way throughout this period) may be suggested by the increased emphasis upon the duties, responsibilities and rights of party members. And finally, there was an emphasis upon the more democratic aspects of the party's structure,[157] an emphasis consistent with the claims about the achievement of socialism. These two strands of discipline and democracy seem graphically to highlight the symbolic importance of the principles of democratic centralism.

THE POST-STALIN PERIOD

The Rules adopted in 1952 just prior to Stalin's death were amended at the XX Congress in 1956 and replaced by a new statute at the XXII Congress in 1961. This edition of the Rules, amended in 1966 and 1971, remained in force until replaced by a new statute at the XXVII Congress in February–March 1986. Both the 1961 and 1986 Rules were the subject of prolonged public discussion in the periods between the publication of the respective drafts and the adoption of the final versions at the two party congresses. There were no changes of consequence between the draft and the adopted version in 1961, but there were some interesting changes in 1986.[158]

The post-Stalin Rules restored a preamble and contained ten sections. In 1961 these dealt with party members and their responsibilities and rights; candidate members; organizational structure and intra-party democracy; higher organs; party organizations at the republican, territory, regional, area, city and district levels; primary party organizations; Komsomol; organization in the army; groups in non-party organizations; and finances. In 1986 the penultimate section was concerned with the party and state and public organizations. Basically the same ground was covered in these Rules as in 1952, the reduction in the number of sections resulting from the consolidation of three sections concerning party organization between the national and lowest levels into one.

The 1961 preamble is almost entirely new, with only a few phrases carried forward from #1 of the 1952 Rules. It echoes the tenor of the new party programme adopted at the same time. However, many of the sentiments expressed in the preamble are to be found in earlier editions of the Rules: the party's uniting of the most conscious part of the working class, kolkhoz peasantry and intelligentsia, its leadership in the achievement of socialism, its unity, discipline and monolithic cohesion which has no room for factions,[159] its following of the tenets of Marxism–Leninism, and its part in the international communist and workers' movement had all been included at various times in the Rules even if some of them had, in the interim, been omitted. But there were a number of elements that were new. Reflecting one of Khrushchev's major innovations, and one which has not disappeared despite the dismantling of many of his changes, is the reference to 'the party of all the Soviet people'. This constituted formal recognition of the implicit assumption behind the formally non-discriminatory recruiting policy introduced in 1939. Furthermore, the party was now said to exist for and to serve the people. In a reference reflecting one of the major thrusts of Khrushchev's approach to the question of Stalin, the CPSU was said to base its work on, *inter alia*, 'unswerving observance of leninist norms of party life, the principle of the collectivity of leadership, the all-round development of intra-party democracy. . .' Provision was also made for the 'creative development' of Marxism–Leninism. The tone of the preamble seemed to suggest a party that was more flexible and open to society that it had been before.

The preamble of the 1986 Rules also reflects the tenor of the party programme introduced at the same time. This is particularly clearly shown in the references to the need for the planned all-round perfection of socialism and the advance to communism on the basis of accelerated socio-economic development, and to 'the world system of socialism', relations with peoples struggling for national and social liberation, and the quest for peace. The preamble also introduces two new bases upon which the work of the party was said to rest. The 1961 preamble had mentioned intra-party democracy, and in 1986 this was joined by democratic centralism and, reflecting a prominent theme of the first year of Mikhail Gorbachev as General Secretary, the need for wide publicity and openness in the party's operations. The preamble also had three other innovations: it referred to the unity of 'the multinational Soviet society', to 'the state of the entire people', and in a provision introduced only in the final draft, to the country having entered the stage of developed socialism. These changes are interesting for the question of ideological development in the Soviet Union, particularly in the light of the omission from the 1986 preamble of the reference to the party being guided by the teaching of Marxism–Leninism and the party programme.[160]

The first section of the Rules dealt with party membership. The definition of membership has been altered through the omission of the 1952 stipulation that a potential member must be a working person who does not exploit the labour of others and actively assists in the implementation of the party Rules and programme. To the other elements of the 1952 definition: Soviet citizenship; acceptance of the programme and Rules; work in a party organization; and implementation of party decisions and payment of membership dues, was added the need to participate in the construction of communism (#1). This provision was carried forward unchanged from the 1961 Rules into those of 1986.

The article on the responsibilities of the party member underwent wholesale revision in 1961. In broad terms, the responsibilities involved active participation in economic work; creation of a living link between the party and the mass of the population; provision of an example through participation in public life; participation in ideological education and struggle; support for socialist internationalism; strengthening of party unity; observance of 'party spirit'; implementation of the party line on personnel questions; observation of party and state discipline; and the strengthening of the Soviet defence might (#2). Although not fully spelled out until 1961, there were suggestions of some of these in the 1952 Rules, but the most significant change was in the expectations that seemed to be involved in this description of the members' responsibilities. Party members were clearly expected to be much more active in all areas of life than any of the previous editions of the Rules seemed to suggest. This was particularly the case in the economic sphere, where the Rules seem to have given party members a much more extensive role in increasing production than was the case in 1952 (1961, #2(a); compare 1952, #3(c)). In an interesting juxtaposition, this increased emphasis upon active involvement seems to have been accompanied by a downgrading of emphasis upon party unity; this headed the list of responsibilities in 1952 but was sixth on the list in 1961.

In the 1986 Rules the broad areas of a member's responsibilities remained substantially unchanged, although they were reorganized and various aspects of the wording changed. There was still a very strong emphasis upon the activity of the party member in all aspects of life, particularly the economic. The most important change was in the perception of the qualities demanded by the party member, with an increased emphasis upon the moral qualities which a party member should display (#2(e) & (h)). This emphasis in part compensates for the omission from the 1986 Rules of the moral code of the communist which had been part of the 1961 Rules (see below); indeed many of the qualities which were demanded in the latter are now referred to in the preamble. Such an emphasis on the need for high moral qualities on the part of the communist is consistent with the post-Brezhnev emphasis upon the need to improve individual performance and, through that, economic performance. The inclusion of 'eyewash', 'bureaucratism' and 'departmentalism' in the list of shortcomings against which the party member must struggle (#2(g)) is consonant with this theme.

The article on the rights of party members was also rewritten in 1961 (and then carried forward virtually unchanged to 1986), but the essence of those rights remained substantially as they had been in 1952: to participate in party elections as voter and candidate, to criticize any communist in a party forum, to participate in a party forum when his/her activities and behaviour were under discussion, and to address questions, proposals or statements to any party instance and get a reply to the substance of the address. Two major innovations were made in 1961. The first made suppression of criticism or persecution of critics grounds for party punishment. The second made the right of free discussion of party policy and activities in party fora subject to the proviso that the organization concerned had not reached a decision on that issue. Once a decision was reached such discussion had to cease (#3). This was a revival of the provision introduced in 1919 (#50) and dropped in 1925.

Admission has remained on an individual basis, only via the candidate stage, and open to all who had reached eighteen years of age. The requirement that youth up to and including the age of twenty enter the party only through the Komsomol, which dated back to the 1922 Rules, was changed to twenty-three by an amendment of 1966 and twenty-five in the 1986 Rules.[161] Some changes to admission procedure have also been introduced. Those wishing to enter the party were to present the recommendations of three members of at least three years' party standing, amended to five years in 1966, who had known the person for at least twelve months through 'common productive and public work'. This reference to 'common productive and public work' was introduced in 1961 and reflects the emphasis upon the communist working in society that was so evident at this time. The question of admission continued to be handled by the general meeting of the PPO, after 1966 admission being by a mandatory two-thirds majority, and confirmed at the district or city level. In 1986 in line with the injunction about increased publicity of party operations, it was declared that admission was to take place at open party meetings, a procedure which was meant to enable non-party members to contribute to the discussion of the person's worth (#4(b)). The effect of these changes was to make entry to the party a more taxing process.[162]

The provisions on the responsibility of those giving recommendations, on party seniority and on registration and transfer of members have remained essentially unchanged from 1952, despite significant changes in the wording of these articles (1952, #6, 7 and 8; 1961 and 1986, #5, 6 and 7). An interesting addition was made in 1986 whereby those recommending individuals for party membership were obliged to give those they were supporting 'assistance in their ideological–political growth' (#5), a provision which again reflects the concern for the ideological/moral qualities of party members, particularly new recruits.

From 1961, failure to pay membership dues has no longer been met with automatic dismissal from the party, but should investigation prove that there are no valid reasons for such delinquency in payment, the member will be considered to have left the party (#8). Misbehaviour or failure to perform their duties rendered both members and candidates subject to a penalty ranging from comradely criticism to expulsion (#9). From 1966 transfer to candidate status was once again forbidden as a form of party punishment.[163] Expulsion has remained the responsibility of the PPO, from 1961 by a mandatory two-thirds majority of those attending the meeting (which could constitute less than a majority of the membership of the organization as a whole). An amendment of 1966 facilitated expulsion by making confirmation of a PPO's decision the responsibility only of a city or district committee, thereby eliminating the requirement for further confirmation at the next higher level. In 1986 provision was also made for disciplinary procedures to be conducted by levels higher than the PPO, provided the latter was informed of this (#9), and for party organizations to maintain a watching brief on the progress that party members subject to disciplinary action were making in rectifying their shortcomings. The right of appeal against expulsion was maintained, but in 1961 a time limit of two months was set for the lodging of such appeals (#10).

The expulsion of members of committees at and above the district level, and after 1961 of auditing commissions also, remained the preserve of the committee of which the person was a member, where a two-thirds vote was necessary to secure expulsion from the party.

However, the 1961 Rules did introduce one innovation in this regard: initial discussions on the performance of a delinquent party member were to be held in the PPO, which could impose lesser punishments than expulsion, but if this was the penalty that was considered appropriate, the final decision could only be taken by the committee. This change thus gave the PPO a bigger role than it had enjoyed in 1952 (1961 and 1986, #11). The 1961 Rules also made party members who broke the criminal code subject to expulsion from the party and prosecution in accordance with the law (#12);[164] in 1952 the misdemeanour was merely to be reported to the authorities (#12). The corresponding provision in the 1986 Rules (#12) refers to the 'dual responsibility' of party members before the state and the party, but it makes no explicit mention of prosecution, merely of expulsion, and therefore seems to constitute a weakening of the position of 1961.

The candidate stage remained fixed at one year and was designed to enable the candidate to become familiar with the party's programme and Rules and to prepare for party entry, and to enable the party to verify the candidate's personal qualities (1961 and 1986, #14). In 1986 it was declared that these qualities were to be verified through practical work and in the carrying out of assignments. The procedure for admission to candidature was identical to that for admission to full membership. The PPO was to examine the worth of the candidate at the end of the period of candidacy, its decision on acceptance or rejection being subject to confirmation at the city or district level. The provision of 1952 allowing a prolongation of candidacy in uncertain cases was omitted in 1961. There was also a significant change of wording here: in 1952 unsuccessful candidates were considered to have been expelled from the party, but in 1961 they were declared simply to have ceased to be a member. They thereby were spared the stigma of expulsion.[165] Candidate members had rights of participation in a purely non-voting, consultatory capacity in party meetings and could not be elected to leading positions or as delegates to congresses and conferences (#17). Full membership dues were payable by the candidate members and they were subject to all the rules of the party in the same way as a full member.

The third section of the Rules was concerned with the party's organizational structure and intra-party democracy. The guiding principle of the party remained democratic centralism, but the elements of this have been changed in two significant ways in the post-Stalin period. In 1961 the second element was changed to make party organs report periodically not just to their party organizations, but also to higher organs (#19). This complemented the fourth element of democratic centralism, the mandatory nature of decisions of higher organs for lower and reflects the notion of ascendant responsibility. In the 1986 Rules a new, fifth, principle was added. This affirmed the collective nature of work in all organizations and the individual responsibility of party members for the implementation of the duties and tasks assigned to them. Both of these themes, collectivism and individual responsibility, were major emphases of the first year of the Gorbachev leadership. The changes of 1961 and 1986 constitute the most important changes to the formula of democratic centralism since its introduction in 1934.

The 1961 Rules spelled out more clearly the territorial-production basis of the party structure than had its predecessor: PPOs were to be formed in places of work and were then united into organizations formed on a territorial basis (#20).[166] The 1952 provisions relating to local autonomy within the bounds of party policy, the supremacy of the assembly at each level of party organization and the election of executive organs by these assemblies were all carried forward in the Rules of the post-Stalin period (#21–23). Two important changes were made in 1986. The first emphasized a quorum for the assembly, consisting of 50 per cent of the membership (#22). The second made provision for the establishment of an apparatus in all committees between the national and district levels inclusive (#23). The tasks of such an apparatus were basically the same as those formerly associated with the CC Secretariat: the conduct of current organizational work, verification of implementation and the rendering of assistance to lower-level organizations in their activities. This was to constitute a bureaucratic mechanism which the relevant party secretaries at all levels could use to carry out their functions, and constitutes formal acknowledgement of the existence of a permanent administrative hierarchy stretching the length of the party. The apparatus was to be set up under terms specified by the CC.

Major changes have occurred in the way the Rules have dealt with the election of party organs. In 1961 the basic procedure remained broadly unchanged,[167] with the exception that a simple majority vote of those participating in the meeting was now declared to be necessary for a candidate to be elected (#24); previously no figure had been given.[168] The 1961 Rules also introduced the principle of the 'systematic renewal' of the composition of party organs. Then followed precise figures on the desired rate of personnel turnover and of length of tenure of office at each level (#25). However, in the name of 'continuity of leadership', individuals characterized by particularly valuable qualities could be exempt from the regular turnover and limited tenure provisions, thereby providing a means for some to escape the main thrust of these provisions and remain in office for extended periods. After the fall of Khrushchev, the provisions specifying turnover levels and tenure limits were abolished in the name of greater efficiency and democracy[169] while the principles of systematic renewal and leadership continuity remained formally in place. The other major change came in 1986 with the qualification of the principle of secret ballot through provision for the possibility of an open ballot for party secretaries, deputy secretaries, party group organizers and delegates to district and city party conferences in small party organizations (#24).

The provision for the expulsion of members of committees and auditing commissions referred to in Section I of the Rules was repeated in a more extended form at this point in the Rules (1961, #26; 1986, #25). Despite some shortening of the article and some changes in terminology, the essential meaning of this provision has remained unchanged in the post-Stalin period.

The article on the right of free and businesslike discussion was partly rewritten in 1961, but its essence remained as it had been in 1952. Free discussion was the right of all, provided it did not threaten the unity of the party (1961, #27; 1986, #26). The Rules do not at this point repeat the earlier provision (#3(b)) that such freedom of discussion existed only until a decision had been made. Important changes were introduced in 1986, most of which were added after the draft Rules had been published. The combined effect of the additions was to reduce the scope for free discussion. No longer was the free and businesslike discussion of party policy declared to be 'the inalienable right of a party member', while the rewriting of the terms under which general party discussion could take place omitted the provision which enabled this to occur in the absence of a firm majority in the CC on a particular issue. Whatever scope may previously have existed in formal terms for a defeated minority in the CC to appeal to the party as a whole, was now gone.

In 1961 a new article was introduced (#28) and carried forward into 1986 (#27) which established collectivity as the highest principle of leadership, essential to the normal functioning of party life. The importance of this principle was established by contrasting it with the negative leadership styles of previous leaders. In 1961 it was counterposed to the cult of personality and associated violations of intra-party democracy; in 1986 these were joined by 'the adoption of volitional, subjective decisions' and the infringement of Leninist norms of party life. These were clear references to the legacies of Stalin and Khrushchev. This article repeated the point made earlier that collective leadership did not eliminate the personal responsibility of individuals for matters entrusted to them. As a confirmation of this, the 1986 Rules added that leadership collectivity assumes supervision over the activities of party organizations and members.

The question of responsibility was also addressed in the following articles of these Rules (1961, #29; 1986, #28) which made it incumbent upon party committees to keep their party organizations informed about their work in the intervals between the regular congresses and conferences. This was a reaffirmation of part of the second element of democratic centralism. In 1986 this provision was expanded. In an addition made to the Rules after the draft was published, committees were instructed that the regular informing of their organizations had to include full details about criticisms made about them and their operations, an injunction clearly aimed against the covering up of abuses that has been so common in party life. Another post-draft addition to this provision was the instruction that committees and PPOs must also keep higher-standing party organs regularly informed about their activities and the situation in their areas. This formally introduced the notion of ascendant responsibility into this provision for the first time and made it completely consistent with all the second element of democratic centralism rather than of only a part, as in 1961.

The post-Stalin Rules have also sought to promote participation by extending the activity of *aktivs* from city and district centres to party organizations at all levels between the district and union republic (1961, #30; 1986, #29). In addition, the 1986 Rules (#30) extended the right to establish commissions and workers' groups from party committees at the area, city and district levels (1961, #52) to committees at all levels. The tasks of the commissions and workers' groups were, *inter alia*, to draw communists into party work.

A number of changes were introduced into the higher organs of the party. The frequency of party congresses was changed from four to five years in 1971 in order to bring such meetings into sequence with the five-year planning period.[170] The validity of special (extraordinary) congresses was now made dependent upon the representation of at least half of all party members (1961 and 1986, #31) compared with the previous requirement of half of all of those represented at the last regular congress. Despite some additions to the wording, the responsibilities of the congress have remained essentially unchanged from the Stalinist period.

For the first time since 1903 the description of the powers of the CC was substantially rewritten in 1961, but the main change has been in the formulations used rather than in the powers themselves (1952, #36; 1961 and 1986, #35). The CC's responsibility for the guidance of all aspects of the party's work between congresses was confirmed: over local party organs; over central state and public organizations through party groups; the creation and supervision of various party bodies; and control over the use of party funds. The CC's control over personnel was made more explicit through the replacement of the reference to the CC distributing the forces of the party by the statement that the CC 'carries out the selection and assignment of leading cadres'.[171] The CC also retained responsibility for the appointment of the editors of leading newspapers and journals, for representing the party as a whole in relations with other parties, for establishing norms of representation at party congresses and for convening such congresses. The additions made to #28 of the Rules in 1986 noted above were also to apply to the CC, highlighting the responsibility of that body to party organizations at lower levels.

The frequency of CC plena continued to be set at six-monthly intervals. For the conduct of its work between plena, the CC was to elect a Presidium (retitled Politburo in 1966) and a Secretariat. The latter was responsible chiefly for personnel matters and for verification of the implementation of party decisions (1961, #39; 1986, #38). In the 1952 Rules both bodies had been 'organized' by the CC, but in 1961 this was changed to make them 'elected' by their parent body. In addition, in 1961 the CC was given responsibility for the establishment of a CC Bureau for the RSFSR, thereby for the first time in the party's history establishing a separate party administration for the Russian Republic.[172] The Bureau was deleted from the Rules in 1966, having been declared redundant by Brezhnev because all important matters relating to the RSFSR were handled in the party's central organs.[173] A major addition was made to this section of the Rules in 1966 when, for the first time, it was declared that the General Secretary was to be elected by the CC (#38). This, the leading position in the party, had not previously been mentioned in the Rules. There was also a major deletion from this section of the Rules in 1961. The CC's right to establish political departments and to despatch party organizers to specific problem areas (1952, #37) was omitted, a significant change because of the implications it had for greater autonomy from the centre on the part of the PPOs.[174]

The two other executive organs provided for in 1952 were carried forward almost unchanged into the post-Stalin period. The Central Auditing Commission retained its watching brief over the central organs of the party, with the description of its tasks being greatly expanded in 1986 compared with 1961 (1961, #37; 1986, #36). The Committee of Party Control continued to focus its attention upon the question of party discipline. Two changes had been made with regard to the Committee of Party Control by amendment in 1956: its right to have representatives in the localities independent of local party organs was eliminated (an important de-Stalinizing measure because it brought the party's disciplinary apparatus at each level more closely under local committee control); and the partial list of infringements of party ethics that had been included in 1952 was abolished.

One other addition was made to this section of the Rules in 1966. This provided for the convocation of a party conference between congresses to discuss urgent questions of party policy, if this was deemed necessary (#40). This restored the provision of 1939 (#37) that was omitted in 1952. The restoration of this to the Rules was justified by reference to the increasing tasks to be faced, the greater role played by the party in communist construction, and party history.[175]

The post-Stalin Rules have considered the republican, territory, regional, area, city and district organizational levels in one section. In general terms, these organizations and their committees were to be guided not just by the decisions of leading party organs and the party itself, but also by the party's programme and Rules (1961 and 1986, #41). The precise responsibilities of these bodies were spelled out in a more extended form in the post-Stalin period than they had been in 1952 (1952, #43; 1961 and 1986, #42). The basic tasks allocated to the committees in 1952 were carried forward, albeit sometimes in different terminology. These bodies retained responsibility for the education and training of communists; the direction of the work of soviets and public organizations; the organization of party groups and enterprises; distribution of party funds; and the rendering of regular reports to higher organs. But the post-Stalin discussion of this issue differed from that of 1952 in three respects. Firstly, the responsibilities in the personnel area were made more explicit, just as in the central organs. Secondly, party organizations were warned not to supplant the public organizations they were meant to guide (this provision was transferred to #60 in 1986).[176] Thirdly, the post-Stalin Rules placed considerably higher emphasis upon these bodies' functions in the general community. They were to be actively involved in the organization of the masses for the achievement of economic goals, they were to organize and supervise cultural–educational work among the masses, they were to attract communists into voluntary public work and, as a stimulus to 'the gradual transition from a socialist state to communist public self-administration', they were to stimulate the initiative and activity of the masses and attract them into the work of public organizations. This emphasis upon party work among the populace clearly reflects the populist leanings of Khrushchev's approach and the continuation of the public participation emphasis, albeit with a greater sense of structure, by his successors.

The 1986 Rules introduced a number of interesting changes to this discussion. Henceforth these organizations were to be concerned, *inter alia*, with increasing the effectiveness of production and, in the conduct of cadre policy, with the moral purity of party cadres. The 1961 reference to mass participation as a 'necessary condition for the gradual transition from a socialist state to communist public self-administration' became a 'necessary condition for the further deepening of socialist democracy'. In addition, a new provision was added, emphasizing the need for Leninist principles and methods of leadership, the unity of ideological, organizational and economic activities, and the strengthening of discipline and order. The 1986 discussion was, therefore, much more businesslike and practically-orientated than that of 1961 and reflects the much more sober outlook of the Gorbachev leadership.

The leading organs of these organizations were discussed in two groups. The highest organ of the regional/territory/republican organization[177] remained the conference/congress and, between such assemblies, the relevant committee (#43). The frequency of meetings of these assemblies had been changed from once every eighteen months in 1952 to every two years in 1956 (in republics with regional divisions this could be extended to four years) (#44). An amendment of 1971 altered the intervals between regional/territory conferences to two–three years, approximately midway between the new five-yearly congresses of the republican parties.[178] Thus the change in frequency of the national congresses necessitated similar changes at lower levels.[179]

The functions of the conference/congress remained essentially the same as in 1952, with the exception that cultural work rather than trade-union work was included among the questions this body could discuss. The 1952 provision that this body was to hear reports from regional/territory/republican bodies other than the committee and auditing commission was omitted in 1961 (1952, #41; 1961 and 1986, #44). Party committees at these levels, which as a result of a 1956 amendment were to meet at four-monthly intervals rather than every two months as in 1952, were empowered to elect bureaux, which were to include the committee secretaries. The size of each bureau and the number of secretaries was no longer specified in the Rules,[180] while the minimum period of party membership required for secretaries remained five years. No specific provision was made for higher level confirmation of these bodies (including the secretaries) at this point in the Rules, as had been done in 1952. Secretariats could be (in 1986 'are') established to examine current questions and to verify the implementation of decisions, and the rights of committee plena to confirm the chairmen of party commissions, heads of committee departments and editors of party newspapers and journals was affirmed (1961 and 1986, #45).

The highest organ of the area, city and district levels was the party conference or general meeting of communists. By amendment in 1956 these were to be convened every two years compared with a frequency of one year for the city and district levels and eighteen months for the area level in 1952. This was changed to two–three years in 1971 to bring them into line with the regional and territory conferences. The responsibilities of these bodies were changed to included discussion of questions of party, economic and cultural construction, but their specific right to approve the reports of the appropriate committee and auditing commission was omitted (1952, #46; 1961 and 1986, #48). The 1961 introduction of the provision that committees at the regional, territory and republican levels led the work and heard the reports of these lower organs (#47) seems to emphasize the subordination of these organs to the next higher level much more than had been the case previously.

The committees at these levels were formally accorded the right to establish norms of representation for the corresponding conference (#48) in the post-Stalin Rules. Meeting in plenary session every three months (a 1956 amendment had changed this from the six-week period for the area committee and month for the district and city committees of 1952), these bodies were entitled to elect an executive organ including the committee secretaries (to be of three years' party standing in 1961, changed to five years in 1986 and confirmed at the regional, territory or republican level), to confirm the heads of committee departments, newspaper editors and, in 1986, the chairman of the party commission (#49). The other powers the committees could exercise have been substantially reduced compared with 1952 (1952, #48 and 51; 1961 and 1986, #50). In 1952 the powers of committees at these levels mirrored those of the region, territory and republic. In 1961 they were restricted to organizing, confirming and leading PPOs (in 1986 to simply establishing and guiding PPOs), hearing the reports of PPOs and keeping a record of membership. They have become effectively the guardians of the PPOs, at least in formal terms. One additional area of responsibility they have gained has been to draw communists and volunteer workers into party and public work on a voluntary basis (1961, #52; 1986, #30), a development reflecting the increased emphasis upon participation noted above.

If the profile of the area, city and district level organizations seems to have declined in the post-Stalin period, that of the primary organizations has expanded. The organizational structure of PPOs has become much more complex in the post-Stalin Rules. PPOs were to be established in places of work where there were at least three communists and, from 1961, also in places of residence if the need arose (1961, #53; 1986, #52).[181] Reflecting changes in the organization of industrial production in the 1960s and 1970s, provision was made in an amendment of 1971 for the possibility of the establishment of a single PPO covering a number of enterprises in the one production combine,[182] a change which introduced an element of ambiguity into the party's formal lines of accountability.[183] Provision was also made for the establishment of sub-units in PPOs that had a large membership (1961 and 1986, #54).

The highest organ of the PPO was to be the party meeting, which was to be held monthly, except for party organizations numbering more than 300 in which case the frequency was not fixed. A 1966 amendment declared that general meetings would be held at two-monthly intervals in PPOs in which there were sub-unit party organizations (1961, #55; 1986, #54). In 1961 primary and sub-unit party organizations were entitled to elect a bureau on an annual (in 1986 two–three year) basis. PPOs were also to elect secretaries, but these were not to be full-time positions in organizations numbering less than 150 members (100 in 1952).[184] If a PPO or sub-unit organization had less than fifteen members, it did not elect a bureau, but only a secretary and deputy secretary who had both to be of one year's party standing. Provision was also made for large PPOs[185] to establish party committees and for the sub-unit organizations within those organizations to be granted the rights of PPOs (1961, #57; 1986, #56).[186] In PPOs with more than a thousand communists, the party committee could be granted the responsibilities of a district committee with regard to personnel matters and, from 1986, could elect a bureau of its own to conduct current work.

The description of the tasks of PPOs was greatly expanded in 1961. In general terms, the PPO was to remain the link between party and masses, working among the latter to unite them around the party, to help realize party policies and struggle for the construction of communism (#58). The responsibilities of the PPO fell into two areas: non-party and party. In the non-party area the PPO was to organize the workers for the satisfactory fulfilment of their economic tasks and an improvement in economic performance, to conduct agitational–cultural activities among the workers, and to lead the struggle against such negative phenomena as bureaucratism, violation of discipline and economic wastefulness. In the party sphere, the PPO was to assist the area, city and district committees in their work and to concern itself with personnel matters. Admission to the party remained the PPO's responsibility, but greater emphasis was placed on its role in the moulding and education of party members. The PPO's responsibility for the political education of party members, for their study of Marxism–Leninism, was not new. What was an innovation in the 1961 Rules was the listing of those qualities which it was the responsibility of the PPO to ensure characterized each communist. These qualities were presented as the moral code of the builder of communism and reflect the ideal party activist: highly principled devotion to the cause of communism and all that was associated with it. This was the profile of the ideal Soviet man which Khruschchev and his immediate successors wanted to emerge.

In 1986 much of this discussion of the tasks of the PPOs was recast (#58). The most striking change compared with 1961 is the absence of the moral code of the builder of communism; although PPOs are to be concerned with their members' 'exemplary conduct in private life', and members must show strong commitment to the accepted values (#58), no profile of the desired member is to be found in these Rules. But the general emphasis on individual responsibility and the need for the highest personal and moral standards and improved labour performance on the part of individual party members, flowed through to the tasks of the PPOs. Through the expansion of the PPOs' powers into the 'conduct of the party's cadre policy' (#58) and 'the selection, placement and education' (#59) of members, the PPOs are in the immediate forefront of the struggle to improve the quality of party members and their work. This is particularly important in the economic sphere, where the PPOs' responsibilities seem to be more specific than they were in 1961 and to bulk much larger in their overall responsibilities. This is in accord with the emphasis during the first year of Gorbachev's tenure as General Secretary on the need for improved performance at the lower levels of the economic structure.

PPOs in some economic areas had enjoyed the right of supervision over administration (effectively the right to supervise the actions of management) for some time. This was expanded in 1961 to include some design, construction and research bureaux (#59); and in 1971 into the cultural, educational and health areas and, more importantly, into government ministries, state committees and other central and local soviet and economic institutions and departments. Provision was made in 1986 for PPOs to create within themselves special commissions to exercise such supervision (#59).[187] The extension of PPO supervision into the state arena in 1971 was a significant change because this was explicitly rejected in the 1961 Rules. It constitutes a significant expansion in the role and power of the PPOs and reflects the desire to have the party more closely involved in economic development.[188] It adds to the impression of a formally heightened role and importance of the PPO in the post-Stalin period. The only area of life in which PPOs were not accorded a right of supervision was the military.

Despite some textual revisions, no changes of major significance were made in the Rules regarding the Komsomol. This organization was to remain an active assistant and reserve of the party, helping to mould youth in line with the values which the party prizes so highly and assisting the party in carrying out the tasks confronting it at all levels. The Komsomol retained the right to keep a check on the actions of non-party bodies and to raise before the party questions about the work of such bodies; in 1986, they gained the right to become directly involved in the resolution of those questions if they involved youth (#64). In 1986 the Komsomol also became responsible for the mobilization of youth 'for the resolution of concrete tasks of productive and social life' (#65). Simultaneous membership of party and Komsomol remained impossible except for occupants of leading positions in the latter body.

The section in the post-Stalin Rules on party organization in the armed forces[189] (omitting the concern for transport[190] and of the navy as a separate force) for the first time gave a broad description of the functions such organizations were meant to carry out (1961, #64; 1986, #67). Guided by the party programme and Rules and working on the basis of instructions confirmed by the CC, they were to ensure the implementation of party policy, unite personnel around the party, politically educate servicemen, strengthen unity between army and people, and help to improve the military efficiency (and in 1986 military preparedness and discipline) of the army by encouraging the right sorts of attitudes and behaviour on the part of military personnel. Significantly, their powers did not extend to supervision over administration; the military chain of command has remained intact. The Chief Political Administration of the Soviet Army and Navy, which exercised the authority of a CC department, was the pinnacle of the party structure in the armed forces. The chain of command extended below this through political administrations of military areas and fleets, to political departments of armies, flotillas (introduced in 1986) and individual formations (1961, #65; 1986, #68). Close links were to be maintained with local party committees outside the military structure (1961, #66; 1986, #69), but there is no suggestion of any control over party organs in the military by local party organs.

The section on party groups in non-party organizations was carried from 1952 into 1961 virtually intact. Party groups, working under the guidance of the appropriate party committee at the district level or above, were convened in all meetings and elected organs of public organizations in order to ensure party leadership of these bodies. The only change from the Stalinist Rules was that there was no provision for the groups to elect a secretary (#67, 68). In 1986 this section was replaced by one dealing with the party's relationship with state and public organizations. While much of the 1961 section was carried forward into 1986, two innovations were made. A new provision (#60) declared that the party, acting within the state constitution,[191] led, directed and co-ordinated the activities of state and public organizations. It also called on the party to ensure that state and public organizations were active in drawing workers into their work and that party bodies did not displace non-party organs. The second innovation occurs in the discussion of the tasks of the party groups. These were to implement party policy in the non-party organizations and strengthen the influence of communists in these bodies (#61).

The final section in the Rules related to party finances. The only change in the 1961 Rules was in the scale of dues payable by members.

The size of dues continued to be determined by level of monthly earnings, but the scale introduced in 1961 broke the earnings up into more and smaller categories, reflecting the currency reform of 1 January 1961;[192] except for the open-ended final category, each one covered a fifty-rouble range compared with a range of 500 roubles in 1952. The changed table represents an effective reduction in the level of dues individuals would have to pay. In 1986 the table was modified again to reduce the levels of payment for many in the lower income brackets. In the 1986 Rules this section also emphatically declared that it was the CC that determined the way in which party funds were to be used.

It is clear from the above discussion that significant changes have been introduced in the post-Stalin Rules. Although the term de-Stalinization was not mentioned, the 1961 party statute was a document conceived in that climate and, despite the rejection of de-Stalinization as a policy by Khrushchev's successors, much of that ethos remained despite the amendments of 1966 and 1971. While the most overt signal of this was the negative reference to the cult of personality, the emphasis which runs through the Rules upon popular involvement in the political process and in economic development reflects a different type of relationship between party and citizenry. The implication is much more one of trust, which contrasts with the emphasis on discipline and unity under Stalin. The party was no longer seen as purely the vehicle for one class, but for society as a whole, a fact reflected in its concern for improved material and cultural standards for the population. Similarly, the expanded attention devoted to the individual party member seems to signal a search for a much more active and innovative membership, an attempt to tap energies and talents which previously were not formally encouraged in the Rules. But at the same time centralized control was not relaxed. Freedom of debate was limited by the stipulation that it must cease once a decision had been taken; the increased time between plenary assemblies underlined the power of the party's executive organs; and accountability to higher organs continued to coexist beside accountability to lower organizations. The formula of democratic centralism continued to apply, and even though many changes introduced by Khrushchev reinforced the democratic side of that equation, some of the changes associated with his name buttressed the centralist side.

If the 1961 Rules are reflective of the optimism and enthusiasm that is usually associated with Khrushchev, then the Rules of 1986 are appropriate for the straitened economic circumstances of that time. The ethos of the Rules is more sober, businesslike and down-to-earth than in 1961. The emphasis on the need for economic development is much more marked in this edition of the Rules than in its predecessors. The main themes of Gorbachev's first year in office, economic growth and development, increased state, labour and production discipline, a deepening of socialist democracy, increased openness, the high moral and political quality of cadres and improvement in their performance, the application of Leninist principles in work, the abolition of bureaucratic obfuscation and shortcomings, and the increased responsibility of all party members and workers, are all echoed in the Rules. They make for a document which is much more sober in tone and tenor than that which went before. But this should not be interpreted as meaning that the latest edition of the Rules represents a significant tilt in a centralist direction and away from the popular involvement and enthusiasm which the Khrushchevian Rules sought to evoke. Popular participation and involvement remain major elements of party life under the current Rules; 'socialist self-administration' remains on the agenda. But in contrast to 1961, they are now harnessed much more closely to the achievement of practical tasks and the overcoming of specific problems. In this way, the Rules do accurately reflect the tenor and approach that has been adopted by the party leadership since Gorbachev's election.

NOTES AND REFERENCES

1. This is not uncommon in state constitutions, particularly in those states with a Westminster-style parliamentary system.
2. In principle, a distinction can be made between the distribution of party forces and the power of confirmation, with the former referring to the despatch of personnel into the lower party apparatus and the latter to the approval of the composition of elected party organs. The distinction did exist in terms of the mobilization of many party members to work under the supervision of lower level party organs, particularly in the 1920s and 1930s. However, the distinction collapses in the case of those leading party positions that were filled through the *nomenklatura* system.
3. In effect, this means that candidates for party office are recommended/ approved by higher party organs before they are presented to the party electorate for election. For studies of this, see Bohdan Harasymiw, 'Nomenklatura: the Soviet Communist Party's leadership recruitment system', *Canadian Journal of Political Science* 2, 4 (1970), pp. 493–512; T. H. Rigby and Bohdan Harasymiw, *Leadership Selection and Patron–Client Relations in the USSR and Yugoslavia* (London: George Allen &

Unwin, 1983); Bohdan Harasymiw, *Political Elite Recruitment in the Soviet Union* (London: Macmillan, 1984).

4. It has been suggested that soundings may be made among the congress delegates about the list of candidates before that list is presented for ratification. For a discussion of this, see Jerry F. Hough and Merle Fainsod, *How the Soviet Union is Governed* (Cambridge, Mass.: Harvard University Press, 1979), pp. 451–5.

5. On the events see Roy Medvedev, *Khrushchev* (Oxford: Basil Blackwell, 1982, trans. Brian Pearce), ch. 11. On the more general point, the CC may have significant input into some questions, but this is likely to be less on an institutional and more on an individual basis.

6. For example, the Australian Constitution only hints at the principles of responsible cabinet government and mentions neither the cabinet nor the prime minister.

7. *Izvestiia tsentral'nogo komiteta rossiiskoi kommunisticheskoi partii (bol'shevikov)*, 1919–1929; *Partiinoe stroitel'stvo*, 1929–1946; *Partiinaia zhizn'*, 1946–1948, 1954–.

8. The most important of these is *Spravochnik partiinogo rabotnika*, nine volumes of which appeared between 1921 and 1935. It reappeared in 1957 and volumes have appeared in 1957, 1959, 1961, 1963, 1964, 1966 and annually since then. Similar publications exist for more specialized groups, for example, *Spravochnik sekretariia pervichnoi partiinoi organizatsii* and *Sputnik partgruporga*.

9. For example, the sketchy treatment in the Rules accorded to party organization in the military was in part rectified at an early stage by CC instructions. See *Spravochnik partiinogo rabotnika*, II (1922), pp. 115–21.

10. *Desiatyi s'ezd RKP(b). Mart 1921 goda. Stenograficheskii otchet* (Moscow, 1963), pp. 571–3 and *Trinadtsatyi s'ezd RKP(b). Mai 1924 goda. Stenograficheskii otchet* (Moscow, 1963), pp. 617–23.

11. *Dvenadtsatyi s'ezd RKP(b). 17–25 aprelia 1923 goda. Stenograficheskii otchet* (Moscow, 1968), pp. 701–6.

12. *Spravochnik partiinogo rabotnika*, IV (1963), pp. 191–200 and P. A. Rodionov, *Kollektivnost' – vysshii printsip partiinogo rukovodstva* (Moscow, 1967), p. 219.

13. See this discussed in Graeme Gill, 'Institutionalisation and Revolution: Rules and the Soviet Political System', *Soviet Studies*, XXXVII, 2 (April 1985) pp. 212–26.

14. See Medvedev, *Khrushchev*, for a discussion of this.

15. For example, the constitution of a state based upon the private ownership of capital will usually reflect different concerns and different institutional configurations from one where socialized ownership is the norm.

16. Recognition of the increased power the central organs could wield in a congress is reflected in the attempt to prevent such domination by giving each delegate, with the exception of members of the Party Council, two votes each. For the reasoning behind this, see the comments of the Bund delegate, V. Goldblatt: 'allowing the committees the right to send only one delegate leads to the representatives of the committees being overwhelmed by representatives of the central institutions. Allow me a little calculation. If we assume that we have 20 committees, the number of

delegates having the right to attend the congress will be 27 (20 delegates from committees and five from the Party Council and 2 delegates from the CC and the Central Organ). A congress is considered valid if more than half, i.e. 14 members are in attendance; an absolute majority, decisive on all questions, is eight; consequently it is sufficient for the central institutions, with their seven votes, to attract one more vote, and they will decide all questions against the remaining committees', *Vtoroi s'ezd RSDRP. Iiul'–avgust 1903 goda. Protokoly* (Moscow, 1959), pp. 284–5. Goldblatt favoured two delegates from each committee, but this was rejected in favour of one delegate with two votes.

17. This is not to suggest that the issue of the definition of a party member was the cause of the dispute. This was merely the trigger for a dispute with deeper roots in questions of theory, personalities and organization. See the discussion in Leonard Schapiro, *The Communist Party of the Soviet Union* (London: Methuen, 1970), pp. 48–54 and J. L. H. Keep, *The Rise of Social Democracy in Russia* (Oxford: Clarendon Press, 1963), ch. IV.

18. For the text of Lenin's draft, see V. I. Lenin, *Polnoe sobranie sochinenii* (Moscow, 1979, 5th edn), vol. 7, pp. 256–8. For the discussion of the Rules, see *Vtoroi s'ezd RSDRP. . .*, pp. 163–74 and 259–316. For some of Lenin's later thoughts on this, see the selection of his writings in V. I. Lenin, *KPSS ob Ustave partii* (Moscow, 1981), Part I. For the draft worked out by the Organizing Committee, see ibid., pp. 181–90.

19. A resolution preceding the Rules declared: 'The general rules of the party are binding for all sections of the party. Exceptions are determined by special appendices hitherto.' There were no special appendices.

20. The only approach to this was #10 which gave each member the right to address the leading party organs, a provision which could be used as a kind of appeal mechanism. But this right was open to anyone who had business with the party and was therefore not the exclusive prerogative of party members.

21. Co-optation required a two-thirds majority in local organs and unanimity in the CC. In 1898 only the CC had enjoyed the right of co-optation.

22. This constitutes an embryonic system of personnel registration.

23. See the discussion of the Rules in *Tret'ii s'ezd RSDRP. Aprel'–mai 1905 goda. Protokoly* (Moscow, 1959), pp. 269–304.

24. The Mensheviks held their own All-Russian Conference at the same time, which adopted a number of decisions including a set of Organizational Rules. These differed substantially from those adopted by the Bolsheviks: no effort was made to define party membership, the focus was directed squarely at the lower level party organs rather than at the apex, there was much greater concern about the way committees actually worked, and a higher level of rank-and-file activity was envisaged. These Rules are translated in Resolutions and Decisions of the Communist Party of the Soviet Union', vol. 1. Ralph Carter Elwood (ed.), *The Russian Social Democratic Labour Party 1898–October 1917* (Toronto: University of Toronto Press, 1974), pp. 69–70.

25. This may reflect Lenin's inability to persuade the Party Council to convene the III Congress, with the result that, formally in party terms, this gathering was illegal.

26. It was originally proposed to give the Petersburg and Moscow party organizations and the Committee of Foreign Organizations two votes each, but this was defeated. *Tret'ii s'ezd RSDRP. . .*, p. 270.
27. Physically the CC was still to be located in Russia while Lenin, the editor of the party newspaper, remained abroad. The degree of accountability such an arrangement would allow was limited. A secret resolution adopted by the congress providing for four-monthly conferences between the CC and its 'foreign section' was one means of trying to overcome this problem. Of course, it also gave Lenin access to the committee. Ibid., pp. 277–8.
28. Ibid., pp. 270, 295 and 297–8. See also Keep, *The Rise of Social Democracy in Russia*, p. 114.
29. *Tret'ii s'ezd RSDRP. . .*, p. 301.
30. Ibid., pp. 278 and 296.
31. In a separate resolution adopted by the congress, periphery organizations were to be kept informed about party affairs and to be consulted about them in so far as this was consistent with 'conspiratorial considerations'. This meant that they had only conditional access. Ibid., pp. 458–9.
32. For example, see ibid., p. 271.
33. The first mention of the term by Lenin was at this time when he declared that the chief task was 'to apply the principles of democratic centralism in party organization, to work tirelessly to make the local organizations the principal organizational units of the party in fact, and not merely in name, and to see to it that all the higher-standing bodies are elected, accountable, and subject to recall,' V. I. Lenin, *Polnoe sobranie sochinenii*, vol. 10, p. 60.
34. Candidates were to enter in the order determined by the congress. But this whole process introduced a strange anomaly: the CC was elected but casual vacancies were filled by people who were appointed as candidates, presumably at the same time as the election, since the congress was not scheduled to meet again until it was time to elect a new CC.
35. *Chetvertyi (ob'edinitel'nyi) s'ezd RSDRP. Aprel' (Aprel'–mai) 1906 goda. Protokoly* (Moscow, 1959), pp. 461–9. There is little evidence of the Menshevik Rules adopted in 1905 in this document.
36. This consisted of the Bolsheviks Lenin and Vasilii Desnitskii and the Menshevik V. N. Krokhmal.
37. *Chetvertyi (ob'edinitel'nyi) s'ezd. . .*, p. 639, and compare V. I. Lenin, *Polnoe sobranie sochinenii*, vol. 13, p. 56.
38. *Chetvertyi (ob'edinitel'nyi)*, pp. 465–8. The Bolsheviks wanted it to be as it had been in the 1905 Rules but they were defeated along factional lines. They were also defeated on a proposal to make provision in the Rules for those changing abode to join a local party organization. This was deemed to be superfluous, a decision which reflects the absence of any recognition of the need to have accurate personnel records. V. I. Lenin, *KPSS ob Ustave partii*, pp. 196–7.
39. All amendments were proposed by Lenin: see *Polnoe sobranie sochinenii*, vol. 21, p. 153.
40. For a discussion of Lenin's attempts in this regard, see R. C. Elwood, 'The

Congress That Never Was. Lenin's Attempt to Call a "Sixth" Party Congress in 1914', *Soviet Studies*, XXXI, 3 (July 1979), pp. 343–63.
41. *Shestoi s'ezd RSDRP (bol'shevikov). Avgust 1917 goda. Protokoly* (Moscow, 1958), pp. 166–77.
42. Ibid., pp. 175–7.
43. Articles 6–9 dealt with district and regional level bodies and their financial obligations to the CC. The chief innovation here was the provision that confirmation of new party organizations was now the responsibility of regional committees and, in their absence, of the CC, rather than regional conferences or two neighbouring organizations as in 1907.
44. It was now declared to be up to party organizations to form the Organizational Committee, a much more specific formulation than that used in 1907.
45. Even where a regional committee was present to exercise its right of confirmation, the CC continued to exercise overall supervision.
46. There is no evidence that this body ever operated in a continuing fashion. It is usually seen as a precursor of the Politburo, but it may be more accurate to see it as the forebear of the Secretariat: the description of its tasks, to be concerned with 'current work', presage the description of the responsibilities of the Secretariat, and its membership (Stalin, Felix Dzerzhinsky, Vladimir Miliutin, Yakov Sverdlov, Matvei Muranov, Andrei Bubnov, Ivan Smilga, Grigorii Sokol'nikov, Moshe Uritsky, Adolph Joffe and Elena Stasova) did not include leading Bolshevik luminaries such as Lenin and Grigorii Zinoviev.
47. *Shestoi s'ezd RSDRP. . .*, p. 174.
48. Although conflict did occur. See Note 38 above.
49. The first congress after the seizure of power was an extraordinary congress, the VII, called to ratify the Brest–Litovsk treaty.
50. Entitled 'On the Organizational Question', *Vos'moi s'ezd RKP(b). Mart 1919 goda. Protokoly* (Moscow, 1959), pp. 423–29. The resolution instructed the CC to make preparations for the following conference to change the Rules.
51. The material gathered at the VIII Congress was passed to the Organization-Instruction Department of the CC which worked through this and produced a draft set of Rules. This evoked many submissions from lower party organs, with the result that a commission (led by Alexander Beloboradov, Elena Stasova and Vladimir Maksimovskii) was formed, which produced the draft presented to the conference, *Vos'maia konferentsiia RKP(b). Dekabr' 1919 goda. Protokoly* (Moscow, 1961), pp. 136–7.
52. In his memoirs, Boris Bazhanov claims to be the author of these Rules. Employed in the Organization-Instruction Department of the CC, Bazhanov claims to have drawn up the Rules and taken them to the Department head, Lazar Kaganovich. He in turn took them through CC Secretary Vyacheslav Molotov to General Secretary Stalin. From Stalin they went, with Lenin's approval, to the Politburo, which in May 1922 authorized the Orgburo to establish a commission to review the Rules. The draft went through this commission (which consisted of Molotov,

Kaganovich, N. V. Lisitsyn, I. M. Okhlopkov and Bazhanov) to the XII Conference which, following the deliberations of an editorial commission (Molotov, Kaganovich, Bazhanov and some regional leaders), formally adopted the Rules. Boriz Bazhanov, *Vospominania byvshego sekretaria stalina* (Paris, Izd. "Tret'ia volna", 1980), pp. 17–21.

53. In fact, the congress only approved the changes to the draft and left the final editorial work to be carried out under CC supervision. The text was finally approved by the CC on 17 June 1926. There were substantial differences between the draft Rules and the text finally adopted; the final version was half as long again as the draft. The main differences are indicated in the footnotes. The draft and the changes will be found in V. I. Lenin, *KPSS ob Ustave partii*, pp. 383–409. For the congress discussion, see *XIV s'ezd vsesoiuznoi kommunisticheskoi partii (b). 18–31 dekabria 1925g. Stenograficheskii otchet* (Moscow–Leningrad, 1926), pp. 876–95.

54. For some indications of concern, see *Vos'moi s'ezd RKP(b)*, p. 423; *Vos'maia konferentsiia RKP(b)*, pp. 157–68; *Desiatyi s'ezd RKP(b)*, pp. 74–5, 220 and 239; *Odinnadtsatyi s'ezd RKP(b). Mart–aprel' 1922 goda. Stenograficheskii otchet* (Moscow, 1961), pp. 167–8 and 647.

55. A party week was a special period when normal entry requirements were waived in an attempt to attract large numbers of recruits into the party.

56. The XI Congress called for much greater attention to be devoted to the candidate stage. *Odinnadtsatyi s'ezd RKP(b)*, p. 549. For Lenin's view, see his letter to Molotov on the eve of the congress: V. I. Lenin, *Polnoe sobranie sochinenii*, vol. 45, pp. 17–21.

57. In the initial draft the period for workers was one month and peasants two months. This was changed by amendment at the conference, chiefly because of the VIII Congress injunction to improve access to the party for members of *both* classes. Also it was considered 'inexpedient' to differentiate between these groups and Red Armymen, *Vos'maia Konferentsiia RKP(b)*, pp. 149–50.

58. This decision was actually embodied in a resolution of the XI Congress, some three months before the formal adoption of the Rules, *Odinnadtsatyi s'ezd RKP(b)*, p. 549. In a move that was consistent with the XI Congress' emphasis on the candidate stage, in 1922 those giving recommendations were made responsible for those they recommended and were made subject to party punishment if their recommendations proved unfounded (#2(b)).

59. This was foreshadowed at the XII Congress in 1923, *Dvenadtsatyi s'ezd RKP(b)*, pp. 703–4. In the draft Rules, people in categories one and two needed recommendations from three members of three years' standing, as in 1922.

60. This stipulation did not appear in the 1925 draft, which virtually repeated the provision of 1922.

61. These additions did not appear in the 1925 draft.

62. This was frequently violated in practice. See, for example, *XIV s'ezd Vsesoiuznoi kommunisticheskoi partii(b)*, p. 878.

63. See T. H. Rigby, *Communist Party Membership in the USSR 1917–1967* (Princeton, New Jersey: Princeton University Press, 1968), ch. 4.

64. *Vos'maia konferentsiia RKP(b)*, p. 139.

65. This created a curious anomaly in all the Rules of this period. This provision seemed to place responsibility for initiating expulsion with the party cell to which the member belonged. However, when the Rules dealt with the cell, this was not mentioned. Instead responsibility for expulsion was accorded to the parish level. This reflects ambiguity not only on the expulsion question, but on the relationship between cell and parish organizational levels as well.

66. Attempts were made to regularize the relationship, but these did not resolve the rivalry. For example, *Izvestiia tsentral'nogo komiteta*, 26, 20 December 1920, 26, p. 17.

67. Even the Democratic Centralist opposition, which was very vocal in support of local autonomy, supported this principle. See N. Osinskii's comments in *Vos'moi s'ezd RKP(b)*, p. 308.

68. The organ is the elected body, the organization is the general party structure and mass membership.

69. Excluding alterations to the individual levels of the formal structure.

70. It is a quirk of the 1925 Rules that while no source of confirmation is given at this point for party committees at these levels, #33 does declare that the executive organs (the presidia or bureaux) of the regional, territory and national communist party central committees were to be confirmed by the CC.

71. The 1925 draft did not mention either of these at this point.

72. This was not included in the draft.

73. The draft had repeated the provision of 1922. The draft had also omitted #29 and part of #30 which gave the congress the power to determine the size of the Central Control Commission and the Central Auditing Commission. The draft had specified a membership of three for the latter.

74. The principle, as opposed to the wording, actually goes back to 1905.

75. *Vos'moi s'ezd RKP(b)*, pp. 27, 164–5, 170 and 187–8.

76. Ibid., pp. 424–5.

77. The 1922 Rules made no other mention of the territory level.

78. In the draft, these reports were to be made on a three-monthly basis.

79. The XIV Congress formally gave the CC the power to replace the editor of *Leningradskaia Pravda*, which, as the voice of the Zinoviev-led Leningrad opposition, had been critical of the party leadership for some time, *XIV s'ezd vsesoiuznoi*, p. 716.

80. *Vos'moi s'ezd RKP(b)*, pp. 424–5.

81. The draft also included a membership size for the Orgburo and Secretariat.

82. This was foreshadowed in a resolution of the XI Congress. *Odinnadtsatyi s'ezd RKP(b)*, pp. 565–6. The wording in the Rules is taken from a CC regulation of 28 December 1921. *Spravochnik partiinogo rabotnika II* (1922), p. 68. For an earlier, broader view of the role of auditing commissions, see the IX Conference resolution, *KPSS v rezoliutsiiakh i resheniiakh s'ezdov, konferentsii i plenumov ts.k.* (Moscow, 1970). vol. 2, pp. 190–1. An auditing commission had been established at the national level in the 1917 Rules and extended to lower levels in 1919. The change in nomenclature in 1922 presumably reflects an attempt at greater precision.

83. In 1925 this section of the Rules did signal the creation of the Central

Control Commission (although the draft did not), but this is dealt with in detail in the section devoted to the control commissions later in the Rules.

84. This was implicit in 1919 (#30) also. At the VIII Conference Anastas Mikoian had argued unsuccessfully for the establishment of territory level organizations. *Vos'maia konferentsiia RKP(b)*, pp. 144–5 and 155.

85. This had been omitted from the draft. Also see Note 77.

86. In 1922 provision was also made for the CC to establish regional bureaux under special circumstances (#31). These were to be considered the equivalent of regional committees. This provision gave the central authorities the right to establish party organs at this level where the necessary party infrastructure may have been lacking.

87. The draft had repeated the provision of 1922, so the expansion in the powers of the conference took place between the draft and the final version.

88. The draft had retained the six-month period.

89. Monthly frequency in the draft.

90. This reflects the concern expressed at the VIII Congress about the weakness of links between the centre and the localities. According to one delegate, the CC received regular reports from only four organizations, *Vos'moi s'ezd RKP(b)*, p. 177.

91. Monthly frequency in the draft.

92. Provincial committees had retained this role in the draft.

93. The same expansion took place here as for the regional conference. There was no mention of the Komsomol in the draft discussion of the provincial committee.

94. This had not been included in the draft.

95. A resolution of the XIII Congress had made this six years. *Trinadtsatyi s'ezd RKP(b)*, p. 617. The 1925 draft had retained the 1922 formulation, 'pre-October'.

96. In the draft the frequency was six months.

97. The draft had made such reports monthly and omitted mention of the district.

98. The draft had also made provision for the provincial committee to convene meetings of representatives of country and district committees every three months. In the adopted version, no timetable was set.

99. This did not appear in the draft Rules.

100. Aryeh L. Unger, *Constitutional Development in the USSR. A Guide to the Soviet Constitutions* (London: Methuen, 1981), p. 91. The administrative divisions of the USSR have undergone various changes over time. These are discussed in Unger's book and in A. I. Lepeshkin, *Sovietskii federalizm* (Moscow, 1977).

101. This was not done at the provincial level until 1922. This was a response to the generalized concern expressed at the VIII Congress about the weakness of the party in the rural areas, a weakness attributed in part to the need for party members to spread their work between a number of different organizations. Involvement in the soviets was particularly important here, *Vos'moi s'ezd RKP(b)*, pp. 177–80.

102. In the draft, two members of the bureau were to be freed from work, the

bureau was to consist of three people while the committee was to number from seven to nine.

103. The 1925 draft did not have the reference to the control commission plenipotentiary or the election of delegates to the provincial conference present in the adopted version of the Rules. Nor did it give the county committee the right to confirm district organizations or to direct the work of the Komsomol. It did, however, specify a three-month frequency for meetings of representatives of parish cells. One unusual provision in the final version of the 1925 Rules was that which made provincial control commission plenipotentiaries responsible to the county committees (#48). During the discussion of the changes to the Rules at the XIV Congress, some felt that the area level should have the same powers as the provincial committees rather than their being equivalent to the county level, *XIV s'ezd vsesoiuznoi*, p. 878.

104. In the 1925 draft, the parish committee was to consist of three to five people and was to serve for three months. No provision was made for a compulsory period of party membership for the secretary. The committee was to meet weekly.

105. This was not included in the draft. The city level of organization was briefly discussed in the section dealing with the provincial level.

106. In the draft they were entitled to send delegates to the provincial conference; no provision was made for those parishes with less than three village cells.

107. This provision was not mentioned in the draft, nor was the area committee as a source of confirmation.

108. This provision did not appear in the draft.

109. The draft stipulated a bureau of three people serving for three months.

110. *Vos'maia konferentsiia RKP(b)*, p. 137. The speaker was Zinoviev.

111. *Vos'moi s'ezd RKP(b)*, pp. 287 and 426.

112. The resolution also declared, 'All decisions of higher echelons are absolutely binding for those below', Ibid., p. 426.

113. *KPSS v rezoliutsiiakh. . .*, vol. 2, pp. 194–5.

114. *Desiatyi s'ezd RKP(b)*, pp. 577–8. See also the resolution of the XI Congress, *Odinnadtsatyi s'ezd RKP(b)*, pp. 562–5.

115. Following the resolution of the XIII Congress, *Trinadtsatyi s'ezd RKP(b)*, pp. 617–23. This survey of their role was not in the 1925 draft, nor was any reference to the area control commission. The draft did, however, devote some attention to the composition of the control commissions; it also ruled out control commissions for regional bureaux.

116. See the speech by Aaron Sol'ts at the X Congress, *Desiatyi s'ezd RKP(b)*, pp. 59–65.

117. Following a resolution of the XII Congress, *Dvenadtsatyi s'ezd RKP(b)*, p. 702.

118. For one discussion of this, see S. L. Dmitrenko, 'Ob'edinenye plenumy TsK i TsKK (1921–1933gg)', *Voprosy Istorii KPSS*, 10 (1965), pp. 73–9.

119. Reflecting the naïve view that the recruitment of workers and peasants into the political structure would help to place a check on bureacratic tendencies in party and state machines. For Lenin's position, see V. I. Lenin, *Polnoe sobranie sochinenii*, vol. 45, pp. 346–8.

120. The major difference was the power given to area and county levels to institute control commission plenipotentiaries to create a 'direct and living link' with lower-level party organs and worker and peasant masses. The sections of the Rules concerned with the control apparatus at the different organizational levels were not in the draft of 1925.
121. A resolution of the XI Congress declared that the CCC had 'insufficiently unified and led the work of local control commissions and orders the future CCC to pay more attention to this side of the matter', *Odinnadtsatyi s'ezd RKP(b)*, p. 562.
122. *Dvenadtsatyi s'ezd RKP(b)*, pp. 241–9 and 698–706.
123. On this see L. Schapiro, *The Communist Party of the Soviet Union*, p. 323.
124. Absolute figures were to be established by instruction in 1919 and 1922. In 1925 this position had been included in the draft but was omitted from the adopted version. Provision was also made for those not on a fixed wage and, from 1922, those who were unemployed or on social security (1919, #57; 1922, #56 and 57; 1925, #88 and 89). For the former, the level of dues in 1919 and 1922 was to be established by provincial committees in conformity with CC instructions. This was included in the 1925 draft but omitted from the final version.
125. The drafting commission in 1919 rejected a proposal to make this figure three in the cities and five in the rural areas because of the paucity of communists in the latter, *Vos'maia konferentsiia RKP(b)*, p. 141.
126. In 1925 this was restricted to questions which were important in principle or upon which co-ordinated statements by communists were necessary. In the draft this had been formulated the same way as in 1922.
127. The reference in the 1925 Rules to people being subject to disciplinary measures 'in accordance with the Rules' did not appear in the draft.
128. The adopted version of the 1925 Rules added to the draft the stipulation that the movement of members into and out of the fraction had to take place in accordance with the rules and regulations of the non-party organ in which the fraction is found.
129. This provision was not in the draft.
130. This question had been the subject of long and heated discussion in the early years of Bolshevik rule. Its inclusion in 1925 followed the reorganization of the system of political control in the army in 1924. For one discussion of the party–army relationship at the local level, which among other things gives some details about the tasks a company cell was meant to carry out, see Merle Fainsod, *Smolensk Under Soviet Rule* (New York: Vintage Books, 1958), pp. 335–42.
131. Unlike secretariats at some lower levels (see Note 155), the CC Secretariat has never had a military department. Andrei Andreev's words in introducing this provision were that the PUR 'must in essence be the military department of the Central Committee', *XIV s'ezd vsesoiuznoi*, p. 880.
132. A brief summary of their responsibilities is in 1925, #80. A more extensive discussion is in the October 1925 CC decision, *Spravochnik partiinogo rabotnika*, V (Moscow, 1926), pp. 476–9.
133. The changed order of their listing reinforces this emphasis.

134. T. H. Rigby, *Communist Party Membership. . .*, p. 222 and V. I. Lenin, *KPSS ob Ustave partii*, p. 411. The resolution on the adoption of the 1939 Rules refers to the way in which 'the basis for the moral and political unity of Soviet society has been created', *XVIII s'ezd vsesoiuznoi kommunisticheskoi partii (b). 10–21 Marta 1939g. Stenograficheskii otchet* (Moscow, 1939), pp. 667–8.
135. E. I. Bugaev and V. M. Leibzon, *Besedy ob ustave KPSS* (Moscow, 1964), p. 83.
136. This was a direct reaction to the experience of the purge years. *XVIII s'ezd vsesoiuznoi. . .*, p. 668.
137. The XVIII Congress resolution declared that henceforth mass party purges were to be abolished, principally because they were a blunt weapon for handling opposition in the party. This did not mean that violators of the programme, Rules or discipline of the party would not be punished, but this would be done on a careful individual basis.
138. A proposal to establish such groups was rejected by the commission which presented the draft to the VIII Conference on the grounds that such bodies were unnecessary because there were sufficient other means of attracting new party recruits. *Vos'maia konferentsiia RKP(b)*, p. 140.
139. For the decision renewing party entry, dated 29 September 1936, see *KPSS v rezoliutsiiakh. . .*, (1985), vol. 6, pp. 369–72. For the decision of 10 December 1932 halting recruitment, see Ibid., (1984), vol. 5, p. 440.
140. Compare this with Lenin's initial formulation, note 33.
141. In 1934 this was referred to in terms of 'from the top to the bottom'; from 1939 'from the bottom to the top'.
142. This particular principle had been applied to the CC in the Rules of 1903 and 1905, but then omitted.
143. This was originally decided at a CC plenum of February–March 1937. *KPSS v rezoliutsiiakh. . .*, (1985) vol. 6, p. 381. However, in March 1938 provision was made for open voting for party secretaries, a clear case of conflict in the formal rules of the party, *Partiinoe stroitel'stvo*, 8 (April 1938), pp. 62–4.
144. Departments of Agriculture and Schools continued to be based on the earlier principle because, according to the resolution of the XVIII Congress, 'of the particular importance of supervising and checking up on the activities of soviet and party organizations in agriculture' and because of the need to 'supervise the organization of popular education in all the republics', *XVIII s'ezd vsesoiuznoi. . .*, p. 671.
145. This was justified in 1939 by the need to concentrate verification functions in a body subordinate to the CC. While the Rules talk about the CC organizing this body, the XVIII Congress resolution talks about the CC electing the control commission.
146. Given the expansion in the powers of the Secretariat over time, the Orgburo was superfluous. At the first CC meeting following the congress, a Presidium Bureau was established for which there was no provision in the newly-adopted Rules, *Khrushchev Remembers* (London: André Deutsch, 1971) Introduction, Commentary and Notes by Edward Crankshaw, trans. Strobe Talbott, vol. 1, pp. 280–1.
147. This was stated even more explicitly in the congress resolution on the

adoption of the Rules, V. I. Lenin, *KPSS ob Ustave partii*, pp. 273–4.
148. For examples of decisions about the establishment of such departments, see the CC decisions of 11 January 1933 (in the MTS and sovkhozy) and 28 November 1934 (in agriculture). *KPSS v rezoliutsiiakh. . .*, (1985), vol. 6, pp. 21–32 and 186–91.
149. These periods were extended by an amendment of 1956.
150. This was changed by amendment in 1956.
151. In practice, they would always have been members.
152. A 1956 amendment declared that it was inadvisable to specify the number of secretaries.
153. This provision, expanded in 1934 compared with 1925, was further expanded in 1939 and amended in 1956.
154. In 1925 a decision was taken, to be phased in over five years, providing for the elimination of the system of dual command which had been instituted during the civil war. Henceforth military commissars were to become deputy or assistant commanders for political affairs; the power to make military decisions was vested with the commander while the political deputy was responsible for political work among the troops. The deputy commander could be a head of a political department. This unity of command was revoked in May 1937 with the restoration of the commissar to his former position, but this was in turn revoked in August 1940. Except for a three-month period in 1941, unity of command has remained the operative principle in the armed forces. Under such a system, the political officers are responsible both to the military command and to higher level political officers, Timothy Colton, *Commissars, Commanders, and Civilian Authority. The Structure of Soviet Military Politics* (Cambridge, Mass.: Harvard University Press, 1979), pp. 9–15 and 25.
155. Ibid., p. 30. This is despite the provision in the 1939 Rules for military departments in CCs of the communist parties of the union republics and in area, regional, territory, city and district committees (#27).
156. This principle dated back to the X Congress in 1921.
157. This is reflected most graphically in the resolution of the XVIII Congress which listed a series of changes to the Rules as evidence of increased intra-party democracy: the ban on co-optation and voting by list, the need to vote by secret ballot on individual candidates, the unlimited right to challenge and criticize candidates, and the compulsory periodic convocation of city *aktivs* and, in the large cities, district *aktivs*, *XVIII s'ezd vsesoiuznoi*, pp. 669–70.
158. On 10 January 1961 a CC plenum set down the agenda for the XXII Congress. Included in that agenda was change of the party Rules. The draft was approved by a CC plenum on 19 June and was then subject to public discussion. Some 30 amendments were made to the original draft, most purely grammatical or terminological and none of major importance. These are discussed in Leonard Schapiro, 'The Party's New Rules', *Problems of Communism*, XI, 1 (January 1962), pp. 28–35. Some 120 000 letters were received by the press during the discussion period and more than half a million people took part in party meetings, V. I. Lenin, *KPSS ob Ustave partii*, pp. 10 and 322–3. The report on the

changes and the discussion will be found in *XXII s'ezd kommunisticheskoi partii sovetskogo soiuza. 17–31 oktiabria 1961 goda. Stenograficheskii otchet* (Moscow, 1962), vol. 3, pp. 3–33 and 46–58. In August 1984 it was announced that the Rules would be amended at the forthcoming congress and a commission was established to prepare the draft, *Pravda*, 25 August 1984. The draft was approved by a CC plenum on 15 October 1985 and published soon after, *Pravda*, 2 November 1985. According to Mikhail Gorbachev, nearly two million people took part in the public discussion of the Rules that followed and, as a result, the CC introduced changes to the draft directed at increasing the vanguard role of communists, improving the preparedness of PPOs, developing intra-party democracy, and ensuring the constant monitoring of the activities of every party organization and every party worker, *Pravda*, 26 March 1986. Certainly, major changes were introduced into the draft; these are to be found in the notes to the 1986 Rules.

159. An amendment of 1966 restored a principle which had been found in the 1939 preamble but omitted from the 1952 Rules: the communist party rids itself of those who infringe the party's programme or Rules or compromise the lofty title of communist.
160. This was to be found in the draft Rules.
161. Leonid Brezhnev justified the 1966 change on the grounds of making admission more exacting, enhancing the role of the Komsomol, and assisting in the selection of the most active section of the youth, *XXIII s'ezd kommunisticheskoi partii sovetskogo souiza. 29 marta–8 aprelia 1966 goda. Stenograficheskii otchet* (Moscow, 1966), vol. 1, p. 97. The desire to make recruitment more restrictive and to improve the quality of those entering the party was also behind the 1986 change. This had been foreshadowed by Victor Grishin at the end of 1984, *Pravda*, 11 September 1984.
162. Provision was also made in 1961 for the admission of former members of communist and workers' parties of other countries.
163. Brezhnev argued that this had not worked in practice and that sufficient other educative measures were available, *XXIII s'ezd kommunisticheskoi. . .*, p. 97.
164. This provision clearly raises the question of the party prejudging the decision of the courts in the trial of a party member.
165. For the symbolic importance of this, see E. I. Bugaev and V. M. Leibzon, *Besedy obustave KPSS*, pp. 84–5.
166. The provision that such organizations could be established at places of residence (#53) was not mentioned at this point in the Rules.
167. The 1961 Rules did omit the provision that explicitly forbade voting by list, but this was suggested by the provision that voting was to take place on candidates individually.
168. According to Frol Kozlov, who delivered the report to the XXII Congress, the change was made because good candidates were being unnecessarily prevented from holding office because they received some three to five votes less than a successful candidate even though they attained an absolute majority. This came about because candidates were elected in order of the number of votes cast for them, the cut-off being

determined by the agreed size of the body to be elected, *XXII s'ezd kommunisticheskoi. . .*, vol. 3, pp. 15–16.

169. *XXIII s'ezd kommunisticheskoi. . .*, pp. 98–9.

170. *XXIV s'ezd kommunisticheskoi partii sovetskogo soiuza. 30 marta–9 aprelia 1971 goda. Stenograficheskii otchet* (Moscow, 1972), vol. 1, p. 123.

171. This control had been made even more explicit by the 1956 amendment which removed from the Rules mention of specific numbers of secretaries to be elected at lower levels and gave the power to decide this to the CC.

172. This was actually established in 1956. Its independence from the central party organs, which previously had been responsible for this region, was minimal: the party First Secretary (Khrushchev) became Chairman of the Bureau and no separate register of party members was established.

173. *XXIII s'ezd kommunisticheskoi. . .*, p. 98.

174. The position of CC Organizer was abolished by a CC decision of 17 August 1956, ostensibly 'to extend democracy within the party still further and to heighten the responsibility of local party organs for the work of large enterprises and the most important institutions'. The Organizer was to be replaced by a permanent secretary of the party organization, *Spravochnik partiinogo rabotnika*, I (Moscow, 1957), p. 429.

175. *XXIII s'ezd kommunisticheskoi. . .*, p. 98.

176. This has been a common theme since the foundation of the Soviet state and reflects the problem of the demarcation of responsibility between two similar administrative structures. The injunction was not applied to the national level, suggesting that substitutionism was not considered a problem here.

177. These are listed in the reverse order in the 1986 Rules.

178. See also the 1966 amendment providing for the convocation of republican party conferences if these were deemed necessary.

179. See the link drawn between the national and lower levels in Brezhnev's report to the XXIV Congress, *XXIV s'ezd kommunisticheskoi. . .*, pp. 123–4.

180. As provided for in the 1956 amendment. See note 171.

181. The 1952 provision for the establishment of party groups in those institutions where there were less than three Communists was eliminated in 1961, perhaps in the belief that such people would be picked up in the newly-created residentially-based PPOs.

182. For a discussion of some of the changes, see Timothy Dunmore, 'Local Party Organs in Industrial Administration: The Case of the Ob'edinenie Reform,' *Soviet Studies*, XXXII, 2 (April 1980), pp. 195–217.

183. The 1973 establishment of production associations created a situation in which one production association might have its constituent enterprises scattered across a number of districts. In this situation, individual enterprise PPOs might each answer to their local district party committees, thereby making the association as a whole not subject to co-ordinated party supervision, or the association might have only one PPO which was subject to the district committee where the head office

of the association was found, with the result that filial enterprises in other districts were not under the supervision of the local district committee. Either supervision on the territorial principle or on the production principle was sacrificed.

184. The provision on full-time secretaries was a significant change from a CC decision of 21 May 1957 which allowed some exceptions to the minimum size of the PPO necessary for full-time staff (at that time 100) and provided for payment of part-time officials, *Spravochnik partiinogo rabotnika*, I (1957), pp. 440–1.

185. Reflecting the smaller size of party organizations in the rural areas, in this provision the relevant membership sizes of rural organizations is smaller than for urban ones.

186. Initially this applied to shop party organizations, but a 1966 amendment extended it to production division party organizations within factory shops.

187. The original decision dates from February 1982, *Spravochnik partiinogo rabotnika*, XXIII (Moscow, 1983), pp. 487–92.

188. See Brezhnev's comments at the XXIV Congress, *XXIV s'ezd kommunisticheskoi. . .*, p. 122.

189. No mention is made specifically of PPOs in the armed forces in this section although they are referred to elsewhere in the Rules (1961, #53; 1986, #52). For a discussion of the level at which PPOs are established, see T. Colton, *Commissars, Commanders and Civilian Authority*, p. 19.

190. Omitted as a result of a 1956 amendment. There were some differences at this point between the draft and the final version adopted in 1961. The major ones were the reference to the Chief Political Administrations of the army and navy as administrations of the Ministry of Defence, and the retention of transport in this section, V. I. Lenin, *KPSS ob Ustave partii*, pp. 321–2 and 420–6.

191. This is the first time the Rules has mentioned constitutional constraints on party action. This brings the Rules into line with the 1977 state constitution in this regard.

192 Under this reform, old roubles were replaced by new ones at a ratio of 10:1. More detailed instructions on dues were issued on 25 May 1962, *Spravochnik partiinogo rabotnika*, IV (Moscow, 1963), pp. 495–507.

The Rules

Decisions of the Congress

Adopted at the I Congress of the RSDRP, March 1898

** 1. The Union of Struggle for the Liberation of the Working Class, the *Rabochaia Gazeta* group and the General Jewish Workers' Union in Russia and Poland merge into a single organization called the Russian Social Democratic Workers' Party; the General Jewish Workers' Union in Russia and Poland enters the party as an autonomous organization, independent in questions concerning especially the Jewish proletariat.

** 2. The executive organ of the party is the Central Committee, elected by the party congress to which it reports on its activities.

3. The Central Committee has responsibility for:

* (a) concern for the regular activities of the party (distribution of the forces and funds, submission and follow up of routine demands etc); the Central Committee is guided in this by the general instructions given by the party congresses;

** (b) the issue and supply of literature to local committees;

** (c) the organization of those enterprises which have general significance for all of Russia (celebration of May 1, publication of leaflets on important occasions, assistance to strikers etc.).

** 4. In especially important cases the Central Committee is guided by the following principles:

** (a) on questions which can be postponed, the Central Committee must seek instructions from the party congress;

** (b) on questions which cannot be postponed, the Central Committee acts independently by unanimous decision, reporting to the next regular or extraordinary party congress.

5. The Central Committee has the right to replenish its membership with new members.

** 6. The party funds, which are at the disposal of the CC, consist of:

** (a) single voluntary payments from local committees at the time of the formation of the party;

** (b) periodic voluntary deductions from the funds of local committees;

91

** (c) special party assessments.

** 7.   Local committees implement the decisions of the Central Committee in that form which they find most suited to local conditions. In exceptional cases local committees have the right to refuse to implement the demands of the Central Committee, having notified the latter of the reasons for the refusal. In all other matters local committees act completely independently, being guided only by the party programme.

** 8.   Through its Central Committee the party enters into relations with other revolutionary organizations, in so far as this does not infringe the principles of its programme and its tactical methods. The party recognizes the right of self-determination for each nationality.

> NOTE   Local committees enter into relations with those organizations only with the knowledge of and at the direction of the Central Committee.

* 9.   The highest organ of the party is the congress of representatives of local committees. Regular and extraordinary congresses are held. Each regular congress sets the date for the following regular congress. Extraordinary congresses are convened by the CC both on its initiative and on the demand of two-thirds of the local committees.

** 10.   The Union of Russian Social Democrats Abroad is part of the party and is its foreign representative.

** 11.   The official organ of the party is *Rabochaia Gazeta*.

(A detailed party programme will be published upon examination of it by local committees.)

Organizational Rules of the RSDRP

Adopted at the II Congress, July–August 1903

*   1.   *A member of the Russian Social-Democratic Workers' Party is anyone who accepts its programme, supports the party financially and renders it regular personal assistance under the leadership of one of its organizations.*

*   2.   The *supreme* organ of the party is the party congress. *It is convened (if possible at least once every two years) by the Party Council. The Party Council must convene a congress if this is demanded by party organizations which together are entitled to half the votes at the congress. The congress is considered valid if organizations which together are entitled to more than half of the decisive votes are represented at it.*

*   3.   *The following have representation at the congress: (a) Party Council; (b) CC; (c) CO; (d) all local committees which have not entered special unions; (e) other organizations which are equivalent in this regard to committees; (f) all unions of committees recognized by the party. All of the aforesaid organizations are represented at the congress by one delegate each with two votes; the Party Council by all of its members, each with one vote.*

*   *Representation of unions is determined by special rules.*
   NOTE 1   *The right of representation is enjoyed only by those organizations which have been confirmed no later than one year before the congress.*
   NOTE 2   *The Central Committee may invite to the congress with a consultative vote delegates of those organizations which do not meet the conditions specified in note 1.*

*   4.   *The congress appoints the fifth member of the Council, the Central Committee and the editorial board of the Central Organ.*

**   5.   *The Party Council is appointed by the editorial board of the Central Organ and the Central Committee, which each send two members to the Council; those members leaving the Council are replaced by the institutions which appointed them, and the fifth member is replaced by the Council itself.*

93

The Party Council is the supreme institution of the party.
The task of the Council is to co-ordinate and unite the activities of
the CC and the editorial board of the CO and to represent the party
in relations with other parties. To the Party Council belongs the
right to renew the CC and the editorial board of the CO if all the
members of one of these institutions are put out of action.

The Council meets whenever this is demanded by one of the
centres, i.e. editorial board of the CO or the CC, or two members
of the Council.

6. *The Central Committee organizes committees, unions of*
committees and all other institutions of the party and guides their
activities, organizes and directs enterprises having general party
significance, distributes the forces and funds of the party *and*
manages the central treasury of the party, sorts out conflict both
between and within different institutions of the party and in
general co-ordinates and directs all the practical activity of the
** *party.*

NOTE   *Members of the CC may not simultaneously be in*
another party organization, except the Party Council.

** 7.   *The editorial board of the Central Organ is responsible for*
ideological leadership of the party.

8. *All organizations in the party autonomously manage all*
matters relating specially and exclusively to that region of party
activity for the management of which they have been created.

* 9.   *Apart from organizations confirmed by the party congress,*
all remaining party organizations are confirmed by the Central
Committee. All decisions of the CC are binding for all party
organizations, which must also give funds set by the CC to the
central treasury of the party.

10.   *Each party member and every person having some kind of*
business with the party has the right to demand that any statement
by him be supplied in its original form to the CC or the editorial
board of the CO, or the party congress.

11.   *Every party organization must supply to the CC and the*
editorial board of the CO all materials on all its activities and all its
personnel.

* 12.   *All party organizations and all collegial institutions of the*
party decide matters by a simple majority vote and have the right of
co-optation. A two-thirds majority is necessary for the co-optation
of new members and the expulsion of members, unless there is a
well-founded objection. Appeal is permitted to the Party Council

on the decision of an organization about co-optation or expulsion of members.

Co-optation of new members into the CC and the editorial board of the CO is by unanimous vote. When unanimity is not achieved in cases of co-optation to the CC or the editorial board of the CO, the question may be appealed to the Council and, in cases of cassation by the Council of a decision of the corresponding collegium, the question is finally decided by a simple majority vote.

The Central Committee and the editorial board of the CO inform one another about newly co-opted members.

** *13. The Foreign League of Russian Revolutionary Social Democrats, as the only foreign organization of the RSDRP, has as its purpose propaganda and agitation abroad, and also assistance to the Russian movement. The League has all the rights of committees with the only exception that it gives support to the movement in Russia only through persons and groups especially appointed by the Central Committee.*

Rules of the Party

Adopted at the III Congress of the RSDRP, April 1905

*   1.   A party member is anyone who accepts its programme, supports the party financially and *participates through personal work in one of its organizations.*

*   2.   The supreme organ of the party is the party congress. It is convened *annually by the CC of the party. The Central Committee* must convene a congress *in the course of two months* if the convocation of a congress is demanded by party organizations which together are entitled to half the votes at the congress. The congress is considered valid if organizations which together are entitled to more than half of the decisive votes are represented at it.

*   NOTE 1   *If the CC refuses to convene a congress on the demand of half of the committees, the congress is convened by an OC, elected at a conference of representatives of committees enjoying full rights. The Organizational Committee enjoys all the rights of the Central Committee with respect to the convening of a congress.*

**   NOTE 2   *A list of newly confirmed organizations is published immediately in the CO of the party with an indication of the date of their confirmation by the Central Committee.*

**   3.   The following have representation at the congress: (a) CC; (b) all local committees which have not entered special unions; (c) other organizations which are equivalent in this regard to committees; (d) all unions of committees recognized by the party. All the aforesaid organizations are represented at the congress by one delegate each with one vote; the CC is represented by two delegates, each having *one* vote; *one of these delegates must be the responsible editor of the Central Organ.*

Representation of unions is determined by special rules.

**   NOTE 1   The right of representation is enjoyed only by those organizations which have been confirmed no later than *half a year* before the congress.

**   NOTE 2   The Central Committee may invite to the congress with a consultative vote delegates of those organizations which do not meet the conditions specified in note 1.

4. The congress *elects* the Central Committee.

* 5. *The Central Committee represents the party in relations with other parties, appoints the responsible editor of the CO from among its ranks*, organizes committees, unions of committees and other institutions of the party and guides their activities; it organizes and directs enterprises having general party significance; it distributes the forces and funds of the party and manages the central treasury of the party; it sorts out conflict both between and within different institutions of the party and in general co-ordinates and directs all the activity of the party.

** 6. All party organizations *which are carrying out integral work (local, district, factory committees, etc.)* autonomously manage all matters relating specially and exclusively to that region of party activity for the management of which they have been created; *the degree of autonomy of groups carrying out particular and special functions (technical, agitational groups, etc.) is determined by the centres which created them.*

* 7. *Any organization confirmed by the congress or CC has the right to publish party literature in its own name. The Central Committee must distribute the publications of any organization if this is requested by five committees enjoying full rights. All party periodicals must, on demand of the CC, publish all its statements.*

* 8. Apart from organizations confirmed by the party congress, other party organizations are confirmed by the CC; *local periphery organizations by local centres.* All decisions of the CC are binding for all party organizations, which must also give to the central treasury *20 per cent of all their income, except the Committee of Foreign Organizations which must give 90 per cent to the CC.*

** 9. *A local committee must be dissolved by the CC if simultaneously two-thirds of the members of the CC and two-thirds of the local workers in party organizations favour dissolution.*

** 10. Each party member and every person having some kind of business with the party has the right to demand that any statement by him be supplied in its original form to the CC or the editorial board of the CO, or the party congress.

** 11. Every party organization must supply to the CC and the editorial board of the CO all materials on all its activities and all its personnel, *presenting to the CC detailed reports on its activities at least once every two weeks.*

** 12.   All party organizations decide matters by a simple majority vote; *autonomous organizations* have the right of co-optation. A two-thirds majority is necessary for the co-optation and expulsion of members. *Committees have the right to place their members in autonomous periphery organizations.* Appeal is permitted to the *Central Committee* on a decision about co-optation or expulsion of members.

Co-optation of members into the CC is by unanimous vote. *In committees and similar organizations, official candidates proposed by the CC or autonomous periphery organizations are co-opted by simple majority vote.*

Organizational Rules

Adopted at the IV (Unified) Congress of the RSDRP, April 1906

1.   A party member is anyone who accepts the party programme, supports the party financially and *belongs to some party organization.*

2.   *All party organizations are built on the principles of democratic centralism.*

3.   *All party organizations are autonomous with regard to their internal activities.* Every confirmed party organization has the right to publish party literature in its own name.

4.   *New party organizations are confirmed by regional conferences or two neighbouring organizations. Supervision over confirmation belongs to the Central Committee.*

5.   *Organizations of one district may unite to form regional unions. The regional centre is elected at regional conferences or congresses.*

6.   All party organizations must contribute *10 per cent* of all their receipts to the CC.

*   7.   The Central Committee *and the editorial board of the CO* are elected at the congress. The CC represents the party in relations with other parties, organizes various party institutions and guides their activities, organizes and directs enterprises having general party significance, distributes the forces and funds of the party and manages the central treasury of the party; it sorts out conflicts both between and within different institutions of the party, and in general co-ordinates all the activity of the party. *During the resolution of questions of a political character the CC is to include the editorial board of the Central Organ. Vacancies occurring in the CC are filled from among the candidate members appointed by the congress in the order determined by the congress. Members leaving the editorial board of the CO are replaced by the CC acting jointly with the remaining members of the editorial board.*

*   8.   The supreme organ of the party is the party congress. Regular congresses are convened annually by the CC. An extraordinary congress must be convened within two months on the demand *of no less than half of all party members.*

If the CC refuses to convene a congress *under these*

conditions, the half of the party which has demanded its convocation has the right to form an OC which enjoys all the rights of the CC with respect to the convening of a congress.

All confirmed party organizations are represented at the congress by one delegate for each 500 members who have participated in the election of delegates. Organizations with no less than 300 electors are entitled to send one delegate. Organizations which do not have a sufficient number of members, may combine with neighbouring organizations to send a common delegate if together they have no less than 500 electors. Elections to the congress take place on democratic principles.

A congress is considered valid if *more than half of all party members are represented at it.*

The convocation of any congress and the agenda are announced by the CC of the party or, in appropriate cases, by the OC no less than one and a half months before the congress.

Organizational Rules

Adopted at the V (London) Congress of the RSDRP, May 1907

*   1. A party member is anyone who accepts the party programme, supports the party financially and belongs to some party organization.

2. All party organizations are built on the principles of democratic centralism.[1]

*   3. All party organizations are autonomous with regard to their internal activities. Every confirmed party organization has the right to publish party literature in its own name.

*   4. New party organizations are confirmed by regional conferences or two neighbouring organizations. Supervision over confirmation belongs to the Central Committee. *In due course the CC publishes in the party press the names of all newly confirmed organizations.*

*   5. Organizations of one district may unite to form regional unions. The regional centre is elected at regional conferences or congresses.

6. All party organizations must contribute 10 per cent of all their receipts to the CC.

*   7. The Central Committee is elected at the congress. The Central Committee represents the party in relations with other parties, organizes various party institutions and guides their activities, *appoints the editorial board of the CO, which works under its supervision*, organizes and directs enterprises having general party significance, distributes the forces and funds of the party and manages the central treasury of the party; it sorts out conflicts both between and within different institutions of the party, and in general co-ordinates all the activity of the party. Vacancies occurring in the CC are filled from among the candidate members appointed by the congress in the order determined by the congress.

**   8. *For discussion of the major questions of party life the CC convenes periodically, at least once every 3–4 months, meetings of representatives of regional unions of individual organizations, the Bund, Social Democrats of Poland and Lithuania and Social Democrats of the Latvian territory, proportional to the number of organized workers taking part in elections to the last party congress, on the basis of one delegate for each 5000.*

All organizations which are not united into regional unions elect delegates in the same way to their conferences. Decisions of the meetings come into force only when confirmed by the CC.[2]

*   9. The supreme organ of the party is the congress. Regular congresses are convened annually by the CC. An extraordinary congress must be convened within two months on the demand of no less than half of all party members.

If the CC refuses to convene a congress under these conditions, the half of the party which has demanded its convocation has the right to form an Organizational Committee which enjoys all the rights of the CC with respect to the convening of a congress.

All party organizations *that have been confirmed 3 months prior to the convocation of the congress* have right of representation at the congress on the basis of one delegate for each full *1000* members participating in the election of delegates. Organizations which do not have a sufficient number of members may combine with neighbouring organizations to send a common delegate, if together they have no less than *1000* electors. Elections to the congress take place on democratic principles.[3]

A congress is considered valid if more than half of all party members are represented at it.

The convocation of any congress and the agenda are announced by the CC of the party or, in appropriate cases, by the OC no less than one and a half months before the congress.

AMENDMENTS TO THE 1907 RULES ADOPTED AT THE VI (PRAGUE) ALL-RUSSIAN CONFERENCE OF THE RSDRP, 5–17 JANUARY 1912

1. To this article was added the provision that co-optation was permissible. This was justified in terms of the December 1908 conference and was not carried forward into the 1917 Rules.
2. The text of #8 was deleted and replaced with the following: 'The CC convokes conferences of representatives of all party organizations as often as possible.' This was omitted from the 1917 Rules.
3. This paragraph was omitted and replaced with the following: 'Norms of representation at future congresses of the party are established by the CC after preliminary discussions with local organizations.' This provision was not carried forward in this form into the 1917 Rules.

Rules of the Russian Social Democratic Workers' Party

Adopted at the VI Congress of the RSDRP(b), August 1917

* 1. A party member is anyone who accepts the party programme, belongs to one of its organizations, *submits to all party decisions and pays membership dues.*

* 2. *New members are admitted by local party organizations on the recommendation of two party members and are confirmed by the next general meeting of members of the organization.*

* 3. *Membership dues are established by local organizations at a rate not less than 1 per cent of earnings.*

New members pay entry dues of 50 kop.

NOTE *Party members who have not paid membership dues for three months without valid reasons are considered to have left the organization, and the general meeting is so informed.*

* 4. *The question of the expulsion of a party member is decided at the general meeting of the local organization of which he is a member. The decision of a general meeting may be appealed to a higher party institution, to the district or regional (in the capital, the city) conference.*

The highest instance is considered to be the party congress.

NOTE *Expulsions of members of the party are reported in the party organs.*

5. All party organizations are built on the principles of democratic centralism.

* 6. All organizations are autonomous with regard to their internal activities. Every organization of the party has the right to publish party literature in its own name.

* 7. Party organizations *are* united by *district and* region. *District* and regional *committees* are elected at *district and* regional conferences.

The borders of districts and regions are determined by district conferences. In case of misunderstanding between neighbouring regions, decision of the question is transferred to the Central Committee.

** 8. New party organizations are confirmed by regional

103

committees and, in their absence, by the Central Committee. Supervision over confirmation belongs to the Central Committee. Each new organization is announced by the CC in the party press.

9. All local organizations must assign to the CC 10 per cent of all *membership dues and other financial receipts which do not have a special purpose.*

** NOTE *In localities where the organization is divided into districts and sub-districts, the local organization is considered to be the district and sub-district committee.*

* 10. The supreme organ of the party is the congress. Regular congresses are convened annually. Extraordinary congresses are *convened by the CC on its own initiative or* on the demand of not less than *one-third of the total number of members represented at the last party congress.* The convocation of a party congress and the agenda are announced not less than 1½ months before the congress. An extraordinary congress is convened within 2 months. The congress is considered valid if no less than half of all party members are represented at it.

Norms of representation at the party congress are set by the CC in agreement with *regional committees in accordance with the principle of proportionality.*

11. If the CC does not convene an extraordinary congress as directed in point 10, the *organizations* which have demanded it have the right to form an Organizational Committee which enjoys all the rights of the CC with respect to the convening of a congress.

12. *The congress: (a) hears and approves the reports of the CC, auditing commission and other central institutions; (b) reviews and changes the party programme; (c) determines the tactical line of the party on current questions, and (d) elects the CC and auditing commission.*

* 13. The Central Committee is elected *annually* at the congress. *For current work the CC chooses from among its members a sub-committee of the Central Committee.*

Plenary sessions of the CC meet at least once every 2 months. The Central Committee represents the party in relations with other parties *and institutions,* organizes the various institutions of the party and guides their activities, appoints the editorial board of the CO, which works under its supervision, organizes and directs enterprises having general party significance, distributes the forces and funds of the party and manages the central treasury of the party.

Vacancies occurring in the CC are filled from among the candidate members *elected* by the congress in the order determined by the congress.

14.   *The auditing commission is elected annually at the party congress; it inspects the treasury and all CC enterprises and presents a report to the next party congress.*

Rules of the Russian Communist Party (Bolsheviks)

Adopted at the Eighth All-Russian Conference of the RKP(B), December 1919

I On party members

1. A party member is anyone who accepts the party programme, *works in* one of its organizations, submits to the decisions of the party and pays membership dues.

** 2. New members are admitted by local party *committees from among candidate members* and are confirmed by the next general meeting of the organization.

** NOTE *In exceptional cases on the recommendation of two party members admitted before October 1917, new members may be admitted from among those who are not candidates. The same exception is allowed during the course of a party week, in accordance with the instructions of the CC.*

* 3. *Any member of one organization who is transferred into the area of work of another organization is admitted into the latter organization with the agreement of the former.*

4. The question of the expulsion of *someone* from the party is decided *by* a general meeting of the organization of which that person is a member. *A decision on expulsion takes effect only when confirmed by the provincial committee, with the person concerned being removed from party work until confirmation of his expulsion.* Expulsions of members of the party are reported in the party *press with an indication of the reason for an expulsion.*

II On candidate members of the party

5. *All persons wishing to enter the ranks of party members pass through a candidate stage, which is intended to acquaint the candidate thoroughly with the programme and tactics of the party and to verify the personal qualities of the candidate.*

** 6. *New members are admitted as candidates on the recommendation of two party members of six months' standing and after verification of their recommendations by the local party committee.*

106

**   7.   *Workers and peasants must remain candidates for no less than two months, others no less than six months.*

8.   *Candidates are allowed to exercise a consultative vote at open general meetings of the party organization.*

9.   *Candidates pay the usual membership dues to the treasury of the local party committee.*

III   On the organizational structure of the party

10.   The guiding principle of the organizational structure of the party is democratic centralism.

11.   *The party is built on the basis of democratic centralism along territorial lines: an organization serving a district is considered to be higher than all the organizations serving parts of that district.*

12.   All *party* organizations are autonomous in *deciding local questions.*

13.   *The highest leading organ of each organization is the general meeting, conference or congress.*

14.   *The general meeting, conference or congress elects a committee which is its executive organ and which leads all the current work of the local organization.*

15.   *The scheme of organization of the party is as follows:*
   - (a) *territory of the RSFSR – All-Russian congress, CC;*
   - (b) *regions and Soviet republics of the RSFSR – regional conferences, regional committees;*
   - (c) *provinces – provincial conferences, provincial committees;*
   - (d) *counties – county conferences, county committees;*
   - (e) *parishes – parish meetings, parish committees;*
   - (f) *enterprises, villages, Red Army units, institutions – general cell meetings, cell bureaux.*

16.   *The order of subordination, accountability, the passage and questioning of all party decisions (from the highest instance to the lowest) is as follows: All-Russian congress, CC, regional conference, regional committee, provincial conference, etc.*

*   17.   *Special departments (national, work among women, among youth, etc.) are formed for special forms of party work. Departments are attached to committees and are directly subordinate to them. The procedure for the organization of departments is set out in special instructions confirmed by the Central Committee.*

18.   *All lower organizations up to the county are confirmed by the county committees with the sanction of the provincial committee, county committees by the provincial committee with the sanction of the regional committee, and in its absence by the CC, provincial committees by regional committees with the sanction of the CC, and in the absence of a regional committee, by the CC directly.*

19.   *Following its final confirmation, every organization has the right to acquire its own press, but only with the sanction of the appropriate higher party body.*

IV   On the central institutions of the party

20.   The supreme organ of the party is the congress. Regular congresses are convened annually. Extraordinary congresses are convened by the Central Committee on its own initiative, or on the demand of not less than one-third of the total number of members represented at the last party congress. The convocation of the party congress and the agenda are announced no later than a month and a half before the congress. An extraordinary congress is convened within two months. A congress is considered valid if *no less than half of all members of the party represented at the last regular congress are represented.*

Norms of representation at the party congress are set by the CC *and the regular pre-congress conference.*

21.   If the Central Committee does not convene an extraordinary congress as provided for in point 1 above [*sic* – means para. 20] the organizations which have demanded it have the right to form an Organizational Committee, which enjoys all the rights of the Central Committee with respect to the convening of a congress.

22.   The congress:
   (a) hears and approves the reports of the CC, auditing commission and other central institutions;
   (b) reviews and changes the party programme;
   (c) determines the tactical line of the party on current questions;
   (d) elects the CC and auditing commission, *etc.*

*   23.   The Central Committee is elected *with a membership of 19 (12 candidates).* In the event of vacancies occurring in the CC, they are filled from among the candidate members elected by the congress in the order determined by the congress.

* 24. The Central Committee represents the party in relations with other parties and institutions, organizes the various institutions of the party and guides their activities, appoints the editorial *boards* of the central *organs* working under its supervision, organizes and directs enterprises having general party significance, distributes the forces and funds of the party and manages the central treasury.

The Central Committee directs the work of the central soviet and public organizations through party fractions.

The Central Committee has no less than *two plenary sessions per month on days fixed beforehand.*

* 25. *The Central Committee forms a Political bureau for political work, an Organizational bureau for organizational work and a Secretariat headed by a secretary who is a member of the Organizational bureau of the CC.*

** 26. *Once every three months the CC convenes a party conference of the provincial and capital committees of the party.*

* 27. *Once a month the CC sends a written report of its activities to provincial and capital committees of the party.*

* 28. *The auditing commission consists of three people, periodically* inspects the treasury and all CC enterprises and presents a report to the next party congress.

V   On regional organizations

29. *With the permission of the CC*, party organizations *may* unite by region. The regional committee is elected at the regional conference. The boundaries of a region are determined by the regional conference *and confirmed by the Central Committee.*

* 30. *Party organizations serving the territory of federative parts of the RSFSR are equal in all respects to regional organizations of the party, i.e. wholly subordinate to the CC RKP(b).*

31. *The regular regional conference is convened by the regional committee every six months, and an extraordinary conference on the decision of the regional committee or half of the total membership of the organizations in the region.*

The norm of representation at the regional conference is established by the regional committee in agreement with the provincial committees in the region.

The regional conference hears and approves the reports of the regional committee, the auditing commission and other regional institutions and elects the committee and auditing commission.

*   32.   *The regional committee is elected at a regular conference.*

For current work a regional committee elects a presidium numbering no less than three people.

The regional committee organizes the various institutions of the party in the region and guides their activities, appoints the editorial board of the regional party organ working under its supervision, organizes and directs enterprises having general significance for the region, distributes forces and funds of the party in the region and manages the regional treasury. The regional committee directs the activity of the executive organs of the soviets through party fractions and every three months presents a detailed report on its activities to the CC RKP.

The regional committee is convened twice a month on a fixed day.

VI   On provincial organizations

*   33.   *The regular provincial party conference is convened by the provincial committee once every three months, a special conference by decision of the provincial committee or one third of the total membership of organizations in the province.*

The provincial conference hears and approves reports of the provincial committee, the auditing commission and other provincial institutions, and elects the committee and the auditing commission.

*   34.   *The provincial committee is elected by the conference and it must include workers from the provincial centre and other major working class centres of the province.*

The provincial committee is convened twice a month on a fixed day.

The provincial committee chooses a presidium of not less than five of its members for the conduct of current work.

35.   *The provincial committee confirms the county or district organizations of the province with the sanction of the regional committee or the CC, organizes the various institutions of the party in the province and guides their activities, appoints the editorial board of the provincial party organ working under its*

supervision, organizes all enterprises having significance for the province, distributes the forces and funds of the party in the province and manages the provincial treasury. The provincial committee directs the activities of the soviet, trade unions and the co-operative organizations through the corresponding party fractions. The provincial committee presents a detailed report on its activities and on the activities of the county committees to the CC each month.

* 36. In the intervals between conferences, provincial committees periodically make informational reports to the general meeting or conference of the city organization, besides which the provincial committees convene monthly provincial meetings of representatives of county and city organizations.

** 37. City committees, subordinated to provincial committees, may be formed in provincial cities only with the permission of provincial committees and the sanction of the CC.

** NOTE   The city committees in Petersburg and Moscow are in all respects equal to provincial committees.

VII On county organizations

* 38. The county conference hears and approves the reports of the county committee and the county auditing commission, and elects the committee and the auditing commission. The conference is convened at least once every three months.

* 39. The county committee, composed of from five to nine persons, is elected at county conferences.

The county committee chooses a presidium of three of its members, of whom the secretary must be freed from all work except party work.

40. The county committee confirms parish organizations and cells in the county with the sanction of the provincial committee, organizes the various institutions of the party in the county and guides their activities, organizes all the enterprises having significance for the county, arranges meetings of representatives of parish cells and manages the county party treasury.

NOTE   The right to publish a party organ and party literature in the county belongs only to the county committee.

* 41. Through the party fraction the county committee directs the work of the county executive committee, the soviet and all parish soviets, as well as trade union organizations, co-operative and other associations in the county.

VIII   On parish organizations

42.   *The highest organ of the parish is the general meeting of party members in the parish.*

NOTE   *In large parishes, where it is difficult to convene a general meeting, a parish conference may be substituted for a general meeting.*

*   43.   *The general meeting of the parish is convened at least once a month. The general meeting: (a) admits and expels party members; (b) elects the parish committee and the auditing commission; (c) discusses and approves the reports of the parish committee and the auditing commission; (d) elects delegates to provincial, county and other conferences; (e) discusses and approves the report of the fraction of the parish executive committee.*

44.   *The parish committee of from three to five members serving for three months is elected at the general meeting (or conference).*

*   45.   *The parish committee directs and guides the work of all organizations in the parish, conducts the registration of all party members, organizes the distribution of literature, arranges meetings, lectures, etc., organizes new cells and presents them to the county committee for confirmation, manages the parish party treasury, presents a monthly report on its activities to the county, provincial, regional and Central committees, and directs the work of the parish Soviet and executive committee through the party fraction.*

**   46.   *The auditing commission inspects the parish treasury once a month.*

IX   On party cells

*   47.   *The basis of party organization is the party cell. The cell is confirmed by the county, city or district committee and has no less than three members.*

**   NOTE   *A cell which has attained major dimensions may, with the permission of the appropriate committee, be divided into several cells, which constitute one sub-district.*

48.   *The cell is the organization which links the worker and*

peasant masses with the leading organ of the party in a given locality. *The tasks of the cell are: (1) execution of party slogans and decisions among the masses; (2) attraction of new members; (3) assistance to the local committee in its organizational and agitational work; (4) active participation, as a party organ, in the economic and political life of the country.*

* 49.   *For the conduct of current work the cell elects a bureau of three members serving for one month.*

X   On party discipline

50.   *The strictest party discipline is the primary duty of all party members and all party organizations. The decisions of party centres must be implemented quickly and exactly. At the same time, inside the party the discussion of all contentious questions of party life is completely free until a decision is adopted.*

51.   *The failure to implement the decisions of higher organizations and other misdemeanours acknowledged as criminal by public opinion in the party, entails: for an organization – censure, appointment of a temporary committee from above and general re-registration (dissolution of the organization); for individual members of the party – party censure, public censure, temporary removal from responsible party and soviet work, temporary removal from all party and soviet work, expulsion from the party and expulsion from the party with a report of the misdemeanour to administrative and judicial authorities.*

** 52.   *For the examination of any kind of disciplinary misdemeanour, each committee has the right to set special meeting days, to form special commissions, without in any way turning the latter into permanent party courts.*

53.   *Disciplinary misdemeanours are examined by committees and general meetings in the normal way through the established authorities.*

XI   On the finances of the party

54.   *The finances of organizations come from membership dues, subsidies from higher party organizations and other receipts.*

55.   Membership dues are set at not less than $^1\!/_2$ per cent of earnings. *There are four categories of membership dues*

depending upon the size of earnings. The first category pays $\frac{1}{2}$ *per cent, second 1 per cent, third 2 per cent and fourth 3 per cent. Absolute figures of assessable earnings are established by instruction.*

56.   New members pay entry dues of 5 *roubles.*

*   57.   *Membership dues for people who do not receive a fixed wage, for example peasants, are established by the local provincial committee in conformity with general norms.*

*   58.   Members of the party who have not paid membership dues for three months without valid reasons are considered to have left the organization, and the general meeting is informed of this.

**   59.   All local organizations must assign to the CC 10 per cent of all membership dues and other financial receipts not set aside for a special use. *Parish organizations assign 60 per cent to the treasury of the county committee, including in it 10 per cent for the CC, the county committee 30 per cent to the treasury of the provincial committee. 10 per cent of all receipts of the provincial committee is sent to the treasury of the CC.*

XII   On fractions in non-party institutions and organizations

*   60.   *In all non-party congresses, meetings, institutions and organizations (soviets, executive committees, trade unions, communes, etc.), where there are not less than three party members, fractions are organized, the task of which is the all-round strengthening of the influence of the party, the execution of its policy in the non-party milieu and party supervision over the work of all of the stated institutions and organizations.*

61.   *When questions concerning a fraction are being discussed in a committee, the fraction sends its representatives to the plenary session of the committee with a consultative vote. Fractions may elect bureaux for current work.*

62.   *Fractions, regardless of their importance, are wholly subordinate to the party. In all questions on which a legal decision of an appropriate party organization exists, fractions must adhere to these decisions strictly and without deviation. The committee has the right to introduce any member into the fraction and to recall any from it, but must inform the fraction of the reasons for such a measure. The fraction is autonomous in questions of its internal life and current work. In the event of an important disagreement between a party committee and a fraction on any*

question within the latter's competence, the committee must examine this question a second time with representatives of the fraction and take a final decision, which is subject to immediate implementation on the part of the fraction.

* 63. *Candidates for all of the most important positions in that institution or organization in which the fraction works are nominated by the fraction together with the appropriate party organization. Transfers from one position to another are carried out in the same way.*

* 64. *All questions having political significance and subject to discussion in the fraction must be discussed in the presence of representatives of the committee. Committees must delegate their representatives when the fraction first makes its request.*

65. *Each question subject to decision by a non-party organization in which a fraction works, must be discussed beforehand in the general meeting or the bureau of the fraction.*

66. *All members of the fraction of a non-party organization must, in the general meeting of that organization, vote unanimously on any question which has been decided in the fraction. Persons violating this rule are subject to the usual disciplinary measures.*

Rules of the Russian Communist Party (Bolsheviks) (Section of the Communist International)

Adopted at the Twelfth All-Russian Conference of the RKP(B), August 1922

I   On party members

1. A party member is anyone who accepts the party programme, works in one of its organizations, submits to the decisions of the party and pays membership dues.

2. New members are admitted *from among the candidates who have passed through a school of political literacy and have served the established period of candidacy.*

The procedure for the admission of candidates as members of the party is as follows:

(a) *Three categories are established: (1) workers and Red Armymen from worker and peasant backgrounds; (2) peasants (except for Red Armymen) and handicraft workers who do not exploit another's labour; (3) others (white collar workers, etc.)*

*

(b) *For admission to the party, persons in categories 1 and 2 must have recommendations from three members of the party of three years' standing; for persons in category 3, recommendations from five members of the party of five years' standing are needed.*

NOTE *Those who give recommendations bear responsibility for those they recommend and in cases of unfounded recommendations, are subject to party punishment up to expulsion from the party.*

(c) *Verification of the recommendation precedes admission and is the responsibility of the local party committee.*

*

(d) *The question of admission to the party is first examined by the cell, is decided by the general meeting of the organization and comes into force upon confirmation by the party committee; for category 1 – by the county committee, for categories 2 and 3 – by the provincial committee. In the*

urban district organizations the decision of the general
district meeting is final for persons in category 1.

*   (e) *Former members of other parties are admitted on the
recommendation of five members of the party of five years'
standing but only with the confirmation of the provincial
committee, regardless of the social position of the person
admitted.*

*   (f) *Youth up to and including 20 years of age (with the
exception of Red Armymen) enter the party only through the
RKSM.*

3.   Any member of one organization who is transferred into
the area of work of another organization is *registered with* the
latter *as one of its members.*

*   NOTE *The transfer of party members within the
boundaries of a province may take place with the agreement
of the provincial committee. Transfer from one province to
another takes place in accordance with the rules established
by the CC of the party.*

*   4.   The question of the expulsion of someone from the party is
decided by a general meeting of the organization of which that
person is a member *or the provincial control commission.* A
decision on expulsion takes effect only when confirmed by the
provincial committee, with the person concerned being removed
from party work until confirmation of his expulsion.

Expulsions of members of the party are reported in the
party press with an indication of the reasons for expulsion.

II   On candidate members of the party

5.   All persons wishing to enter the ranks of party members
pass through a candidate stage, which is intended to acquaint the
candidate thoroughly with the programme and tactics of the
party and to verify the personal qualities of the candidate.

6.   *The procedure for admission to candidate membership
(division into categories, the character of the recommendations
and their verification, decision of the organization on admission
and confirmation by the party committee) is absolutely identical to
that for admission to membership of the party.*

7.   *For workers and for Red Armymen of worker and peasant
backgrounds, the candidate stage is no less than six months, for*

peasants and handicraft workers, one year and for others, two years.

   NOTE   *Former members of other parties, regardless of their social position, pass through a two-year candidate stage.*

   8.   Candidates are allowed to exercise a consultative vote at open general meetings of that party organization *to which they belong*.

   9.   Candidates pay the usual membership dues to the treasury of the local party committee.

III   On the organizational structure of the party

   10.   The guiding principle of the organizational structure of the party is democratic centralism.

   11.   The party is built on the basis of democratic centralism along territorial lines: an organization serving a district is considered to be higher than all the organizations serving parts of that district.

   12.   All party organizations are autonomous in deciding local questions.

   13.   The highest leading organ of each organization is the general meeting, conference or congress.

   14.   The general meeting, conference or congress elects a committee which is its executive organ and which leads all the current work of the local organization.

   15.   The scheme of organization of the party is as follows:

*   (a) territory of the RSFSR – All-Russian congress, Central Committee;
*   (b) regions and Soviet republics in the RSFSR – *regional bureau of the CC (or* regional conferences *and congresses of national communist parties*, regional committees *and the CC of the national communist party*);
   (c) provinces   –   provincial   conferences,   provincial committees;
   (d) counties – county conferences, county committees;
*   (e) parishes – parish meetings, parish committees;
   (f) enterprises, villages, Red Army units, institutions – general cell meetings, cell bureaux.
*   16.   The order of subordination, accountability, the passage and questioning of all party decisions (from the highest instance

to the lowest) is as follows: All-Russian congress, CC, regional conference, regional committee, provincial conference, etc.

* 17. Special departments (national, work among women, etc.) are formed for special forms of party work. Departments are attached to committees and are directly subordinate to them. The procedure for the organization of departments is set out in special instructions confirmed by the Central Committee.

** 18. All lower organizations up to the county are confirmed by the county committee with the sanction of the provincial committee, county committees by the provincial committee with the sanction of the regional committee, and in its absence by the CC, provincial committees by regional committees with the sanction of the CC, and in the absence of a regional committee, by the Central Committee directly.

* 19. Following its final confirmation, every organization has the right to acquire its own press, but only with the sanction of the appropriate higher party body.

IV On the central institutions of the party

* 20. The supreme organ of the party is the congress. Regular congresses are convened annually. Extraordinary congresses are convened by the CC on its own initiative, or on the demand of not less than one-third of the total number of members represented at the last party congress. The convocation of the party congress and the agenda are announced no later than a month and a half before the congress. An extraordinary congress is convened within two months. A congress is considered valid if no less than half of all members of the party represented at the last regular congress are represented.

Norms of representation at the party congress are set by the CC and the regular pre-congress conference.

* 21. If the Central Committee does not convene an extraordinary congress as provided for in point 20, the organizations which have demanded it have the right to form an Organizational Committee, which enjoys all the rights of the Central Committee with respect to the convening of a congress.

22. The congress:

(a) hears and approves the reports of the CC, auditing commission and other central institutions;

(b) reviews and changes the programme of the party;

(c) determines the tactical line of the party on current questions;

(d) elects the CC and auditing commission, etc.

23.   The congress elects the Central Committee *and determines its size.*

In the event of vacancies occurring in the CC, they are filled from among the candidate members elected by the congress in the order determined by the congress.

* 24.   The Central Committee represents the party in relations with other parties and institutions, organizes the various institutions of the party and guides their activities, appoints the editorial boards of the central organs working under its supervision, organizes and directs enterprises having general party significance, distributes the forces and funds of the party and manages the central treasury.

The Central Committee directs the work of the central soviet and public organizations through party fractions.

The Central Committee has no less than *one plenary session every two months. Candidate members of the CC participate in plenary sessions of the CC with the right of a consultative vote.*

* 25.   The Central Committee forms a Political bureau for political work, an Organizational bureau *of from 5–7 members for the general leadership of* organizational work, and *for current work of an organizational and executive character,* a Secretariat *consisting of three members of the CC who will work continually in the Secretariat.*

* 26.   *Once a year in the interval between party congresses, the CC convenes an All-Russian party conference of representatives of territory, regional and provincial committees of the party, CCs of the national communist parties, regional bureaux of the CC, and the political sections of the Red Army and Navy.*

** 27.   Once every *two months* the CC sends a written report of its activities to provincial committees of the party.

* 28.   The *Central* Auditing Commission consists of three members *of at least ten years' party standing.*

The Central Auditing Commission inspects: (a) the speed and correctness of the conduct of business in the central organs of the party and the proper functioning of the apparatus of the Secretariat of the CC RKP; (b) the treasury and enterprises of the CC RKP.

V　On regional organizations

*　29.　With the permission of the CC *RKP* party organizations may unite by region. The boundaries of a region are determined by the regional conference and confirmed by the Central Committee.

*　30.　Party organizations serving the territory of federative parts of the RSFSR are equal to regional *(or provincial)* organizations of the party, i.e. wholly subordinate to the CC RKP.

*　31.　The regional committee *(or the CC of a national communist party)* is elected at the regional conference *(or congress of the national communist party)*.

In places where there are regional economic organs (economic councils, etc.) or in districts a long way from the centre, regional bureaux are created by special decision of the CC; they are appointed by the CC RKP and their membership is in each case established by the Central Committee. Regional bureaux of the CC are responsible only to the CC RKP.

*　32.　The regular regional conference *(or congress of the national communist party)* is convened by the regional committee *(CC of the national communist party)* every six months *(in some regions this period may be extended to one year with the agreement of the CC RKP)*; an extraordinary conference is convened by decision of the regional committee *(CC of the national communist party)* or *half* of the total membership of the organizations in the region.

The norm of representation at the regional conference *(congress of the national communist party)* is established by the regional committee *(CC of the national communist party)* in agreement with the provincial committees in the region.

The regional conference *(congress of the national communist party)* hears and approves the reports of the regional committee *(CC of the national communist party)*, the auditing commission and other regional institutions, and elects the regional committee and auditing commission *(CC, CCC of the national communist party)*.

*　33.　The regional committee chooses a *bureau of not less than five persons* for the conduct of current work.

The regional committee *(regional bureau of the CC)* organizes the various institutions of the party in the region and guides their activities, appoints the editorial board of the regional party organ working under its supervision, organizes and directs enterprises having general significance for the region, distributes the forces and funds of the party in the region and manages the regional treasury. The regional committee *(regional bureau of the CC)* directs the activity of the executive organs of the soviets through party fractions and presents a *monthly* report on its activities to the CC RKP.

The regional committee *(regional bureau of the CC) is convened no less than once a month.*

VI   On provincial organizations

* 34.   The regular provincial party conference is convened by the provincial committee once every *six* months, a special conference by decision of the provincial committee or one-third of the total membership of organizations in the province.

The provincial conference hears and approves reports of the provincial committee, the auditing commission and other provincial institutions, and elects the committee and the auditing commission.

* 35.   The provincial committee is elected by the conference and it must include workers from the provincial centre and other major working-class centres of the province.

The provincial committee is convened *at least once a month.* For the conduct of current work the provincial committee chooses a *bureau* of 5 of its members, *although in case of need this number may be increased, but only with the agreement of the CC (or in the regions, the regional committee).*

No less than three members of the bureau must be assigned only to party work.

Secretaries of a provincial committee must be of pre-1917 October revolution party standing and be confirmed by a higher party instance (the sanction of which is necessary for an exception to the requirement on party standing).

* 36.   The provincial committee confirms the county or district organizations of the province with the sanction of the regional committee or the CC, organizes the various institutions of the party in the province and guides their activities, appoints the editorial board of the provincial party organ working under its supervision, organizes all enterprises having significance for the province, distributes the forces and funds of the party in the province and manages the provincial treasury. The provincial

committee directs the activities of the soviet, trade unions and co-operative associations through the corresponding party fractions. The provincial committee presents a detailed report on its activities and on the activities of the county committees to the CC each month. *Regional committees of autonomous regions are equivalent to provincial committees.*

* 37. In the intervals between conferences, provincial committees periodically make informational reports to the general meeting or conference of the city organization; besides which *at least once every three months* provincial committees convene provincial meetings of representatives of county committees and *district* committees *(which are directly subordinate to the provincial committee).*

38. *When the need arises, district organizations are instituted in provincial towns, with the rights of county organizations and subordinated directly to the provincial committee.*

VII On county organizations

* 39. The county conference hears and approves the report of the county committee and the county auditing commission, and elects the committee and the auditing commission. The conference is convened *once every 6 months.*

* 40. The county committee, composed of from *7 to 9* people, is elected at county conferences. The county committee chooses a *bureau* of three of its members, of whom *no less than two comrades* must be freed from all work except party work.

The secretary must be of 3 years' party standing and must be confirmed by a higher party instance (the sanction of which is necessary for an exception to the requirement on party standing).

* 41. The county committee confirms parish organizations and cells in the county with the sanction of the provincial committee, organizes the various institutions of the party in the county and guides their activities, organizes all the enterprises having significance for the county, arranges meetings of representatives of parish cells *at least once every three months* and manages the county party treasury.

NOTE The right to publish a party organ and party literature in the county belongs only to the county committee *(with the permission of the provincial committee).*

42.   Through the party fraction the county committee directs the work of the county executive committee, as well as trade union organizations, co-operative and other associations in the county.

VIII   On parish organizations

43.   The highest organ of the parish is the general meeting of party members in the parish.
>   NOTE   In large parishes, where it is difficult to convene a general meeting, a parish conference may be substituted for a general meeting.

*   44.   The general meeting of the parish is convened at least once a month. The general meeting: (a) decides questions of admission and expulsion of party members *and presents those decisions for confirmation to higher party committees*; (b) elects the parish committee; (c) discusses and approves the report of the parish committee; (d) elects delegates to provincial, county and other conferences; (e) discusses and approves the report of the fraction of the parish executive committee.

*   45.   The parish committee of from three to five members serving for three months is elected at the general meeting or conference.

46.   The parish committee directs and guides the work of all organizations in the parish, conducts the registration of all party members, organizes the distribution of literature, arranges meetings, lectures, etc., organizes new cells and presents them to the county committee for confirmation, manages the parish party treasury, presents a monthly report on its activities to the county committee, and directs the work of the parish executive committee through the party fraction.

IX   On party cells

47.   The basis of party organization is the party cell. The cell is confirmed by the county or district committee and has no less than three party members.

48.   The cell is the organization which links the worker and peasant masses with the leading organ of the party in a given locality. The tasks of the cell are: (1) execution of party slogans and decisions among the masses; (2) attraction of new members; (3) assistance to the local committee in its organizational and

agitational work; (4) active participation, as a party organ, in the economic and political life of the country.

* 49.   For the conduct of current work the cell elects a bureau of three members serving for 3 months.

The secretary of a cell must be of no less than one year's party standing. Exceptions are allowed only with the sanction of the county committee (or the district committee).

X   On control commissions

* 50.   *In order to strengthen the unity and authority of the party in the centre, the regions and the provinces, control commissions are organized through elections at the congress and regional and provincial conferences, and report to the organs which have elected them. In the centre control commissions are elected with 5 members and 2 candidates of 10 years' standing, in the regions from 3 to 5 members and 2 to 8 candidates, and in the provinces 3 members and 2 candidates of pre-February revolution standing.*

Members of the control commissions have the right to participate with a consultative vote in all meetings of corresponding party committees and in all types of other meetings and gatherings of the corresponding party organizations.

Decisions of control commissions cannot be countermanded by corresponding party committees, but come into force with the agreement of the latter and are implemented by the latter.

In case of disagreement the question is transferred to a joint meeting. If agreement with the committee is not achieved, the question is transferred for settlement to the corresponding party conference or higher control commission.

** NOTE   *Control commissions are not created for CC regional bureaux. If there is a protest about the decision of a provincial control commission, the matter is transferred into the CCC along with the findings of the regional bureau of the CC.*

XI   On party discipline

51.   The strictest party discipline is the primary duty of all party members and all party organizations. The decisions of party centres must be implemented quickly and exactly. At the same

time inside the party the discussion of all contentious questions of party life is completely free until a decision is adopted.

* 52.   The failure to implement the decisions of higher organizations and other misdemeanours acknowledged as criminal by public opinion in the party, entails: for an organization – censure, appointment of a temporary committee from above and a general re-registration (dissolution) of the organization; for individual members of the party – party censure, public censure, temporary removal from responsible party and soviet work, temporary removal from all party and soviet work, expulsion from the party, and expulsion from the party with a report of the misdemeanour to administrative and judicial authorities. *Transfer to candidate status is not permitted as a measure of party punishment.*

* 53.   Disciplinary misdemeanours are examined by committees, general meetings *and control commissions* in the normal way through the established authorities.

XII   On the finances of the party

54.   The finances of organizations come from membership dues, subsidies from higher party organizations and other receipts.

* 55.   Membership dues *for members and candidates* are set at not less than ½ per cent of earnings. There are four categories of membership dues depending upon the size of earnings. The first category pays ½ per cent, second 1 per cent, third 2 per cent and fourth 3 per cent. Absolute figures of assessable earnings are established by instruction.

* 56.   Membership dues for people who do not receive a fixed wage, for example peasants, are established by the local provincial committee in conformity with *instructions of the Central Committee.*

57.   The unemployed and those on social security (invalids, the aged) are completely exempt from payment of membership dues.

58.   Entry dues of *3 per cent of earnings* are paid by party members and candidates, *and no one is exempt from them.*

59.   Members *and candidates* of the party who have not paid membership dues for three months without valid reasons are

considered to have left the *party*, and the general meeting is informed of this.

XIII   On fractions in non-party organizations

*   60.   In all non-party congresses, meetings and *elected organs* (soviets, executive committees of soviets, *committees and councils of* trade unions, *boards of cooperatives*, etc.) where there are not less than three party members, fractions are organized, the task of which is the all-round strengthening of the influence of the party, the execution of its policy in the non-party milieu and party supervision over the work of all the stated institutions and organizations.

*   61.   When questions concerning a fraction are being discussed in a committee, the fraction sends its representatives to the plenary session of the committee with a consultative vote. Fractions may elect bureaux for current work.

62.   Fractions, regardless of their importance, are wholly subordinate to the *appropriate* party *organizations*. In all questions on which legal decisions of an appropriate party organization exist, fractions must adhere to these decisions strictly and without deviation. The committee has the right to introduce any member into the fraction and to recall any from it, but must inform the fraction of the reasons for such a measure. The fraction is autonomous in questions of its internal life and current work. In the event of an important disagreement between a party committee and a fraction on any question within the latter's competence, the committee must examine this question a second time with representatives of the fraction and take a final decision, which is subject to immediate implementation on the part of the fraction.

63.   Candidates for all the most important positions in those organizations in which the fraction works are nominated by the fraction together with the appropriate party organization. Transfers from one position to another are carried out in the same way.

64.   All questions having political significance and subject to discussion in the fraction must be discussed in the presence of representatives of the committee.

65.   Each question subject to decision by a non-party organization in which a fraction works, must be discussed

beforehand in the general meeting or the bureau of the fraction.
66.   All members of the fraction in a non-party organization
must, in the general meeting of that organization, vote
unanimously on any question which has been decided in the
fraction. Persons violating this rule are subject to the usual
disciplinary measures.

Rules of the All-Union Communist Party (Bolsheviks) (Section of the Communist International)

Adopted at the XIV Congress of the AUCP(b), December 1925

I On party members

    1. A party member is anyone who accepts the party programme, works in one of its organizations, submits to the decisions of the party and pays membership dues.

    2. New members are admitted from among the candidates who have passed through a school of political literacy and have served the established period of candidacy.

    The procedure for the admission of candidates as members of the party is as follows:

**   (a) Three categories are established: (1) workers and Red Armymen from worker and peasant backgrounds; (2) peasants (except for Red Armymen) and handicraft workers who do not exploit another's labour; (3) others (white collar workers, etc).

The first category is divided into two groups:

In the first group of the first category are the industrial workers occupied continuously in paid physical labour.

In the second group of the first category are non-industrial workers, Red Armymen from worker and peasant backgrounds, and farm labourers.

**   (b) *For admission to the party persons of the first group of the first category present two recommendations from party members of one year's standing; persons of the second group of the first category – two recommendations from party members of two years' standing*; persons of the second category – three recommendations from party members of *two years'* standing; persons of the third category – five recommendations from party members of five years' standing.

*   NOTE *When komsomol members of the first and second categories are admitted to the party, the recommendation of* the committee of the *VLKSM* is equal to the recommendation of one party member.

*(c) Former members of other parties are admitted *in exceptional cases* on the recommendation of five party members of five years' standing, *only through a production cell*, with compulsory confirmation by the *CC*, regardless of the social position of the person admitted.

NOTE *The CC may grant to individual territory party committees and to the CCs of the national communist parties the right of final confirmation of former members and other parties.*

(d) Verification of the recommendation precedes admission and is the responsibility of the local party committee.

*(e) The question of admission to the party is first examined by the cell, is decided by the general meeting of the organization and comes into force upon confirmation by the party committee; for the first category – by the county *and district* committees *(in the towns and industrial centres)*; for the second and third – by the *area committee or the* provincial committee. In the urban district organizations the question of admission to the party is decided by the general meeting of party members. *When there are more than 1000 members and candidates in urban districts, admission is brought about by the plenum of the district committee, without the sanction of the general meeting.*

*(f) Youth up to and including 20 years of age (with the exception of Red Armymen) enter the party only through the *VLKSM.*

3.   Those who give recommendations bear responsibility for those they recommend and in cases of unfounded recommendations, are subject to party punishment up to expulsion from the party.

*4.   *Seniority of party membership of those candidates admitted as party members is counted from the day on which the general meeting of the appropriate cell decides to confirm the given comrade as a party member.*

5.   Any member of one organization who is transferred into the area of work of another organization is registered with the latter as one of its members.

NOTE   The transfer of party members *from one*

organization to another is conducted in accordance with the rules established by the CC of the party.

* 6.   The question of the expulsion of someone from the party is decided by a general meeting of the organization of which that person is a member *and is confirmed by the provincial (area) control commission, or directly [decided] by the provincial (area) control commission.* A decision on expulsion takes effect only *upon agreement with it* by the provincial *(area)* committee, with the person concerned being removed from party work *from the day of expulsion by the general meeting or the PCC (area control commission).* Expulsions of members of the party are reported in the party press with an indication of the reasons for expulsion.

II   On candidate members of the party

* 7.   All persons wishing to enter the ranks of party members pass through a candidate stage, which is intended to acquaint the candidate thoroughly with the programme and tactics of the party and to verify the personal qualities of the candidate.

8.   The procedure for admission to candidate membership (division into categories, the character of the recommendations and their verification, decision of the organization on admission and confirmation by the party committee) is absolutely identical to that for admission to membership of the party.

* 9.   The candidate stage is established as follows: *for the first category, not less than 6 months*; for the second category, not less than 1 year, and for the third category, not less than 2 years.

*   NOTE   Former members of other parties, regardless of their social position, pass through a 2-year candidate stage.

* 10.   Candidates of the party take part in open meetings of that organization of which they are a member. Candidate members of the party participating in party meetings do not have the right of a decisive vote, participating only with a consultative vote.

11.   Candidates pay the usual membership dues to the treasury of the local party committee.

III   On the organizational structure of the party

12.   The guiding principle of the organizational structure of the party is democratic centralism.

13.   The party is built on the basis of democratic centralism

along territorial lines; an organization serving a district is considered to be higher than all the organizations serving parts of that district.

14.　All party organizations are autonomous in deciding local questions.

15.　The highest leading organ of each organization is the general meeting, conference or congress.

16.　The general meeting, conference or congress elects a committee which is its executive organ and which leads all the current work of the local organization.

17.　The scheme of organization of the party is as follows:

　　(a)　Territory of the *USSR* – All-*Union* Congress – CC.

*　　(b)　Regions, republics, provinces – regional (*territory*) conferences, congresses of national communist parties, provincial congresses – regional committees (*territory committees*), CCs of national communist parties, provincial committees.

**　　(c)　*Areas*, counties – *area and* county conferences – *area and* county committees.

**　　(d)　Parishes *(districts)* – parish *(district) conferences* – parish *(district)* committees.

*　　(e)　Enterprises, villages, Red Army units, institutions – general meetings of the cell – cell bureaux.

*　18.　The order of subordination, accountability, the passage and questioning of all party decisions (from the highest instance to the lowest) is as follows: All-*Union* congress, CC, regional *(territory)* conference, regional *(territory)* committee, *conference of the national communist party, CC of the national communist party*, provincial conference, etc.

**　19.　Special departments are formed for special forms of party work. Departments are attached to committees and are directly subordinate to them. The procedure for the organization of departments is set out in special instructions *of* the CC.

20.　Following its final confirmation, every organization has the right to acquire its own press, but only with the sanction of the appropriate higher party *organization*.

IV　On the central institutions of the party

*　21.　The supreme organ of the party is the congress. Regular congresses are convened annually.[1] Extraordinary congresses

are convened by the Central Committee on its own initiative, or on the demand of not less than one-third of the total number of members represented at the last party congress. The convocation of the party congress and the agenda are announced no later than a month and a half before the congress. An extraordinary congress is convened within two months.

A congress is considered valid if no less than half of all members of the party represented at the last regular congress are represented.

Norms of representation at the party congress are set by the Central Committee.

22. If the Central Committee does not convene an extraordinary congress as provided for in point 21, the organizations which have demanded it have the right to form an organizational committee, which enjoys the rights of the Central Committee with respect to the convening of a congress.

*   23. The congress: (a) hears and approves the reports of the Central Committee, *Central Control Commission, Central* Auditing Commission and other central institutions; (b) reviews and changes the programme *and Rules* of the party; (c) determines the tactical line of the party on current questions; (d) elects the Central Committee, *the Central Control Commission* and the *Central* Auditing Commission, etc.

24. The congress elects the Central Committee and determines its size. In the event of vacancies occurring in the Central Committee, they are filled from among the candidate members elected by the congress in the order determined by the congress.

*   25. *In the intervals between congresses the Central Committee guides all the work of the party*, represents the party in relations with other parties, *organizations* and institutions, organizes the various institutions of the party and guides their activities, appoints the editorial boards of the central organs working under its supervision *and confirms the editors of party organs of major local organizations*, organizes and directs enterprises having *social* significance, distributes the forces and funds of the party and manages the central treasury.

The Central Committee directs the work of the central soviet and public organizations through party fractions.

The Central Committee has no less than one plenary session every two months. Candidate members of the CC participate in plenary sessions of the CC with the right of a consultative vote.

26.   The Central Committee *organizes* a Political Bureau for political work, an Organizational Bureau for the general leadership of organizational work, and a *Secretariat for current work of an organizational and executive character*.

** 27.   Once during the intervals between party congresses the Central Committee convenes an All-*Union* party conference of representatives of *local party organizations*.

28.   *The Central Committee regularly informs party organizations about its work*.

** 29.   *The size of the Central Control Commission is determined by the congress of the party which elects it*.

* 30.   *The size of the Central Auditing Commission is determined by the congress of the party which elects it*; those elected must be of no less than 10 years' party standing.

The Central Auditing Commission inspects (a) the speed and correctness of the conduct of business in the central organs of the party and the proper functioning of the apparatus of the Secretariat of the CC *AUCP(b)*; (b) the treasury and enterprises of the CC *AUCP(b)*.[2]

V   On regional (territory) organizations

** 31.   With the permission of the CC *AUCP(b)* party organizations may unite in regional *(territory) unions*. The boundaries of a region *(territory)* are determined by the regional *(territory)* conference and confirmed by the CC.

** 32.   Party organizations serving the territory of *national republics (and regions) of the USSR* and RSFSR are equal to regional (or provincial) organizations of the party, i.e. wholly subordinate to the CC *AUCP(b)*.

** 33.   The regional *(territory)* committee (or the CC of a national communist party) is elected at the regional *(territory)* conference (or congress of the national communist party).

** NOTE   *Presidiums or bureaux of territory and equivalent committees are confirmed by the CC AUCP(b)*.

** 34.   In places where there are regional economic organs (economic councils, etc.) or in districts a long way from the centre, regional bureaux are created by special decision of the

CC; they are appointed by the CC and their membership is in each *individual* case established by the CC. Regional bureaux of the CC are responsible only to the CC *AUCP(b)*.

*   35.   The regular regional *(territory)* conference (or congress of the national communist party) is convened by the regional *(territory)* committee (CC of the national communist party) *annually*; an extraordinary conference is convened by decision of the regional *(territory)* committee (CC of the national communist party) or *one-third* of the total membership of the organizations in the region *(territory)*.

The norm of representation at the regional *(territory)* conference (congress of the national communist party) is established by the regional *(territory)* committee (CC of the national communist party).

The regional *(territory)* conference (congress of the national communist party) hears and approves the reports of the regional *(territory)* committee (CC of the national communist party), *the control commission*, the auditing commission and other regional *(territory)* institutions, *discusses questions of party, soviet, economic and trade union work in the region (territory) or republic* and elects the regional *(territory)* committee, *the regional (territory) control commission* and the auditing commission (CC, CCC and *CAC* of the national communist party).

*   36.   The regional *(territory)* committee chooses a bureau of not less than 5 persons for current work.

The regional *(territory)* committee *(CC of the national communist party)* organizes the various institutions of the party in the region *(territory)* and guides their activities, appoints the editorial board of the regional *(territory)* party organ working under its supervision, organizes and directs *its own* enterprises having general significance for the region, distributes the forces and funds of the party in the region *(territory)* and manages the regional *(territory) party* treasury. The regional *(territory)* committee *(CC of the national communist party)* directs the activity of the organs of the soviets, *trade unions, co-operative and other organizations* through party fractions, *and also directly guides the work of the VLKSM organizations* and presents to the CC *detailed reports on its activities at the time and in the form established by the CC AUCP(b).*

The *plenum* of the regional *(territory)* committee *(or the CC of the national communist party)* is convened no less than once *every two months*.

VI   On provincial organizations

** 37.   The regular provincial party conference is convened by the provincial committee at least once *a year*, special conferences by decision of the provincial committee or one-third of the total membership of organizations in the province.

The provincial conference hears and approves the reports of the provincial committee, *the provincial control commission*, the auditing commission and other provincial institutions, *discusses questions of party, soviet, economic and trade union work in the province*, elects the *provincial* committee, *the provincial control commission*, the auditing commission *and delegates to the All-Union congress*.

** 38.   The provincial committee is elected by the conference and it must include workers from the provincial centre and other major working-class centres of the province.

The provincial committee is convened at least once a month. For the conduct of current work the provincial committee chooses a bureau of *not less than 5 people*.

No less than 3 members of the bureau must be assigned only to party work.

The secretary of a provincial committee must be of *7 years'* party standing and be confirmed by a higher party instance (the sanction of which is necessary for an exception to the requirement on party standing).

** 39.   The provincial committee confirms the county *and* district organizations of the province with the sanction of the regional (territory) committee or the CC, organizes the various institutions of the party in the province and guides their activities, appoints the editorial board of the provincial party organ working under its supervision, organizes all *its own* enterprises having significance for the province, distributes the forces and funds of the party in the province and manages the provincial treasury.

The provincial committee directs the activities of the soviets, trade unions, co-operative associations *and other organizations* through the corresponding fractions, *and also at first hand directs the work of the komsomol.* The provincial committee presents reports on its activities to the CC *at the time and in the form established by the CC.* Regional committees of autonomous *republics and* regions are equivalent to provincial committees.

** 40. In the intervals between conferences, provincial committees periodically make informational reports to the general meeting or conference of city *or county (district)* organizations; besides which provincial committees convene *expanded plena or* provincial meetings of representatives of county committees and district committees (which are directly subordinate to the provincial committee).

** 41. When the need arises, district organizations are instituted in provincial towns, with the rights of county organizations and subordinated directly to the provincial committee.

VII   On area organizations

** 42.   *The area party conference is convened by the area committee at least once a year, an extraordinary conference by decision of the area committee or one-third of the total membership of organizations in the area.*

The area conference hears and approves reports of the area committee, control commission, auditing commission and other area institutions, elects the area committee, control commission, auditing commission and delegates to the All-Union congress of the party.

** 43.   *The area committee elected by the conference must include both workers from the area centre and the other major working-class centres of the area.*

** 44.   *The area committee is convened at least once a month. The area committee chooses a bureau numbering no less than 5 of its members for current work.*

No less than 3 people in the bureau must be assigned only to party work.

The secretary of an area committee must be of 5 years' party standing and be confirmed by a higher party instance (the sanction of which is necessary for an exception to the requirement on party standing).

** 45.   *The area committee confirms district organizations and party cells (district organizations must then be confirmed by* *regional (territory) committees or the CC of the national communist party), organizes the various institutions of the party in the area and guides their activities, appoints the editorial board of the area party organ working under its guidance and supervision, organizes all its own enterprises having significance for the area, distributes the forces and funds of the party in the area and manages the area treasury. The area committee directs the activities of the soviets, trade unions, co-operative and other associations through the corresponding fractions, and also at first hand directs the work of the komsomol. The area committee presents to the regional (territory) committee (or the CC of the national communist party) reports on its activities at the time and in the form established by the CC.*

** 46. *In the intervals between conferences, area committees periodically make informational reports to the general meeting or conference of the city or district organizations; besides which area committees convene expanded plena or area meetings of representatives of district committees and major cells (which are directly subordinate to the area committee).*

** 47. *With the permission of a higher party committee, district organizations equivalent to the district committees of provincial cities may be established in large area cities.*

VIII   On county organizations

** 48.   The county conference hears and approves the reports of the county committee, auditing commission *and the plenipotentiary of the provincial control commission, discusses questions of party, soviet, economic and trade union work of the county,* elects the committee, auditing commission *and delegates to the provincial conference.* The conference is convened once every six months.

** 49.   The county committee is elected at the county conference. The county committee chooses a bureau of *not more than 5–7* of its members, of whom no less than *3* comrades must be freed from all work except party work.

The secretary *of the county committee* must be of 3 years' party standing and be confirmed by a higher party instance (the sanction of which is necessary for an exception to the requirement on party standing).

** 50.   The county committee confirms parish *and district* organizations and cells in the county with the sanction of the provincial committee, organizes the various institutions of the party in the county and guides their activities, organizes all *its own* enterprises having significance for the county, arranges meetings of representatives of parish cells and manages the county party treasury.

**   NOTE   The county party committee may publish party literature and a party organ only with the approval of the provincial committee.

**   51.   Through party fractions, the county committee directs the work of the county executive committee, as well as trade union organizations, co-operative and other associations in the county *and also at first hand directs the work of the organizations of the komsomol.*

IX   On parish (district) organizations

**   52.   The highest organ in the parish is the general meeting of party members in the parish.

**   NOTE   In large parishes *(districts)*, where it is difficult to convene a general meeting, a parish *(district)* conference may be substituted for the general meeting. *Such conferences are convened at least once every 3 months.*

**   53.   The general meeting of the parish *(district)* is convened at least once a month; the general meeting: (a) decides questions of admission and expulsion of party members and presents those decisions for confirmation to higher party committees; (b) discusses and approves the report of the parish *(district)* committee; (c) elects the parish *(district)* committee; (d) elects delegates to county and other conferences; (e) discusses and approves the report of the fraction of the parish *(district)* executive committee.

**   54.   The parish *(district)* committee is elected by the *parish (or district)* party meeting or conference and serves for 6 months.

    The secretary of the parish committee must be of one year's party standing.

**   NOTE   *No parish committee is organized in parishes where there are less than three village cells; in these parishes the county committees may entrust the cells of the parish centres with implementation of certain of the duties of the parish organization.*

** 55. *The parish (district) committee is convened at least once every two weeks.*

** 56. The parish *(district)* committee directs and guides the work of all organizations in the parish *(district)*, conducts the registration of all party members, organizes the distribution of literature, arranges meetings, lectures, etc., organizes new cells and presents them to the county *(area)* committee for confirmation, manages the parish *(district)* party treasury, presents a monthly report on its activities to the county *(area)* committee, and directs the work of the parish *(district)* executive committee through the party fraction.

X   On party cells

** 57. The basis of party organization is the party cell. The cell is confirmed by the *area*, county or district committee and has no less than three party members.

** 58. *In major enterprises with a large number of workers, cells by shop (shop cells) may be organized in the general factory cell covering the whole enterprise, in each individual case with the approval of the area committee (county committee) or the district committee (in cities).*

* 59. The cell is the organization which links the worker and peasant masses with the leading organ of the party in a given locality. The tasks of the cell are (1) execution of party slogans and decisions among the masses; (2) attraction of new members *and their education*; (3) assistance to the local committee in its organizational and agitational work; (4) active participation, as a party organ, in the economic and political life of the country.

* 60. For the conduct of current work the cell elects a bureau serving for *six* months.

The secretary of a cell must be of no less than one year's party standing; exceptions are allowed only with the sanction of the *area committee* (county committee) or the district committee *(in cities)*.

XI   On control commissions

** 61. In order to *assist the party in the task of* strengthening the unity and authority of the *AUCP(b)*, *of attracting into the ranks of the party the best part of the working class, of struggling with* *infringements by party members of the programme and Rules of the AUCP(b), for ensuring in all respects the party line in the activities of soviet organs and in the development of measures for the improvement and strengthening of the soviet and economic apparatus*, control commissions are organized through elections at the congress and *regional*, territory, provincial *and area* conferences and report to the organs which have elected them.

**   NOTE   *Area Control Commissions are organized with the approval of the Central Committee and the CCC AUCP(b).*

**   62. Decisions of control commissions cannot be countermanded by corresponding party committees, but come into force *only* with the agreement of the latter and are implemented by the latter.

In case of disagreement the question is transferred to a joint meeting. If agreement with the committee is not achieved, the question is transferred for settlement to the corresponding party conference, higher control commission, *or congress of the party*.

A   *On the Central Control Commission*

**   63. *The CCC is elected mainly from among workers and peasants having the necessary party, soviet, economic or direct production experience. Members of the CCC intended for work directly in the CCC or RKI must be of no less than 10 years' party standing, members of the CCC working in local organs must be of no less than 7 years' party standing, and workers from the bench and peasants, 5 years' standing.*

**   64. *Members of the CCC may not simultaneously be members of the CC and may not occupy administrative and economic posts.*

**   NOTE   *Exceptions are allowed in each case with the special permission of the CC AUCP(b) and the Presidium of the CCC.*

**   65. *A plenum of the CCC is convened once every 3 months. For the leadership of all the current work of CCC organs in the periods between plena, a Presidium of 21 members and 9 candidates is formed, as is its executive organ, the secretariat; also formed for the examination of violations of party ethics, the Rules and programme of the AUCP(b) is a party collegium of the Central Control Commission.*[3]

**   66. *At party congresses and conferences – all-union, national communist party, territory, regional, provincial, area, county and others, and also at plena, meetings, sessions and assemblies,* *members of the CCC participate with the right of a consultative vote. At plena of the CC AUCP(b) only members and candidates of the CCC Presidium are present. In those cases when joint plena of the CC and CCC are convened, members of the CCC participate with the right of a decisive vote.*

The Presidium of the CCC delegates 3 members and 3 deputies for participation in the Politburo of the CC and 5 members and 5 deputies[4] for participation in sessions of the Orgburo and Secretariat of the CC with the right of a consultative vote.

** 67. *The CCC has the right to assign tasks within the limits of its competence to all members of the party and to all party organizations.*

B   On the Control Commissions of the national communist parties, regions (territories), provinces and areas

** 68. *The number of members and candidates of the CCC of a national communist party, of regional (territory), provincial and area control commissions is determined by the CCC AUCP(b) depending upon the power of the organization, the economy of the district and other features.*

Control commission members and candidates are elected mainly from among workers and peasants who are the most steadfast in party matters; for the CCC of the national communist party and regional (territory) control commissions – no less than 7 years' party standing, and for other control commissions – no less than 5 years' party standing and having the appropriate party, soviet and trade union experience, capable of achieving real party and soviet supervision.

** NOTE *Exceptions are allowed with the agreement of the Presidium of the CCC AUCP(b) and the CC AUCP(b).*

** 69. *Members of the control commission may not simultaneously be members of party committees and may not occupy responsible administrative posts.*

** NOTE *Exceptions are allowed with the permission of the CCC AUCP(b).*

** 70. *The plenum of the control commission elects a presidium and party collegium and nominates the membership of the collegium of the RKI.*

** 71. *Members and candidates of the control commission*

participate with the right of a consultative vote in sessions of the
appropriate party committee plena, party conferences and
meetings in their organizations.

   The presidium of the control commission delegates some of
its members to participate with the right of a consultative vote in
sessions of the appropriate bureaux of party committees.

** 72.   In the case of a divergence between the decisions of the
control commission and the party committee, a joint session is
arranged. If agreement is not obtained the question is transferred,
in the case of the CCC of the national communist party, the
regional (territory) control commission and the provincial control
commission which is not under the CCC of a national communist
party or a regional (territory) control commission, into the CCC
AUCP(b); in the case of provincial control commissions and
regional control commissions under the CCC of a national
communist party or a territory control commission, into the
corresponding CCC of the national communist party or district
(territory) control commission.

** 73.   The control commission has the right to assign tasks within
the limits of its competence to all members of the party and to all
party organizations.

C   On plenipotentiaries of Control Commissions

** 74.   In order to bring about a direct and living link between
the organs of the control commission and the lower party
organizations and the wide worker and peasant masses, the
institution of control commission plenipotentiaries in area and
county party organizations is formed.

** 75.   Area and county party conferences propose as control
commission plenipotentiaries primarily those workers and
peasants who are the most steadfast in party matters and are of no
less than 5 years' party standing; they are confirmed by the
corresponding control commission.

**   NOTE   It is desirable that control commission members be
proposed as plenipotentiaries.

** 76.   In the biggest districts of major political and economic
significance control commission plenipotentiaries are freed from
all except party work, in all other districts they do this as well as
their other work.

** 77.   Control commission plenipotentiaries have the right to *participate in sessions of the appropriate party committee, party conferences, meetings and sessions of the control commission with the right of a consultative vote.*

XII   On party organizations in the Red Army

*   78.   *General leadership of party work in the Red Army and the Red Fleet is carried out by the Political Administration of the RKKA, as the military department of the CC. The PUR exercises its leadership through its appointed political departments (fronts, areas, fleets, armies, divisions), military commissars and party commissions elected at the corresponding army conferences.*

Cells and party collectives in the Red Army and Fleet work on the basis of special instructions confirmed by the CC.

*   79.   *Heads of political departments of areas, fleets and armies must be of 7 years' party standing and heads of political departments of divisions and brigades of 4 years' party standing.*

**   80.   *Party commissions handle questions of the admission and expulsion of party members and candidates and also watch for infringements of the programme and Rules of the party. Members of the commission must be of 5 years' party standing.*

**   81.   *Party members and candidates in the Red Army and Fleet are appointed and transferred by the appropriate political organs.*

The procedure for agreement with party organs on the transfer of leading party workers in the army (commanding and political staff) is set by CC instructions.

*   82.   *Political organs must maintain close ties with local party committees through the constant political participation in the local party committees of the leaders of political organs and military commissars, and also through the systematic hearing in party committees of reports of the heads of political organs and military commissars on political work in the military units. Local party committees and control commissions lead the work of party commissions with regard to admission to candidate status, transfer from candidacy to party membership and the struggle against violations of the party rules through the systematic hearing of reports on the organization of this work in division and area party commissions and through the issuing of appropriate directives to the latter.*

XIII   On party discipline

*   83.   The strictest party discipline is the primary duty of all party members and all party organizations. The decisions of party centres must be implemented quickly and exactly. At the same time inside the party the discussion of all contentious questions of party life is completely free until a decision is adopted.

*   84.   The failure to implement the decisions of higher organizations and other misdemeanours acknowledged as criminal by public opinion in the party, entails: for an organization – censure, appointment of a temporary committee from above and general re-registration (dissolution of the organization); for individual members of the party – *some type of* censure *(admonition, reproof, etc.)*, public censure, temporary removal from responsible party and soviet work, expulsion from the party, expulsion from the party with a report of the misdemeanour to administrative and judicial authorities. Transfer to candidate status is not permitted as a measure of party punishment.[5]

**   85.   Disciplinary misdemeanours are examined by general meetings and control commissions in the normal way through established authorities.

XIV   On the finances of the party

*   86.   The finances of organizations come from membership dues, subsidies from higher party organizations and other receipts.

**   87.   Membership dues for *party* members and candidates are set at not less than ½ per cent of earnings. There are four categories of membership dues depending upon the size of earnings: 1st category pays ½ per cent, 2nd – 1 per cent, 3rd – 2 per cent, 4th – 3 per cent.

**   88.   Membership dues for people who do not receive a fixed wage, for example peasants, are established by local provincial committees.

**   89.   The unemployed and those on social security (invalids and the aged) are completely exempt from payment of membership dues.

*   90.   Entry dues of 3 per cent of earnings are collected upon entry to candidature, and no one is exempt from payment.

91.   Members and candidates of the party who have not paid membership dues for three months without valid reasons are considered to have left the party, and the general meeting is informed of this.

** 92.   *The procedure for collecting membership dues and party deductions is set out in a special instruction.*

XV   On fractions in non-party organizations

* 93.   In all congresses, meetings and elected organs (soviet trade union, co-operative, etc.) where there are no less than 3 party members, fractions are organized, the task of which is the all-round strengthening of the influence of the party, the execution of its policy in the non-party milieu and party supervision over the work of all of the stated institutions and organizations.

Fractions may elect bureaux for current work.

** 94.   When questions concerning a fraction *of some organization* are being discussed in a *party* committee, the fraction sends its representatives to the session of the *appropriate* committee with a consultative vote.

* 95.   Fractions, regardless of their importance, are wholly subordinate to the appropriate party organizations. In all questions on which legal decisions of an appropriate party organization exist, fractions must adhere to these decisions strictly and without deviation. The committee has the right to introduce any member into the fraction and to recall any from it, but must inform the fraction of the reasons for such a measure, *while the recall and introduction of a new member must take place in accordance with the rules and regulations of the non-party organ in which the fraction works.* The fraction is autonomous in questions of its internal life and current work.

In the event of an important disagreement between a party committee and a fraction on any question within the latter's competence, the committee must examine this question a second time with representatives of the fraction and take a final decision which is subject to immediate implementation on the part of the fraction.

** 96.   Candidates for all the most important positions in those organizations in which the fraction works are nominated by the fraction together with the appropriate party organization.

Transfers from one position to another are carried out in the same way.

** 97.   All questions having political significance and subject to discussion in the fraction must be discussed in the presence of representatives of the committee.

** 98.   Questions subject to decision in that non-party organization where a fraction works *and which are important in principle, and also all those questions on which co-ordinated statements of communists are necessary*, must be discussed beforehand in the general meeting or bureau of the fraction.

** 99.   All members of the fraction in a non-party organization must, in the general meeting of that organization, vote unanimously on any question which has been decided in the fraction. Persons violating this rule are subject to the usual disciplinary measures *in accordance with the Rules*.

** 100.   *Fractions in non-party organs do not maintain direct contact with fractions in lower level organs. When a fraction has to carry out its decision according to the party line, this is done through the appropriate party committee (signed by the secretary of the committee and a member of the bureau of the fraction).*

AMENDMENTS TO THE 1925 RULES ADOPTED AT THE XV CONGRESS OF THE AUCP(b), 2–19 DECEMBER 1927

1. The frequency was changed to two years in 1927. It became three in 1934.
2. A new section of the Rules was inserted at this point:
   'All-Union discussion may be considered necessary only if:
   (a) this necessity is recognized as an extreme measure by several local party organizations at the province or regional level;
   (b) there is no sufficiently firm majority in the CC on the most important questions of party policy;
   (c) in spite of a firm majority in the CC supporting a particular point of view, the CC considers it necessary to verify the correctness of its policy through discussion in the party.
   In all these cases an all-union discussion may be begun and carried out only after a corresponding decision of the CC.'
   With the exception of the final sentence, which was omitted, the substance of this amendment was carried forward into the 1934 Rules.
3. An amendment declared that plena were to be convened at three-monthly intervals between congresses, and omitted mention of the Presidium guiding work only between plenar, and of the secretariat. The amendment, like the section of which it became part, omitted in 1934.
4. This was changed to 4 and 4 in 1927.

5. An amendment made the failure to answer truthfully questions of the control commissions grounds for immediate expulsion from the party. This provision was carried forward into the 1934 Rules.

Rules of the All-Union Communist Party (Bolsheviks) (Section of the Communist International)

Adopted at the XVII Congress of the AUCP(b), February 1934

* *The All-Union Communist Party (Bolsheviks) is a section of the Communist International, and is the leading organized detachment of the proletariat of the USSR, the highest form of its class organization.*

The party exercises leadership of the proletariat, the working peasantry and all the working masses in the struggle for the dictatorship of the proletariat, for the victory of socialism.

The party leads all the organs of the proletarian dictatorship and ensures the successful construction of socialist society.

The party is a united, militant organization, bound together by conscious, iron, proletarian discipline. The party's strength is its solidarity, unity of will and unity of action, which are incompatible with deviations from the programme, with violations of party discipline and with fractional groupings inside the party.

The party demands from its members active and selfless work for the implementation of the programme and Rules of the party, the carrying out of all the decisions of the party and its organs, the preservation of the unity of the ranks of the party and the strengthening of fraternal international relations both among the working nationalities of the USSR and with the proletariat of all the countries of the world.

I   On party members and their responsibilities

1. A party member is anyone who accepts the party programme, works in one of its organizations, submits to the decisions of the party and pays membership dues.

2. *A party member must:*

   (a) *observe the strictest party discipline, actively participate in the political life of the party and the country, carry out the policy of the party and the decisions of party organs;*

*   (b) *tirelessly work at increasing his ideological competence, at mastering the fundamentals of Marxism–Leninism and the most important political and organizational decisions of the party and explain these to the non-party masses;*

*   (c) *as a member of the ruling party in the Soviet state, be a model in the maintenance of labour and state discipline, in mastering the techniques of his work, and continually increasing his productive and practical qualifications.*

*   3.   *Admission to party membership is made exclusively on an individual basis.* New members are admitted from among the candidates who have completed the established candidate stage, a school of political literacy *and who have mastered the programme and Rules of the party.*

Workers, kolkhozniks, Red Armymen, those who study or are employed, those who have stood out in the work of groups of sympathizers, in soviets, trade union, komsomol, co-operatives and in delegations to meetings are admitted as members of the party after receipt of references from those organizations where they worked or are working.

The procedure for the admission of candidates as members of the party is as follows:

**   (a) *Four categories are established: (1) industrial workers with industrial experience of at least 5 years; (2) industrial workers with less than 5 years' industrial experience, agricultural workers, Red Armymen of worker and kolkhoznik origin and engineering–technical workers working directly in a shop or section; (3) kolkhozniks, members of handicraft–industry artels and primary-school teachers; (4) other employees.*

**   (b) *For admission to the party persons of the first category present three recommendations from party members of five years' party standing; persons of the second category – five recommendations from party members of five years' party standing; persons of the third category – five recommendations from party members of five years' party standing and the recommendation of a representative of the political department of the MTS or district committee; persons of the fourth category – five recommendations from party members of ten years' party standing.*

*   NOTE   During admission to party membership from the komsomol, for all categories the recommendation of *a* *district* committee of the VLKSM is equivalent to the recommendations of *two* members of the party.

* (c) Former members of other parties are admitted in exceptional cases on the recommendation of five party members: *three of ten years' party standing and two of pre-revolutionary party standing*, and only through an *industrial primary organization*, with compulsory confirmation by the CC *AUCP(b)*, regardless of the social position of the applicant.

** NOTE The CC may grant to individual territory *and regional committees* and to the CCs of the national communist parties the right of final confirmation *of party membership* of former members of other parties.

(d) Verification of the recommendation precedes admission and is the responsibility of the local party committee.

* (e) The question of admission to the party is first examined by the *primary party organization*, is decided by the general meeting of the organization and comes into force upon confirmation *for the first and second categories by the district committee or the city committee, for the third and fourth categories by the regional committee, the territory committee or the CC of the national communist party*.

(f) Youth up to and including 20 years of age enter the party only through the VLKSM.

* 4. Those who give recommendations bear responsibility for those they recommend and in cases of unfounded recommendations, are subject to party punishment up to expulsion from the party.

5. Seniority of party membership of those candidates admitted as party members is counted from the day on which the general meeting of the appropriate *primary party organization* decides to confirm the given comrade as a party member.

6. Any member of one organization who is transferred into the area of work of another organization is registered with the latter as one of its members.

NOTE The transfer of party members from one organization to another is conducted in accordance with the rules established by the CC of the party.

* 7. Members and candidates of the party who have not paid membership dues for three months without valid reasons are

considered to have left the party, and the general meeting *of members of the primary organization* is informed of this.

*   8.   The question of the expulsion of someone from the party is decided by a general meeting of that organization of which the person is a member and is confirmed *for those in the first and second categories by the regional or territory committee, for those in the third and fourth categories by the district or city committee,* while from the day of expulsion by the general meeting of the party organization or party committee the given person is removed from party work. Expulsions of members of the party are reported in the party press with an indication of the reasons for the expulsion.

**   9.   *On the basis of periodic decisions of the CC AUCP(b), purges are conducted for the systematic cleansing of the party from:*

> *alien class and hostile elements;*
>
> *double-dealers who deceive the party and conceal from it their real views and who wreck party policy;*
>
> *overt and covert violators of the iron discipline of the party and state;*
>
> *degenerates in league with bourgeois elements;*
>
> *careerists, self-seekers and bureaucratic elements;*
>
> *moral decadents who, through their improper conduct fail to uphold the dignity of the party, who stain the banner of the party;*
>
> *passive individuals who do not carry out the responsibilities of party members and have not mastered the programme, Rules and most important decisions of the party.*

II   On candidate members of the party

*   10.   All persons wishing to enter the *party* pass through a candidate stage, which is intended to acquaint the candidate thoroughly with the programme, *Rules and* tactics of the party, and to verify the personal qualities of the candidate.

*   11.   The procedure for admission to candidate membership (division into categories, the character of the recommendations and their verification, decision of the organization on admission and confirmation by the party committee) is absolutely identical to that for admission to membership of the party.

*   12. The candidate stage is established as follows: for the first category, *one year*; *for the second, third and fourth categories, two years.*

**   NOTE Former members of other parties, regardless of their social position, pass through a 3-year candidate stage.

13. Candidate members of the party take part in meetings of that organization of which they are a member with the right of a consultative vote.

14. Candidates pay the usual membership dues to the treasury of the local party committee.

III On groups of sympathizers

**   15. *In order to organize around the AUCP(b) the non-party activists closest to the party, those who have shown in deed and work their devotion to the party but who are still not ready to join the party, groups of sympathizers of the AUCP(b) are formed attached to the primary party organizations, unconditionally subordinated to all of the decisions of party organs.*

**   16. *Admission to the groups of sympathizers comes about through decisions of factory, institution and other party committees, political departments of MTSs, sovkhozes and railway transport, with the recommendation of two party members.*

**   17. *Those organized into groups of sympathizers of the AUCP(b) must attend all open party meetings, at which they enjoy the right of a consultative vote, actively struggle for the implementation of decisions of the party and government, systematically work under the leadership of party organizations towards raising their ideological–political level.*

IV On the organizational structure of the party

18. The guiding principle of the organizational structure of the party is democratic centralism, which means:

    (a) *the election of all leading organs of the party from the top to the bottom;*

    (b) *the periodic report of party organs to their party organizations;*

    (c) *strict party discipline and the subordination of the minority to the majority;*

*   (d) *the unconditionally binding character of decisions of higher organs for lower organs and all party members.*

* 19.   The party is built on the basis of democratic centralism along territorial–*production* lines: an organization serving a district is considered to be higher than all the organizations serving parts of that district, *or an organization serving a whole branch of production or administration is considered to be higher than all the organizations serving parts of that branch.*

20.   All party organizations are autonomous in deciding local questions, *in so far as those decisions do not contradict decisions of the party.*

21.   The highest leading organ of each organization is the general meeting, conference or congress.

22.   The general meeting, conference or congress elects a committee which is its executive organ and which leads all the current work of the organization.

23.   The scheme of organization of the party *is as follows*:

*   (a) territory of the USSR – All-Union congress – CC *AUCP(b)*;

*   (b) regions, *territories*, republics – regional and territory conferences, congresses of national communist parties – regional committees, territory committees, CCs of national communist parties;

       (c) *cities, districts – city and district conferences – city and district committees*;

*   (d) enterprises, villages, *kolkhozes, MTSs*, Red Army units, institutions – general meetings, *conferences of primary party organizations – primary party committees (factory and plant committees, party bureaux of Red Army units, etc).*

** 24.   The order of subordination, accountability, the passage and questioning of party decisions (from the highest instance to the lowest) is: All-Union congress, CC *AUCP(b)*, regional/territory conference, conference *or congress* of the national communist party, regional and territory committee, CC of the national communist party, *city/district conference, city/district committee, etc.*

* 25.   *For practical work in the implementation of party directives and decisions (and verification of their implementation by soviet-economic organs and lower party organizations), integral production-branch departments are formed in regional*

committees, territory committees, CCs of the national communist parties and the CC AUCP(b).

In the CC AUCP(b):

(a) *Agricultural, (b) Industrial, (c) Transport, (d) Planning–Finance–Trade, (e) Politico-administrative, (f) Leading party organs, (g) Culture and propaganda of Leninism, (h) Institute of Marx–Engels–Lenin (and also 2 sectors – Administration of Affairs and Special).*

In regional committees, territory committees and CCs of the national communist parties:

(a) Agricultural, (b) Industrial–transport, (c) Soviet–trade, (d) Culture and propaganda of Leninism, (e) Leading party organs (city and district) and Special sector.

In each production-branch department is concentrated all the work of a given branch: organization of party work; distribution and training of cadres; mass agitational work; production propaganda; supervision of the implementation of party decisions by appropriate soviet-economic organs and party organizations.

26.   Following its final confirmation, every *party* organization has the right to acquire its own press, but only with the sanction of the appropriate higher party organization.

V   On the central organizations of the party

27.   The supreme organ of the party is the congress. Regular congresses are convened *at least once every three years.* Extraordinary congresses are convened by the Central Committee on its own initiative, or on the demand of not less than one-third of the total number of members represented at the last party congress. The convocation of the party congress and the agenda are announced not less than a month and a half before the congress.

Extraordinary congresses are convened within two months.

A congress is considered valid if no less than half of all members of the party represented at the last regular congress are represented.

Norms of representation at the party congress are set by the Central Committee.

28.   If the Central Committee does not convene an extraordinary congress as provided for in point 27, the

organizations which have demanded the convocation of an extraordinary congress have the right to form an organizational committee, which enjoys the rights of the Central Committee with respect to the convening of *an extraordinary* congress.

29. The congress:

* (a) hears and approves the reports of the Central Committee, *Party* Control Commission, Central Auditing Commission and other central organizations;

(b) reviews and changes the programme and Rules of the party;

(c) determines the tactical line of the party on *basic* questions *of current policy*;

* (d) elects the Central Committee, *Party* Control Commission, Central Auditing Commission and *nominates the membership of the Commission of Soviet Control for submission to the TsIK and SNK of the USSR for confirmation*.

* 30. The congress elects the Central Committee *and other central organizations* and determines their sizes. In the event of vacancies occurring in the Central Committee, they are filled from among those candidates elected by the congress in the order determined by the congress.

31. The Central Committee has no less than one plenary session every *four* months. Candidate members of the CC participate in plenary sessions of the CC with the right of a consultative vote.

32. The Central Committee organizes a Political Bureau for political work, an Organizational Bureau for the general leadership of organizational work, and a Secretariat for current work of an organizational and executive character.

33. In the intervals between congresses the Central Committee guides all the work of the party, represents the party in relations with other parties, organizations and institutions, organizes the various institutions of the party and guides their activities, appoints the editorial boards of the central organs working under its supervision and confirms the editors of party organs of major local organizations, organizes and directs enterprises having social significance, distributes the forces and funds of the party and manages the central treasury.

The Central Committee directs the work of the central soviet and public organizations through party *groups in them*.

*   34.   *In order to strengthen Bolshevik leadership and political work, the Central Committee has the right to establish political departments and to assign party organizers from the CC to lagging sectors of socialist construction which have especially important significance for the national economy and the country as a whole, and also in so far as the political departments complete their urgent tasks, to convert them into normal party organs constructed along the production–territorial principle.*

    Political departments have the rights of the corresponding production party committees and are led directly by the CC AUCP(b) through production-branch departments of the CC or through specially organized political boards and political sectors.

35.   The Central Committee regularly informs party organizations about its work.

*   36.   *The Party Control Commission:*

    (a) *supervises the implementation of decisions of the party and the CC AUCP(b);*

    (b) *calls to account those guilty of violations of party discipline;*

    (c) *calls to account those guilty of violations of party ethics.*

37.   The Central Auditing Commission inspects: (a) the speed and correctness of the conduct of business in the central organs of the party and the proper functioning of the apparatus of the Secretariat of the CC AUCP(b); (b) the treasury and enterprises of the CC AUCP(b).

VI   On territory, regional and republican organizations of the party

*   38.   *The highest organ of the regional/territory/republican party organization is the regional/territory party conference/congress of the national communist party and in the interval between them the regional/territory committee/CC of the national communist party. In their activities they are guided by the general decisions of the All-Union Communist Party and its leading organs.*

*   39.   The regular territory/regional conference/congress of the national communist party is convened by the territory/regional committee/CC of the national communist party *once every one and a half years*, and an extraordinary one is convened by decision of the territory/regional committee/CC of the national communist party or on the demand of one-third of the total membership of organizations in the territory/region/*republic*.

Norms of representation at the territory/regional conference/congress of the national communist party are established by the territory/regional committee/CC of the national communist party.

The territory/regional conference/congress of the national communist party hears and approves the reports of the territory/regional committee/CC of the national communist party, the auditing commission and other territory/regional institutions, discusses questions of party, soviet, economic and trade union work in the territory/region/republic and elects the territory/regional committee *(in the republics – the CC of the national communist party)*, the auditing commission *and delegates to the All-Union congress of the party.*

* 40. *For current work, the territory/regional committee, and in the republics the CC of the national communist party, chooses executive organs of not more than 11 people, confirmed by the CC AUCP(b), and two secretaries, the first and second. Secretaries must be of no less than 12 years' party standing.*

* 41. The territory/regional committee/CC of the national communist party organizes the various institutions of the party in the territory/region/*republic* and guides their activities, appoints the editorial board of the territory/regional party organ working under its supervision, *guides the party groups in non-party organizations*, organizes and directs its own enterprises having general significance for the region/*territory*/*republic*, distributes the forces and funds of the party *within its organization* and manages the territory/regional/*republican* party treasury.

* 42. The plenum of the territory/regional committee/CC of the national communist party is convened at least once every *three* months.

* 43. *Party organizations of national and other regions and autonomous republics in territories and republics work under the guidance of territory committees or CCs of national communist parties and in their internal life are guided by the regulations contained in chapter VI of the Rules of the party on territory, regional and republican organizations.*

VII   On city and district (rural and urban) organizations of the party

* 44. *The city/district party conference is convened by the city/district committee at least once a year, an extraordinary*

conference by decision of the city/district committee or on the demand of one-third of the total membership of organizations in the city/district organization.

The city/district conference hears and approves reports of the city/district committee, auditing commission and other city/district institutions, elects the city/district committee, auditing commission and delegates to the territory/regional conference or congress of the national communist party.

* 45.   The secretary of a city committee must be of 10 years' party standing and the secretary of a district committee of 7 years' party standing. Secretaries of city and district committees are confirmed by the regional committee, territory committee or CC of the national communist party.

* 46.   The city/district committee elects a bureau of 5–7 people, organizes and confirms primary party organizations in enterprises, in sovkhozes, MTSs, kolkhozes and institutions, conducts the registration of all communists, organizes the various institutions of the party in the city/district and guides their activities, appoints the editors of the city/district party organ working under its guidance and supervision, guides the party groups in non-party organizations, organizes its own enterprises having general city/district significance, distributes the forces and funds of the party in the city and district, and manages the city/district treasury. The city/district committee presents to the territory/regional committee/CC of the national communist party a report on its activities at the time and in the form established by the CC AUCP(b).

47.   In large cities district organizations subordinate to the city committee are established with the permission of the CC AUCP(b).

VIII   On primary organizations of the party

* 48.   The basis of the party is the primary party organizations. Primary party organizations are formed in factories, plants, sovkhozes and other economic enterprises, in kolkhozes, MTSs, Red Army units, in villages, in institutions, etc. where there are no less than 3 party members. In enterprises, in kolkhozes, in institutions, etc. where there are less than 3 party members, candidate or party-komsomol groups are formed, headed by a party organizer chosen by district committees, city committees or *political departments. Primary party organizations are confirmed by district/city committees or appropriate political departments.*

*   49.   *In large enterprises, institutions, kolkhozes, etc. with a large number of communists (from 100 members to 3000 and above) inside the general primary party organization embracing the whole enterprise, institution, etc., party organizations may be formed in shops, units, departments, etc., in each particular case with the approval of the district/city committee or appropriate political department. In their turn, within shop, unit and other organizations, party groups may be formed by brigades or units of the enterprise, etc.*

50.   The *primary party organization* links the worker and peasant masses with the leading organs of the party. Its tasks are:

(a) *agitational and organizational work among the masses for party slogans and decisions;*

*   (b) attraction of *sympathizers* and new members and their *political* education;

*   (c) assistance to the *district committee/city committee or political department* in its *daily* organizational and agitational work;

(d) *mobilization of the masses in enterprises, in sovkhozes, kolkhozes, etc. for the implementation of the production plan, the strengthening of labour discipline and the development of shock work;*

(e) *struggle with slackness and the uneconomic management of affairs in the enterprises, in sovkhozes, kolkhozes and daily care for the improvement of the living conditions of the workers and kolkhozniks;*

*   (f) active participation, as a party organ, in the economic and political life of the country.

*   51.   For the conduct of current work the *primary party organization* elects a *party committee (factory party committee, plant party committee, etc.) of not more than 11 people serving for one year, and a shop organization elects a party organizer, who is confirmed by the primary party committee.*

In party organizations with less than 15 members and candidates, party committees are not formed but party organizers are chosen. In primary party committees having no more than 100 party members, party work is conducted, as a rule, by workers who have not been freed from work in production. In party committees with up to 1000 party members there must be 2–3 paid workers who are freed from work in production. In party committees with up to 3000 members or more there may be 4–5 comrades freed from production.

Secretaries of *primary party committees* must be of no less than 3 years' party standing *and party organizers two years' party standing.*

IX On party organizations in the Red Army

*   52.   General leadership of party work in the Red Army, the Red Fleet *and Aviation* is carried out by the Political Administration of the RKKA, which exercises the authority of a military department of the CC *AUCP(b)*. The PUR exercises its leadership through its appointed political departments, military commissars and party commissions elected at corresponding army conferences.

Party organizations in the Red Army, Fleet and *Aviation* work on the basis of special instructions confirmed by the CC *AUCP(b)*.

*   53.   Heads of political departments of areas, fleets and armies must be of *10* years' party standing, and heads of political departments of divisions and brigades of *6* years' party standing.

*   54.   Political organs must maintain close ties with local party committees through the constant participation in the local party committees of the leaders of political organs and military commissars *(assistants for political affairs)*, and also through the systematic hearing in party committees of reports of the heads of political organs and military commissars *(assistants for political affairs)* on political work in military units.

X On party groups in non-party organizations

*   55.   In all congresses, meetings and elected organs of *non-party* soviet, trade union, co-operative and *other mass organizations* where there are no less than 3 party members, *party groups* are organized, the task of which is the all-round strengthening of the influence of the party and the execution of its policy in the non-party milieu, *the strengthening of iron party and soviet discipline, the struggle with bureaucratism, and the verification of the implementation of party and soviet directives.*

The *group* elects a *secretary* for current work.

* 56. *Groups*, regardless of their importance, are wholly subordinate to the appropriate party organizations *(CC AUCP(b), territory committee, regional committee, CC of the national communist party, city committee and district committee). On all questions groups must adhere strictly and without deviation to decisions of leading party organizations.*

XI On intra-party democracy and party discipline

* 57. *The free and businesslike discussion of questions of party policy in individual organizations or in the party as a whole is the inalienable right of every party member, stemming from intra-party democracy. Only on the basis of intra-party democracy can Bolshevik self-criticism be developed and party discipline, which must be conscious and not mechanical, be strengthened. But wide discussion, especially discussion on an all-union scale, of questions of party policy, must be organized in such a way that it cannot lead to attempts by an insignificant minority to impose its will on the enormous majority of the party or to attempts to form fractional groupings, which destroy the unity of the party, to attempts at schism which could shake the strength and steadfastness of the dictatorship of the proletariat to the joy of the enemies of the working class. Therefore wide* discussion on an all-union scale may be considered necessary only if: (a) this necessity is recognized as an extreme measure by several local party organizations at the regional or republican level; (b) if there is no sufficiently firm majority in the CC on the most important questions of party policy; (c) if, in spite of a firm majority in the CC holding a definite point of view, the CC considers it necessary to verify the correctness of its policy through discussion in the party. *Only upon fulfilment of these conditions can the party be guaranteed against the misuse of intra-party democracy on the part of anti-party elements, only under these conditions can it be assured that intra-party democracy serves the cause and will not be used in a way harmful to the party and the working class.*

* 58. *The preservation of the unity of the party, the ruthless struggle with the smallest attempts at fractional struggle and schism, the strictest party and soviet discipline are the primary responsibility of all party members and all party organizations. In order to implement strict discipline inside the party and in all soviet* *work and to achieve the utmost unity with the elimination of any fractionalism, the CC AUCP(b) has the right in cases of the violation of discipline or the revival or toleration of fractionalism to apply all measures of party punishment up to expulsion from the party, and in relation to members of the CC, transfer to candidate status and, as an extreme measure, expulsion from the party. For the application of such an extreme measure to members of the CC, candidate members of the CC and members of the Party Control Commission, a plenum of the CC must be convened with invitations to all candidate members of the CC and all members of the Party Control Commission. If such a general meeting of the most responsible leaders of the party by a two-thirds vote recognizes the need for the transfer of members of the CC or the Party Control Commission to candidate status or expulsion from the party, such a measure must be implemented immediately.*

59.   The decisions of party and soviet centres must be implemented quickly and exactly. The failure to implement decisions of higher organizations and other misdemeanours acknowledged as criminal by public opinion in the party, entails: for organizations – censure and general re-registration (dissolution of the organization); for individual members of the party – some type of censure (admonition, reproof, etc.), public censure, temporary removal from responsible party and soviet work, expulsion from the party, expulsion from the party with a report of the misdemeanour to administrative and judicial authorities.

**   60.   Members of the party who refuse truthfully to answer the questions of the Party Control Commission are subject to immediate expulsion from the party.

XII   On the finances of the party

61.   The finances *of the party and its* organizations come from membership dues, *income from party enterprises* and other receipts.

62.   *Monthly membership dues for party members and candidates are established in the following scale:*

> *Earnings*
> *up to 100 roubles*   *20 kopecks*
> *101–150r*   *60k*

151–200r	*1 rouble*
201–250r	*1r 50k*
251–300r	*2r*
301–500r	*2 per cent of earnings*
above 500r	*3 per cent of earnings*

63.   Entry dues of *2 per cent* of earnings are collected upon entry to candidature.

Rules of the All-Union Communist Party (Bolsheviks) (Section of the Communist International)

Adopted at the XVIII Congress of the AUCP(b), March 1939

** The All-Union Communist Party (Bolsheviks) is a section of the Communist International, is the leading organized detachment of the *working class* of the USSR, the highest form of its class organization. *The party is guided in its work by the theory of Marxism–Leninism.*

The party exercises leadership of the *working class*, peasantry and *intelligentsia, of all the Soviet people* in the struggle for the *strengthening* of the dictatorship of the *working class, for the strengthening and development of the socialist structure, for the victory of communism.*

The party is the leading nucleus of all the organizations of the workers, both public and state, and ensures the successful construction of *the communist* society.

The party is a united, militant organization, bound together by conscious discipline *equally binding on all members of the party.* The party's strength is its solidarity, unity of will, and unity of action, which are incompatible with deviations from the programme *and Rules*, with violations of party discipline, with fractional groupings, *with double-dealing. The party cleanses its ranks from persons who violate the programme of the party, Rules of the party, and discipline of the party.*

The party demands from its members active and selfless work for the implementation of the programme and Rules of the party, the carrying out of all the decisions of the party and its organs, the preservation of the unity of the ranks of the party and the strengthening of fraternal international relations both among the working nationalities of the USSR and with the proletariat of all the countries of the world.

I Party members, their responsibilities and rights

* 1. A Party member is anyone who accepts the party

165

programme, works in one of its organizations, submits to the decisions of the party and pays membership dues.

2.   A party member must:

        (a) tirelessly work at increasing his *consciousness*, at mastering the fundamentals of Marxism–Leninism;

        (b) observe the strictest party discipline, actively participate in the political life of the party and the country, carry out the policy of the party and the decisions of party organs;

        (c) be a model in the maintenance of labour and state discipline, in mastering the techniques of his work, and continually increasing his productive and practical qualifications;

        (d) *daily strengthen links with the masses, promptly respond to the enquiries and needs of the workers, explain to the non-party masses the meaning of party policies and decisions.*

3.   *A party member has the right:*

        (a) *to participate in free and businesslike discussion of practical questions of party policy in party meetings or in the party press;*

        (b) *to criticize any party worker at party meetings;*

        (c) *to vote in elections and be elected to party organs;*

        (d) *to demand personal participation in all cases when a decision is to be made on his personal activities or behaviour;*

        (e) *to address any question and statement to any party instance up to the CC AUCP(b).*

4.   Admission to party membership is made exclusively on an individual basis. New members are admitted from among the candidates who have completed the established candidate stage. Workers, *peasants and intelligentsia who are conscious, active and devoted to the cause of communism are admitted as members of the party.*

Persons who have reached eighteen years are admitted to the party.

The procedure for the admission of candidates as members of the party is as follows:

        (a) *Those entering the party present recommendations of three party members of no less than three years' party standing and who have worked with them for no less than one year.*

*   FIRST NOTE   During admission to party membership from the komsomol, the recommendation of a district committee of the VLKSM is equivalent to the recommendation of *one* party member.

*   SECOND NOTE   *Members and candidate members of the CC AUCP(b) refrain from giving recommendations.*

(b) The question of admission to the party *is discussed and* decided by the general meeting of the *primary party organization*, the decision of which comes into force upon confirmation *by the district committee, and in cities where there is no district division, by the city committee of the party. During discussion of the question of admission to the party, the participation of those who gave the recommendations is optional.*

(c) Youth up to and including 20 years of age enter the party only through the VLKSM.

*   (d) Former members of other parties are admitted *as members of the party* in exceptional cases on the recommendation of five party members: three of ten years' party standing and two of pre-revolutionary party standing, and only through a *primary party organization*, with compulsory confirmation by the CC AUCP(b).

5.   Those who give recommendations bear responsibility for *the high quality of their recommendations.*

6.   Seniority of party membership of those candidates admitted as party members is counted from the day on which the general meeting of the appropriate primary party organization decides to confirm the given comrade as a party member.

7.   Any member of one organization who is transferred into the area of work of another organization is registered with the latter as one of its members.

*   NOTE   The transfer of party members from one organization to another is conducted in accordance with the rules established by the CC of the party.

8.   Members and candidates of the party who have not paid membership dues for three months without valid reasons are considered to have left the party, *on which the primary party organization takes the appropriate decision, which is confirmed by the district committee or the city committee of the party.*

*   9.   The question of the expulsion of someone from the party is decided by a general meeting of *the primary party organization* of which the *expelled* person is a member and is confirmed by the *district committee or city committee of the party. A decision of a district committee or a city committee about expulsion from the party takes effect only when it has been confirmed by the regional or territory committee of the party or the CC of the communist party of a union republic.*

* 10. *Prior to the confirmation by a regional or territory committee or CC of the communist party of a union republic of a decision on expulsion from the party, the party card remains in the hands of the party member and he has the right to attend closed party meetings.* Expulsions of members of the party are reported in the *local* party press *by the regional or territory committee or the CC of the communisty party of a union republic*, along with an indication of the reasons for expulsion. *The reinstatement of illegally expelled members is published in the same way.*

* 11. *During decision of a question of expulsion from the party or of reinstatement of an expelled person to the rights of party member, maximum care and comradely concern must be maintained and a thorough investigation made of the validity of the charges laid against the party member.*

For petty misdemeanours (absence from meetings, non-payment of membership dues on time, etc.) measures of party education and influence as provided for in the Rules must be employed, and not expulsion from the party, which is the highest measure of party punishment.

* 12. *Appeals of those expelled from the party must be examined by the appropriate party organs no later than two weeks from the date of their receipt.*

II   Candidate members of the party

13.   All persons wishing to enter the party pass through a candidate stage, which is necessary to acquaint the candidate with the programme, Rules and tactics of the party, and to *guarantee the verification by a party organization* of the personal qualities of the candidate.

14.   The procedure for admission to candidate membership (individual admission, presentation of recommendations and their verification, decision of the *primary* organization on admission and confirmation) is absolutely identical to that for admission to membership of the party.

15. The candidate stage is fixed at *one year*.

16. Candidate members of the party take part in meetings of that organization of which they are a member with the right of a consultative vote.

17. Candidate *members of the party* pay the usual membership dues to the treasury of the local party committee.

III   Structure of the party. Intra-party democracy

18. The guiding principle of the organizational structure of the party is democratic centralism, which means:

    (a) the election of all leading organs of the party from the bottom to the top;

    (b) the periodic report of party organs to their party organizations;

    (c) strict party discipline and the subordination of the minority to the majority;

    (d) the unconditionally binding character of decisions of higher organs for lower.

19. The party is built along territorial–production lines: a *party* organization serving a district is considered to be higher than all the *party* organizations serving parts of that district, or a *party* organization serving a whole branch of *work* is considered to be higher than all the party organizations serving parts of that branch *of work*.

20. All party organizations are autonomous in deciding local questions in so far as those decisions do not contradict decisions of the party.

21. The highest leading organ of each *party* organization is the general meeting *(for primary organizations)*, the conference (for example, *for district and regional organizations)* and the congress *(for the communist parties of the union republics, for the AUCP(b))*.

22. The general meeting, conference or congress elects a *bureau or* committee which is its executive organ and which leads all the current work of the organization.

23. *The use of voting lists is forbidden in elections to party organs. Voting must take place by separate candidate, with all members of the party assured the unlimited right to challenge candidates and to criticize them. Elections of candidates are conducted by closed (secret) ballot.*

* 24. *In all republican, territory and regional centres, and also in all the more or less significant industrial centres, aktvis of city party organizations are convened for discussion of the most important decisions of the party and government. Aktivs must be convened not for show and formal–celebratory approval of these decisions, but for real discussion of them.*

In large centres not only city but also district party aktivs must be convened.

* 25. The free and businesslike discussion of questions of party policy in individual organizations or in the party as a whole is the inalienable right of every party member, stemming from intra-party democracy. Only on the basis of intra-party democracy can Bolshevik self-criticism be developed and party discipline, which must be conscious and not mechanical, be strengthened. But wide discussion, especially discussion on an all-union scale of questions of party policy, must be organized in such a way that it cannot lead to attempts by an insignificant minority to impose its will on the enormous majority of the party or to attempts to form fractional groupings, which destroy the unity of the party, to attempts at schism which could shake the strength and steadfastness of the dictatorship of the *working class*. Therefore wide discussion on an all-union scale may be considered necessary only if:

   (a) this necessity is recognized as an extreme measure by several local party organizations at the regional or republican level;

   (b) there is no sufficiently firm majority in the CC *AUCP(b)* on the most important questions of party policy;

   (c) if, in spite of a firm majority in the CC *AUCP(b)* holding a definite point of view, the CC *AUCP(b)* considers it necessary to verify the correctness of its policy through discussion in the party. Only upon the fulfilment of these conditions can the party be guaranteed against the misuse of intra-party democracy on the part of anti-party elements, only under these conditions can it be assured that intra-party democracy serves the cause and will not be used in a way harmful to the party and the working class.

** 26. The scheme of organization of the party:

**   (a) *for the party as a whole* – All-Union congress, CC AUCP(b), *All-Union conference*;

**   (b) for the region, territory and union republic – regional and territory conferences, congresses of the communist parties *of the union republics*, regional committees, territory committees, CCs of the communist parties of the *union republics*;

** (c) *for the area – area conferences, area committees*;

** (d) for the city and district – city and district conferences, city and district committees;

** (e) for the enterprise, village, kolkhoz, MTS, units of the Red Army *and Navy*, and for institutions – general meetings, conferences of primary party organizations, *bureaux of primary party organizations*.

** 27. For practical work in the implementation of party decisions in the CC AUCP(b) *there exist the following administrations and departments:*

(a) *Administration of cadres; (b) Administration of propaganda and agitation; (c) Organizational–instruction department;* (d) Agricultural department; (e) *School department.* In area committees, regional committees, territory committees and CCs of the communist parties of the *union republics: (a) Cadres department, (b) Propaganda and agitation department,* (c) *Organizational–instruction department,* (d) Agricultural department, (e) *Military department. In city and district committees of the party:* (a) *Cadres department, (b) Propaganda and agitation department, (c) Organizational–instruction department, (d) Military department.*

The responsibility of the military department is to render assistance to the military organs in the registration of reservists, the organization of the call-up, mobilization in case of war, in the organization of anti-aircraft defence, etc.

Leadership of the agitation and propaganda sections and the cadres sections in regional committees, territory committees and CCs of the communist parties of the union republics must be entrusted to special secretaries.

** 28. Following its final confirmation, every party organization has the right to acquire its own press, but only with the sanction of the appropriate higher party organization.

IV   Higher organs of the party

* 29. The supreme organ of the *AUCP(b)* is the congress of the

AUCP(b). Regular congresses are convened at least once every three years. Extraordinary congresses are convened by the Central Committee *of the AUCP(b)* on its own initiative, or on the demand of not less than one third of the total number of members represented at the last party congress. The convocation of the party congress and the agenda are announced not less than a month and a half before the congress. An extraordinary congress is convened within two months.

A congress is considered valid if no less than half of all members of the party represented at the last regular congress are represented. Norms of representation at the party congress are set by the Central Committee *of the AUCP(b)*.

* 30. If the Central Committee of the *AUCP(b)* does not convene an extraordinary congress as provided for in point 29, the organizations which have demanded the convocation of an extraordinary congress have the right to form an organizational committee, which enjoys the rights of the Central Committee *of the AUCP(b)* with respect to the convening of an extraordinary congress.

31. The congress:

*   (a) hears and approves the reports of the Central Committee *of the AUCP(b)*, Central Auditing Commission and other central organizations;

    (b) reviews and changes the programme and Rules of the party;

    (c) determines the tactical line of the party on basic questions of current policy;

*   (d) elects the Central Committee of the AUCP(b) and the Central Auditing Commission.

* 32. The congress elects the Central Committee *of the AUCP(b) and the Central Auditing Commission* and determines their sizes. In the event of vacancies occurring in the Central Committee *of the AUCP(b)*, they are filled from among the candidate members of the CC elected by the congress.

* 33. The Central Committee *of the AUCP(b)* has no less than one plenary session every four months. Candidate members of the CC *AUCP(b)* participate in plenary sessions of the CC *AUCP(b)* with the right of a consultative vote.

* 34. The Central Committee *of the AUCP(b)* organizes a Political bureau for political work, an Organizational bureau for the general leadership of organizational work, a Secretariat for current work of an organizational–executive character, *and a Party Control Commission for the verification of the implementation of decisions of the party and the CC AUCP(b).*

35. The Party Control Commission:

**   (a) supervises the implementation of decisions of the party and the CC AUCP(b) *by party organizations and soviet economic organs;*

**   (b) *verifies the work of local party organizations;*

*   (c) calls to account those guilty of violations of the *programme* and *Rules of the AUCP(b)* and party discipline.

* 36. In the intervals between congresses the Central Committee *of the AUCP(b)* guides all the work of the party, represents the party in relations with other parties, organizations and institutions, organizes the various institutions of the party and guides their activities, appoints the editorial boards of the central organs working under its supervision and confirms the editors of party organs of major local organizations, organizes and directs enterprises having social significance, distributes the forces and funds of the party and manages the central treasury.

The Central Committee *of the AUCP(b)* directs the work of the central soviet and public organizations through party groups in them.

** 37. *In the intervals between party congresses the Central Committee of the AUCP(b) at least once a year convenes an All-Union party conference of representatives of local party organizations for the discussion of pressing questions of party policy.*

Delegates to the All-Union conference are elected at plena of the regional committees, territory committees and CCs of the communist parties of the union republics.

The procedure for elections and the norms of representation at the All-Union conference are set by the CC AUCP(b).

Members of the CC AUCP(b), if they are not plenipotentiary delegates from local organizations, participate in the work of an All-Union conference with the right of a consultative vote.

** 38. *The All-Union conference has the right to change part of the membership of the CC AUCP(b), i.e. the right to remove from the CC AUCP(b) individual members of the CC AUCP(b) who have not ensured the fulfilment of those responsibilities they have assumed as members of the CC AUCP(b), and to replace them with others, but not more than one-fifth of the CC AUCP(b)* *elected by the congress of the party. The All-Union conference replenishes the membership of the CC AUCP(b) from among the candidates elected by the party congress, and to replace them elects a corresponding number of new candidate members of the CC AUCP(b).*

** 39. *Decisions of the All-Union conference are confirmed by the CC with the exception of decisions on the replacement of members of the CC AUCP(b) and the election of new candidate members of the CC AUCP(b), which do not require confirmation by the CC AUCP(b). Decisions of the All-Union conference which are confirmed by the CC AUCP(b) are binding for all party organizations.*

* 40. In order to strengthen Bolshevik leadership and political work, the Central Committee *of the AUCP(b)* has the right to establish political departments and to assign party organizers from the *CC AUCP(b)* to lagging sectors of socialist construction which have especially important significance for the national economy and the country as a whole, and also, in so far as the political departments complete their urgent tasks, to convert them into normal party organs constructed along the production-territorial principle.

Political departments *work on the basis of special instructions confirmed by the CC AUCP(b).*

41. The Central Committee regularly informs party organizations about its work.

* 42. The Central Auditing Commission inspects: (a) the speed and correctness of the conduct of business in the central organs of the party and the proper functioning of the apparatus of the Secretariat of the CC AUCP(b); (b) the treasury and enterprises of the CC AUCP(b).

V Regional, territory and republican organizations of the party

* 43. The highest organ of the regional/territory/republican party organization is the regional/territory party conference/congress of the communist party of the *union republic*, and in the interval between them, the regional committee/territory committee/CC of the communist party of the *union republic*. In their activities they are guided by the decisions of the All-Union Communist Party (Bolsheviks) and its leading organs.

* 44. The regular regional/territory conference/congress of the communist party of the *union republic* is convened by the regional/territory committee/CC of the communist party of the *union republic* once every one and a half years, and an extraordinary one is convened by decision of the regional/ territory committee/CC of the communist party of the *union republic* or on the demand of one third of the total membership of organizations in the regional/territory/republican *party organization*.

The norms of representation at the regional/territory conference/congress of the communist party of the *union republic* are established by the regional/territory committee/CC of the communist party of the *union republic*.

The regional/territory conference/congress of the communist party of the *union republic* hears and approves the reports of the regional/territory committee/the CC of the communist party of the *union republic*, the auditing commission and other regional/territory/*republican* organizations, discusses questions of party, soviet, economic and trade union work in the region/territory/republic and elects the regional committee/ territory committee/CC of the communist party of the *union republic*, the auditing commission and delegates to the All-Union congress of the party.

* 45. For current work the regional/territory committee/CC of the communist party of the union republic chooses *corresponding* executive organs of not more than 11 people *and 4–5 secretaries, including the first secretary, the second secretary, the secretary for cadres and the secretary for propaganda,* confirmed by the CC AUCP(b). Secretaries must be of no less than *five* years' party standing.

* 46. The regional/territory committee/CC of the communist party of the *union republic* organizes the various institutions of the party in the region/territory/republic and guides their activities, appoints the editorial board of the regional/territory/ *republican* party organ working under its supervision, guides the party groups in non-party organizations, organizes and directs its own enterprises having general significance for the region/ territory/republic, distributes the forces and funds of the party within its organizations and manages the regional/territory/ republican party treasury.

* 47. The plenum of the regional/territory committee/CC of the

communist party of a *union republic* is convened at least once every three months.

48. Party organizations of autonomous republics and also national and other regions in territories and *union* republics work under the guidance of territory committees or CCs of the communist parties of the *union republics* and in their internal life are guided by the regulations contained in chapter V of the Rules of the party on regional, territory and republican organizations.

VI Area organizations of the party

49. *Area party organizations are formed in regions, territories and republics having areas.*

The highest organ of the area party organization is the area party conference, which is convened by the area committee at least once every one and a half years. An extraordinary conference is convened on decision of the area committee or on the demand of one-third of the total membership of organizations in the area organization. The area conference hears and approves the reports of the area committee, auditing commission and other area party organizations, elects the area committee of the party, the auditing commission and delegates to the regional/territory conference or the congress of the communist party of the union republic.

* 50. *The area committee elects a bureau of no more than 9 people and 4 secretaries of the area committee, including the first secretary, the second secretary, the secretary for cadres and the secretary for propaganda. Secretaries must be of three years' party standing. Secretaries of the area committee are confirmed by the regional committee/territory committee/CC of the communist party of the union republic.*

* 51. *The area committee organizes the various institutions of the party in the area and guides their activities, appoints the editorial board of the area party organ working under its leadership and supervision, guides the party groups in non-party organizations, organizes its own enterprises having area significance, distributes the forces and funds of the party in the area and manages the area party treasury.*

VII City and district (rural and urban) organizations of the party

52. The city/district party conference is convened by the

city/district committee at least once a year, an extraordinary conference by decision of the city/district committee or on the demand of one third of the total membership of organizations in the city/district organization.

The city/district conference hears and approves reports of the city/district committee, auditing commission and other city/district organizations, elects the city/district committee, auditing commission and delegates to the territory/regional conference or congress of the communist party of the union republic.

* 53. The city/district committee elects a bureau of 7–9 people *and three secretaries of the city/district committee of the party.* Secretaries of the city/district committee must be of no less than *three* years' party standing. Secretaries of the city and district committees are confirmed by the regional committee, territory committee or the CC of the communist party of the *union republic.*

* 54. The city/district committee organizes and confirms primary party organizations in enterprises, in sovkhozes, MTSs, kolkhozes and institutions, conducts the registration of communists, organizes the various institutions of the party in the city/district and guides their activities, appoints the *editorial board* of the city/district party organ working under its guidance and supervision, guides the party groups in non-party organizations, organizes its own enterprises having general city/district significance, distributes the forces and funds of the party in the city and district, and manages the city/district *party* treasury. The city/district committee presents to the regional/territory committee/CC of the communist party of the *union republic* a report on its activities at the time and in the form established by the CC AUCP(b).

* 55. *The plenum of the city/district committee is convened at least once every one and a half months.*

* 56. In large cities district organizations subordinate to the city committee are established with the permission of the CC AUCP(b).

VIII Primary organizations of the party

* 57. The basis of the party is the primary party organizations. Primary party organizations are formed in factories, plants, sovkhozes, MTSs and other economic enterprises, in kolkhozes, units of the Red Army *and Navy*, villages, institutions, *educational institutions*, etc., where there are no less than 3 party members. In enterprises, in kolkhozes, in institutions, etc. where there are less than 3 party members, candidate or party–komsomol groups are formed, headed by a party organizer chosen by the district/city committee or the political department.

Primary party organizations are confirmed by district/city committees or appropriate political departments.

58.　In enterprises, institutions, kolkhozes, etc. where there are more than 100 *members and candidates of the party* inside the general primary party organization embracing the whole enterprise, institution, etc., party organizations may be formed in shops, units, departments, etc., in each particular case with the approval of the district/city committee or appropriate political department.

In shop, unit, etc. organizations, *and also in primary party organizations numbering less than 100 members and candidates*, party groups by brigades or units of the enterprise may be formed.

* 59.　*In large enterprises and institutions numbering more than 500 members and candidates of the party, factory party committees may be formed, in each case with the approval of the CC AUCP(b), with the shop party organizations in these enterprises being granted the rights of a primary party organization.*

60.　The primary party organization links the masses of workers, peasants and *intelligentsia* with the leading organs of the party.

Its tasks are:

* 　　　(a) agitational and organizational work among the masses for *the fulfilment of* party slogans and decisions, *with the maintenance of leadership of the factory press*;

　　　(b) attraction of new members into the party and their political education;

　　　(c) assistance to the district committee, city committee or political department in *all its practical work*;

* 　　　(d) mobilization of the masses in enterprises, sovkhozes, kolkhozes, etc. for the implementation of the production plan, the strengthening of labour discipline and the development of *socialist competition and* shock work;

(e) struggle with slackness and the uneconomic management of affairs in enterprises, in sovkhozes, kolkhozes and daily care for the improvement of the *cultural*–living conditions of the workers, *employees* and kolkhozniks;

(f) active participation in the economic and political life of the country.

* 61. *To increase the role of primary party organizations in productive enterprises, including sovkhozes, kolkhozes and MTSs, and their responsibility for the state of work of the enterprises, these organizations are granted the right of supervision over the activities of the administration of the enterprise.*

Party organizations in people's commissariats, which cannot exercise supervision functions because of the special conditions of work of soviet institutions, must draw attention to deficiencies in the work of the institution, take note of shortcomings in the work of the people's commissariat and its individual workers and send its information and analysis to the CC AUCP(b) and the leaders of the people's commissariat.

Secretaries of primary party organizations in people's commissariats are confirmed by the CC AUCP(b).

All communists who are workers in the central apparatus of a people's commissariat enter one party organization for the whole people's commissariat.

* 62. For the conduct of current work the primary party organization elects a *bureau* of no more than 11 people for a term of one year.

Bureaux of primary party organizations are formed in party organizations having no less than 15 party members.

In party organizations numbering less than 15 party members, *bureaux* are not formed, *but a secretary of the primary party organization is elected.*

To promote the rapid training and education of party members in the spirit of collective leadership, shop party organizations numbering no less than 15 but no more than 100 party members are granted the right to elect a bureau of the shop party organization consisting of from 3 to 5 people, while those numbering more than 100 party members elect a bureau of from 5 to 7 people.

In primary party organizations having no more than 100 party members, party work is conducted, as a rule, by workers who have not been freed from production.

In *primary party organizations* with up to 1000 party members, there *are* 2–3 paid workers, and in those with up to 3000 members and more, there *are* 4–5 comrades freed from work in production.

Secretaries of primary and *shop party organizations* must be of no less than *one* year's party standing.

IX   Party and Komsomol

*   63.   *The VLKSM carries out its work under the leadership of the AUCP(b). The CC VLKSM is the leading organ of the komsomol, and is subordinated to the CC AUCP(b). The work of local organizations of the VLKSM is directed and supervised by the corresponding republican, territory, regional, city and district party organizations.*

64.   *Members of the VLKSM who become members or candidates of the party leave the komsomol at the moment of their entry to the party if they do not occupy leading posts in komsomol organizations.*

65.   *The VLKSM is the active assistant of the party in all state and economic construction. Komsomol organizations must be in deed the active champions of party directives in all spheres of socialist construction, especially where there are no primary party organizations.*

*   66.   *Komsomol organizations have the right of wide initiative in discussing and raising before appropriate party organizations all questions about the work of enterprises, kolkhozes, sovkhozes and institutions, with the aim of the elimination of shortcomings in their activities and giving them the necessary assistance in the improvement of their work, in the organization of socialist competition and shock working, in the conduct of mass campaigns, etc.*

X   Party organizations in the Red Army, Navy and in transport

*   67.   Leadership of party work in the *Worker–Peasant* Red Army is carried out by the Political Administration of the RKKA, which exercises the authority of a Military department of the CC AUCP(b), *and similarly in the Worker–Peasant Navy and in transport – the Political Administration of the Navy and the Political Administration of Transport exercise the authority of the*

*Navy department and the corresponding transport department of
the CC AUCP(b).*

*The Political Administration of the RKKA, the Political
Administration of the Navy and the Political Administration of
Transport* exercise their leadership through their appointed
political departments, military commissars *party organizers*, and
party commissions, elected at corresponding army, *navy and
railway conferences.*

Party organizations in the Red Army, *Navy and in transport*
work on the basis of special instructions confirmed by the CC
AUCP(b).

68.   Heads of political administrations of areas, fleets and
armies *and heads of political departments of the railways must be
of 5* years' party standing, and heads of political departments of
divisions and brigades of 3 years' party standing.

*   69.   Political organs must maintain close ties with local party
committees through the constant participation in local party
committees of the leaders of political organs and military
commissars and also through the systematic hearing in party
committees of reports of the heads of political organs and
military commissars on political work in military units *and
political departments in transport.*

XI   Party groups in non-party organizations

70.   In all congresses, meetings and elected organs of soviet,
trade union, co-operative and other mass organizations where
there are no less than 3 party members, party groups are
organized, the task of which is the all-round strengthening of the
influence of the party and the execution of its policy *among
non-party people*, the strengthening of party and *state* discipline,
the struggle with bureaucratism, and the verification of the
implementation of party and soviet directives. The group elects
a secretary for current work.

71.   *Party* groups are subordinate to the appropriate party
organizations (CC AUCP(b), CC of the communist party of a
union republic, territory committee, regional committee, *area
committee*, city committee and district committee).

On all questions groups must strictly and without deviation
be guided by the decisions of leading party organs.

XII Penalties for violations of party discipline

** 72. The preservation of the unity of the party, the ruthless struggle with the smallest attempts at *double-dealing*, fractional struggle and schism, *the maintenance of party and state* discipline is the primary responsibility of all party members and all party organizations.

** 73. The decisions of party and soviet centres must be implemented quickly and exactly. The failure to implement the decisions of higher organizations and other misdemeanours acknowledged as criminal by public opinion in the party, entails: for organizations – censure and general re-registration (dissolution of the organization); for individual members of the party – some type of censure (admonition, reproof, etc.), public censure, temporary removal from responsible party and soviet work, expulsion from the party, expulsion from the party with a report of the misdemeanour to administrative and judicial authorities.

** 74. In cases of the violation of *party and state* discipline, the revival or toleration of *double-dealing* and fractionalism *on the part of members of the CC AUCP(b)*, the CC AUCP(b) has the right to expel them from membership of the CC AUCP(b) and, as an extreme measure, expulsion from the party.

For the application of such an extreme measure to members of the CC *AUCP(b)* and candidate members of the CC AUCP(b), a plenum of the CC *AUCP(b)* must be convened with invitations to all candidate members of the CC *AUCP(b)*. If such a general meeting of the most responsible leaders of the party by a two-thirds vote recognizes the need for the expulsion of members of the CC *AUCP(b) from the CC AUCP(b)* or from the party, such a measure must be implemented immediately.

XIII Finances of the party

75. The finances of the party and its organizations come from membership dues, income from party enterprises and other receipts.

* 76. Monthly membership dues for party members and candidates are established in the following scale:

Earnings

up to 100 roubles	20 kopecks
101–150r	60k
151–200r	1 rouble
201–250r	1r 50k
251–300r	2r
301–500r	2 per cent of earnings
above 500r	3 per cent of earnings

The scale of membership dues for party members and candidates who do not have a set salary is determined by the CC AUCP(b).
77.   Entry dues of 2 per cent of earnings are collected upon entry to candidature.

Rules of the Communist Party of the Soviet Union

Adopted at the XIX Congress of the CPSU, October 1952

I The party. Members of the party, their responsibilities and rights

 *   1. *The Communist Party of the Soviet Union is a voluntary militant union of single-minded communists, organized from the people of the working class, toiling peasantry and labouring intelligentsia.*

Having organized a union of the working class and the toiling peasantry, the Communist Party of the Soviet Union achieved in the Great October Socialist Revolution of 1917 the overthrow of the power of the capitalists and land-owners, the organization of the dictatorship of the proletariat, the liquidation of capitalism, the destruction of the exploitation of man by man and ensured the construction of a socialist society.

The chief tasks of the Communist Party of the Soviet Union now are to build a communist society through the gradual transition from socialism to communism, continuously to raise the material and cultural level of society, to educate members of society in the spirit of internationalism and the establishment of fraternal links with workers of all countries, and to strengthen by all means the active defence of the Soviet Motherland from the aggressive acts of its enemies.

 *   2. *Any working person who does not exploit the labour of another, is a citizen of the Soviet Union*, accepts the programme *and Rules* of the party, *actively assists their implementation*, works in one of the organizations *of the party and carries out* all decisions of the party *may be* a member of the Communist Party *of the Soviet Union.*

A party member pays the *established* membership dues.

3. A member of the party must:

 *   (a) *in all ways guard the unity of the party, as the chief condition of the strength and power of the party;*

**   (b) *be an active fighter for the implementation of party decisions. It is insufficient for a party member merely to agree with party decisions; a party member must struggle for the realization of those decisions. A passive and formal*

184

attitude on the part of communists to decisions of the party weakens the readiness for battle of the party and is therefore incompatible with continuance in its ranks;

(c) *be an example in labour, master the techniques of his work, and continually increase his productive and practical skill, in all ways protect and strengthen public socialist property, as the sacred and inviolable basis of the Soviet system;*

(d) daily strengthen links with the masses, promptly respond to the enquiries and needs of the workers, explain to the non-party masses the meaning of party policies and decisions, *remembering that the strength and invincibility of our party is its vital and unbreakable link with the people;*

(e) work at increasing his consciousness, at mastering the fundamentals of Marxism–Leninism;

(f) *observe party and state discipline, which are equally binding for all members of the party. In the party there cannot be two disciplines – one for the leaders and another for the rank-and-file. The party has one discipline, one law for all communists regardless of service and the positions they occupy. Violation of party and state discipline is a greater evil, inflicting damage on the party, and is therefore incompatible with continuance in its ranks;*

(g) *develop self-criticism and criticism from below, expose shortcomings in work and bring about their removal, struggle against a façade of well-being and raptures over successes in work. The suppression of criticism is a grave evil. Thus whoever stifles criticism, who substitutes for it ostentation and eulogy, can have no place in the ranks of the party;*

(h) *report shortcomings in work, regardless of the persons involved, to the leading party organs up to the Central Committee of the party. A party member has no right to conceal an unfavourable state of affairs, to go along with incorrect actions inflicting damage on the interests of the party and state. Thus whoever interferes with the fulfilment of this responsibility by a party member must be strictly punished as a violator of the party's will;*

(i) *be truthful and honest before the party, and not allow the concealment and distortion of the truth. Untruthfulness of a communist before the party and the deception of the party is a grave evil and is incompatible with continuance in the ranks of the party;*

** (j) *observe party and state secrecy, display political vigilance, remembering that the vigilance of communists is necessary in all sectors and in all situations. Disclosure of party and state secrets is a crime before the party and incompatible with continuance in its ranks;*

* (k) *in any post entrusted by the party, without deviation carry out the instructions of the party on the correct selection of cadres on the basis of their political and practical qualities. Violations of these instructions, selection of workers on the basis of friendly relations, personal loyalty, localist ties and kinship is incompatible with continuance in the party.*

4. A party member has the right:

** (a) to participate in free and businesslike discussion of questions of party policy in party meetings or in the party press;

* (b) to criticize any party worker at party meetings;

(c) to vote in elections and be elected to party organs;

(d) to demand personal participation in all cases when a decision is to be made on his personal activities or behaviour;

* (e) to address any question and statement to any party instance up to the CC of the *Communist Party of the Soviet Union.*

5. Admission to party membership is made exclusively on an individual basis. New members are admitted from among the candidates who have completed the established candidate stage. Workers, peasants and intelligentsia who are conscious, active and devoted to the cause of communism are admitted as members of the party.

Persons who have reached eighteen years are admitted to the party.

The procedure for the admission of candidates as members of the party is as follows:

* (a) Those entering the party present recommendations of three party members of no less than three years' party standing and who have worked with them for no less than one year.

FIRST NOTE During admission to *the party of members of the VLKSM,* the recommendation of a district committee of the VLKSM is equivalent to the recommendation of one party member.

SECOND NOTE Members and candidate members of the CC of the *Communist Party of the Soviet Union* refrain from giving recommendations.

(b) The question of admission to the party is discussed and decided by the general meeting of the primary party organization, the decision of which comes into force upon confirmation by the district committee, and in cities where there is no district division, by the city committee of the party.

During discussion of the question of admission to the party, the participation of those who gave the recommendations is optional.

(c) Youth up to and including 20 years of age enter the party only through the VLKSM.

* (d) Former members of other parties are admitted as members of the party on the recommendation of five party members: three of ten years' party standing and two of pre-revolutionary party standing, and only through a primary party organization, with compulsory confirmation by the CC of the *Communist Party of the Soviet Union.*

* 6. Those who give recommendations bear responsibility for the high quality of their recommendations.

* 7. Seniority of party membership of those candidates admitted as party members is counted from the day on which the general meeting of the appropriate primary party organization decides to confirm the given comrade as a party member.

** 8. Any member of one organization who is transferred into the area of work of another organization is registered with the latter as one of its members.

** NOTE The transfer of party members from one organization to another is conducted in accordance with the rules established by the CC of the *Communist Party of the Soviet Union.*

* 9. Members and candidates of the party who have not paid membership dues for three months without valid reasons are considered *automatically* to have left the party, on which the primary party organization takes the appropriate decision, which is confirmed by the district committee or the city committee of the party.

* 10.   The question of the expulsion of *a communist* from the party is decided by a general meeting of the primary party organization of which the expelled person is a member and is confirmed by the district committee or city committee of the party. A decision of a district committee or a city committee about expulsion from the party takes effect only when it has been confirmed by the regional or territory committee of the party or the CC of the communist party of a union republic.

   Prior to the confirmation by a regional or territory committee or CC of the communist party of a union republic of a decision on expulsion from the party, the party card remains in the hands of the party member and he has the right to attend closed party meetings.

* 11.   *A primary party organization cannot take a decision on the expulsion from the party or the transfer to candidate status of a communist if he is a member of the CC of the Communist Party of the Soviet Union, the CC of the communist party of a union republic, a territory committee, regional committee, area committee, city committee or district committee of the party.*

   The question of the expulsion of a member of the CC of the communist party of a union republic, a territory committee, regional committee, area committee, city committee or district committee of the party from that party committee, and also expulsion from party membership or transfer to candidate status is decided at the plenum of the corresponding committee, if the plenum accepts the need for this by a two-thirds vote.

* 12.   *The question of the expulsion of a member of the CC of the Communist Party of the Soviet Union from the CC, and also expulsion from party membership or transfer to candidate status is decided by the party congress, and in the intervals between congresses, by the plenum of the CC of the Communist Party of the Soviet Union by a two-thirds majority of members of the CC plenum. A person expelled from the CC is automatically replaced by a candidate member of the CC in the order established by the congress when electing candidate members of the CC.*

* 13.   *In those cases when a party member has committed a misdemeanour punishable in a court of law,* he is expelled from the party with a report on the misdemeanour to the administrative and judicial authorities.

* 14.   During decision of a question of expulsion from the party, maximum care and comradely concern must be maintained and a

thorough investigation made of the validity of the charges laid against the party member.

For petty misdemeanours measures of party education and influence *(admonition, reproof, etc.)* must be employed, and not expulsion from the party, which is the highest measure of party punishment.

Should the necessity arise as a measure of party punishment a party organization may transfer a party member to candidate status for a period of not more than one year. The decision of a primary party organization on the transfer of a party member to candidate status is subject to confirmation by the district committee or city committee of the party. Upon expiration of the established period, the person transferred to candidate status is admitted to party membership in accordance with the regular procedure, and he retains his former party seniority.

* 15.   Appeals of those expelled from the party, *and also decisions of party organizations on expulsion from the party*, must be examined by the appropriate party organs no later than *twenty days* from the day of their receipt.

II   Candidate members of the party

* 16.   All persons wishing to enter the party pass through a candidate stage, which is necessary to acquaint the candidate with the programme, Rules and tactics of the party, and to guarantee the verification by a party organization of the personal qualities of the candidate.

* 17.   The procedure for admission to candidate membership (individual admission, presentation of recommendations and their verification, decision of the primary organization on admission and its confirmation) is absolutely identical to that for admission to party membership.

* 18.   The candidate stage is fixed at one year.

The party organization must help candidates prepare for entry to party membership. On the expiry of the candidate stage the party organization must examine at a party meeting the question of the candidate member of the party. If the candidate has not been able to prove himself sufficiently for reasons which the party organization considers valid, the primary party organization may prolong his candidate stage for a period of not more than one year. In those cases when the course of the candidate stage has made it clear that in his personal qualities the candidate is not worthy of admission to membership of the party, the party organization takes a decision on the expulsion of him from party candidature. The decision of a primary party organization on the prolongation of the candidate stage or on expulsion from candidature comes into force after confirmation by the district committee or city committee of the party.

19.   Candidate members of the party take part in meetings of that organization of which they are a member with the right of a consultative vote.

*   20.   Candidate members of the party pay the usual membership dues to the treasury of the local party committee.

III   Structure of the party. Intra-party democracy

21.   The guiding principle of the organizational structure of the party is democratic centralism, which means:

    (a) the election of all leading organs of the party from the bottom to the top;

    (b) the periodic report of party organs to their party organizations;

    (c) strict party discipline and the subordination of the minority to the majority;

    (d) the unconditionally binding character of decisions of higher organs for lower.

*   22.   The party is built along territorial–production lines: a party organization serving a district is considered to be higher than all the party organizations serving parts of that district, or a party organization serving a whole branch of work is considered to be higher than all the party organizations serving parts of that branch of work.

*   23.   All party organizations are autonomous in deciding local questions, in so far as those decisions do not contradict decisions of the party.

*   24.   The highest leading organ of each party organization is the general meeting (for primary organizations), the conference (for example, for district and regional organizations) and the congress (for the communist parties of the union republics and for the *Communist Party of the Soviet Union*).

*   25.   The general meeting, conference or congress elects a

bureau or committee which is its executive organ and which leads all the current work of the organization.

* 26.   The use of voting lists is forbidden in elections to party organs. Voting must take place by separate candidate, with all members of the party assured the unlimited right to challenge candidates and to criticize them. Elections of candidates are conducted by closed (secret) ballot.

** 27.   *In city and district centres* aktivs of city *and district* party organizations are convened for discussion of the most important decisions of the party and government. Aktivs must be convened not for show and formal celebratory approval of these decisions, but for real discussion of them.

* 28.   The free and businesslike discussion of questions of party policy in individual organizations or in the party as a whole is the inalienable right of every party member, stemming from intra-party democracy. Only on the basis of intra-party democracy can self-criticism be developed and party discipline, which must be conscious and not mechanical, be strengthened.

But wide discussion, especially discussion on an all-union scale, of questions of party policy, must be organized in such a way that it cannot lead to attempts by an insignificant minority to impose its will on the majority of the party or to attempts to form fractional groupings, which destroy the unity of the party, to attempts at schism which could shake the strength and steadfastness of the *socialist structure.*

Wide discussion on an all-union scale may be considered necessary only if:

* (a) this necessity is recognized as an extreme measure by several local party organizations at the regional or republican level;

* (b) there is no sufficiently firm majority in the CC of the *Communist Party of the Soviet Union* on the most important questions of party policy;

** (c) in spite of a firm majority in the CC holding a definite point of view, the Central Committee considers it necessary to verify the correctness of its policy through discussion in the party.

Only upon the fulfilment of these conditions can the party be guaranteed against the misuse of intra-party democracy on the part of anti-party elements, only under these conditions can it be assured that intra-party democracy serves the cause and will not be used in a way harmful to the party and the working class.

IV Higher organs of the party

* 29. The supreme organ of the *Communist Party of the Soviet Union* is the *party* congress. Regular congresses are convened at least once every *four* years. Extraordinary congresses are convened by the Central Committee of the *party* on its own initiative, or on the demand of not less than one-third of the total number of members represented at the last party congress. The convocation of the party congress and the agenda are announced not less than a month and a half before the congress. An extraordinary congress is convened within two months.

A congress is considered valid if no less than half of all members of the party represented at the last regular congress are represented.

Norms of representation at the party congress are set by the Central Committee.

30. If the Central Committee of the *party* does not convene an extraordinary congress as provided for in point 29, the organizations which have demanded the convocation of an extraordinary congress have the right to form an organizational committee, which enjoys the rights of the Central Committee of the *party* with respect to the convening of an extraordinary congress.

31. The congress;

* (a) hears and approves the reports of the Central Committee of the *party*, Central Auditing Commission and other regional organizations;

(b) reviews and changes the programme and Rules of the party;

* (c) determines the tactical line of the party on basic questions of current policy;

* (d) elects the Central Committee of the *Communist Party of the Soviet Union* and the Central Auditing Commission.

* 32. The congress elects the Central Committee of the *party* and the Central Auditing Commission and determines their sizes. In

the event of vacancies occurring in the Central Committee, they are filled from among the candidate members of the CC elected by the congress.

33. The Central Committee of the *Communist Party of the Soviet Union* has no less than one plenary session every *six* months. Candidate members of the CC participate in plenary sessions of the Central Committee with the right of a consultative vote.

* 34. The Central Committee of the *Communist Party of the Soviet Union* organizes a *Presidium for leadership of the work of the CC between plena*, and a Secretariat for *leadership* of current work, *chiefly the organization of verification of the implementation of decisions of the party and the selection of cadres.*

35. *The Central Committee of the Communist Party of the Soviet Union organizes a Committee of Party Control attached to the CC.*

The Committee of Party Control attached to the CC of the party:

* (a) *verifies the observance of party discipline by members and candidate members of the party,* calls to account *communists* guilty of violations of the programme and Rules of the *party* and of party *and state* discipline, *and also those who infringe party ethics (deception of the party, dishonesty and insincerity before the party, slander, bureaucratism, domestic dissoluteness, etc.);*

(b) *examines appeals against decisions of CCs of the communist parties of the union republics and territory and regional committees of the party on expulsions from the party and party punishments;*

** (c) *has in the republics, territories and regions its representatives independent from the local party organs*[1]

* 36. In the intervals between congresses the Central Committee of the *Communist Party of the Soviet Union* guides all the work of the party, represents the party in relations with other parties, organizations and institutions, organizes the various institutions of the party and guides their activities, appoints the editorial boards of the central organs working under its supervision and confirms the editors of party organs of major local organizations, organizes and directs enterprises having social significance, distributes the forces and funds of the party and manages the central treasury.

The Central Committee directs the work of the central soviet and public organizations through party groups in them.

** 37.   In order to strengthen leadership and political work, the Central Committee of the *party* has the right to establish political departments and to assign party organizers from the CC to *individual* sectors of socialist construction which have especially important significance for the national economy and the country as a whole, and also, in so far as the political departments complete their tasks, *to abolish them or* convert them into normal party organs constructed along the production–territorial principle.

Political departments work on the basis of special instructions confirmed by the Central Committee.

38.   The Central Committee *of the Communist Party of the Soviet Union* regularly informs party organizations about its work.

* 39.   The Central Auditing Commission inspects: (a) the speed and correctness of the conduct of business in the central organs of the party and the proper functioning of the apparatus of the Secretariat of the CC; (b) the treasury and enterprises of the Central Committee of the *party*.

V   Regional, territory and republican organizations of the party

* 40.   The highest organ of the regional/territory/republican party organization is the regional/territory party conference/congress of the communist party of the union republic, and in the interval between them, the regional committee/territory committee/CC of the communist party of the union republic. In their activities they are guided by the decisions of the *Communist Party of the Soviet Union* and its leading organs.

* 41.   The regular regional/territory conference/congress of the communist party of the union republic is convened by the regional/territory committee/CC of the communist party of the union republic once every one and a half years,[2] and an extraordinary one is convened by decision of the regional/ territory committee/CC of the communist party of the union republic or on the demand of one third of the total membership of organizations in the regional/territory/republican party organization.

The norms of representation at the regional/territory

conference/congress of the communist party of the union republic are established by the regional/territory committee/CC of the communist party of the union republic.

The regional/territory conference/congress of the communist party of the union republic hears and approves the reports of the regional/territory committee/CC of the communist party of the union republic, the auditing commission and other regional/territory/republican organizations, discusses questions of party, soviet, economic and trade union work in the region/territory/republic and elects the regional/territory committee/CC of the communist party of the union republic, the auditing commission and delegates to the *congress of the Communist Party of the Soviet Union.*

*   42.   Regional/territory committees/CCs of the communist parties of the union republics *elect* corresponding executive organs of not more than 11 people, including *3* secretaries, confirmed by the CC of the *party.*[3] Secretaries must be of no less than five years' party standing.

Secretariats are established in regional/territory committees of the party/CCs of the communist parties of the union republics for the examination of current questions and verification of implementation. The secretariat reports to the appropriate bureau of the regional committee, territory committee or CC of the communist party of the union republic on decisions that have been adopted.

**   43.   The regional/territory committee/CC of the communist party of the union republic organizes the various institutions of the party in the region/territory/republic and guides their activities, *ensures the undeviating implementation of party directives, the development of criticism and self-criticism and the education of communists in the spirit of an uncompromising attitude to shortcomings, guides members and candidate members of the party in the study of Marxism–Leninism, organizes the communist education of workers,* appoints the editorial board of the regional/territory/republican party organ working under its supervision, *directs the activities of the regional/territory/republican soviets and public organizations through party groups in them,* organizes and directs its own enterprises having general significance for the region/territory/republic, distributes the forces and funds of the party within its organization, manages the regional/territory/republican party treasury, *systematically*

*informs and at specified times presents reports to the Central
Committee on its activities.*

*   44.   The plenum of the regional/territory committee/CC of the communist party of a union republic is convened at least once every *two* months.[4]

*   45.   Party organizations of autonomous republics, and also national and other regions in territories and union republics, work under the guidance of territory committees or CCs of the communist parties of the union republics and in their internal life are guided by the regulations contained in chapter V of the Rules of the party on regional, territory and republican organizations.

VI   Area organizations of the party

*   46.   Area party organizations are formed in regions, territories and republics having areas.

The highest organ of the area party organization is the area party conference, which is convened by the area committee at least once every one and a half years.[5] An extraordinary conference is convened on decision of the area committee or on the demand of one-third of the total membership of organizations in the area organization.

The area conference hears and approves the reports of the area committee, auditing commission and other area party organizations, elects the area committee of the party, the auditing commission and delegates to the regional/territory conference or the congress of the communist party of the union republic.

*   47.   The area committee elects a bureau of no more than 9 people, *including* 3 secretaries of the area committee. Secretaries must be of three years' party standing. Secretaries of the area committee are confirmed by the regional committee/territory committee/CC of the communist party of the union republic.

The plenum of the area committee is convened at least once every month and a half.[6]

*   48.   The area committee organizes the various institutions of the party in the area and guides their activities, *ensures the undeviating implementation of party directives, the development of criticism and self-criticism and the education of communists in the spirit of an uncompromising attitude to shortcomings, guides* *members and candidate members of the party in the study of Marxism–Leninism, organizes the communist education of workers*, appoints the editorial board of the area party organ working under its leadership and supervision, *directs the activities of the area soviet and public organizations through party groups in them,* organizes its own enterprises having area significance, distributes the forces and funds of the party in the area, and manages the area party treasury.

VII   City and district (rural and urban) organizations of the party

*   49.   The city/district party conference is convened by the city/district committee at least once a year,[7] an extraordinary conference by decision of the city/district committee or on the demand of one third of the total membership of organizations in the city/district organization.

    The city/district conference hears and approves reports of the city/district committee, auditing commission and other city/district organizations, elects the city/district committee, auditing commission and delegates to the territory/regional conference or congress of the communist party of the union republic.

*   50.   The city/district committee elects a bureau of 7–9 people, *including* three secretaries of the city/district committee of the party.[8] Secretaries of the city/district committee must be of no less than three years' party standing. Secretaries of the city/district committees are confirmed by the regional committee/territory committee/CC of the communist party of the union republic.

*   51.   The city/district committee organizes and confirms primary party organizations in enterprises, in sovkhozes, MTSs, kolkhozes and institutions, *guides their activities and keeps the records of communists, ensures the implementation of party directives, the development of criticism and self-criticism and the education of communists in the spirit of an uncompromising attitude to shortcomings, organizes the study of Marxism–Leninism by members and candidate members of the party, manages the communist education of workers*, appoints the editorial board of the city/district party organ working under its guidance and supervision, *guides the activities of the city/district soviets and public organizations through party groups in them,* distributes the forces and funds of the party in the city and district, and manages the city/district party treasury. The city/district committee presents to the regional/territory committee/CC of the communist party of the union republic a report on its activities at the time and in the form established by the Central Committee of the *party*.

* 52.   The plenum of the city/district committee is convened at least once *a month*.[9]

* 53.   In large cities district organizations subordinate to the city committee are established with the permission of the CC of the *Communist Party of the Soviet Union*.

VIII   Primary organizations of the party

* 54.   The basis of the party is the primary party organizations.

Primary party organizations are formed in factories, plants, *in* sovkhozes, MTSs and other economic enterprises, in kolkhozes, units of the *Soviet* Army and Navy, villages, institutions, educational institutions, etc. where there are no less than 3 party members.

In enterprises, in kolkhozes, in institutions, etc. where there are less than 3 party members, candidate or party-komsomol groups are formed, headed by a party organizer chosen by the district/city committee or the political department.

Primary party organizations are confirmed by district/city committees or appropriate political departments.

The highest organ of the primary party organization is the party meeting, which is convened at least once a month.

* 55.   In enterprises, institutions, kolkhozes, etc. where there are more than 100 members and candidates of the party inside the general primary party organization embracing the whole enterprise, institution, etc., party organizations may be formed in shops, units, departments, etc., in each particular case with the approval of the district/city committee or appropriate political department.

In shop, unit, etc. organizations, and also in primary party organizations numbering less than 100 members and candidates, party groups by brigades or units of the enterprise may be formed.[10]

* 56.   In large enterprises and institutions numbering more than *300* members and candidates of the party, party committees may be formed, in each case with the approval of the Central Committee of the *party*,[11] with the shop party organizations in these enterprises and *institutions* being granted the rights of a primary party organization.

** 57. The primary party organization links the masses of workers, peasants and intelligentsia with the leading organs of the party. Its tasks are:

**   (a) agitational and organizational work among the masses for the fulfilment of party *appeals* and decisions, with the maintenance of leadership over the *lower-level press (factory newspapers, wall newspapers, etc.)*;

**   (b) attraction of new members into the party and their political education;

**   (c) *organization of the political education of members and candidates of the party and supervision over their achievement of a minimum knowledge of Marxism–Leninism*;

**   (d) assistance to the district committee, city committee or political department in all its practical work;

**   (e) mobilization of the masses in enterprises, *in* sovkhozes, kolkhozes, etc. for the implementation of the production plan, the strengthening of labour discipline and the development of socialist competition;

**   (f) struggle with slackness and the uneconomic management of affairs in enterprises, in sovkhozes, kolkhozes and daily care for the improvement of the cultural–living conditions of the workers, employees and kolkhozniks;

**   (g) *development of criticism and self-criticism and the education of communists in the spirit of an uncompromising attitude to shortcomings*;

**   (h) active participation in the economic and political life of the country.

* 58. To increase the role of primary party organizations in productive *and trading* enterprises, including sovkhozes, kolkhozes and MTSs, and their responsibility for the state of work of the enterprises, these organizations are granted the right of supervision over the activities of the administration of the enterprise.

    Party organizations in *ministries* which cannot exercise supervision functions because of the special conditions of work of soviet institutions, must draw attention to deficiencies in the work of the institution, take note of shortcomings in the work of the *ministry* and its individual workers and send its information and analysis to the CC and the leaders of the *ministry*.

Secretaries of primary party organizations in *ministries* are confirmed by the Central Committee of the *party*.

All communists who are workers in the central apparatus of a *ministry* enter one party organization for the whole *ministry*.

* 59.   For the conduct of current work the primary party organization elects a bureau of no more than 11 people for a term of one year.

Bureaux of primary party organizations are formed in party organizations having no less than 15 party workers.

In party organizations numbering less than 15 party members, bureaux are not formed, but a secretary of the primary party organization is elected.

To promote the rapid training and education of party members in the spirit of collective leadership, shop party organizations numbering no less than 15 but no more than 100 party members are granted the right to elect a bureau of the shop party organization consisting of from 3 to 5 people, while those numbering more than 100 party members elect a bureau of from 5 to 7 people.

In primary party organizations having no more than 100 party members, party work is conducted, as a rule, by workers who have not been freed from production.

Secretaries of primary and shop party organizations must be of no less than one year's party standing.

IX   Party and Komsomol

* 60.   The VLKSM carries out its work under the leadership of the *Communist Party of the Soviet Union*. The CC VLKSM is the leading organ of the komsomol, and is subordinated to the CC of the *Communist Party of the Soviet Union*. The work of local organizations of the VLKSM is directed and supervised by the corresponding republican, territory, regional, city and district party organizations.

61.   Members of the VLKSM who become members or candidates of the party leave the komsomol at the moment of

their entry to the party if they do not occupy leading posts in komsomol organizations.

*   62.   The VLKSM is the active assistant of the party in all state and economic construction. Komsomol organizations must be in deed the active champions of party directives in all spheres of socialist construction, especially where there are no primary party organizations.

*   63.   Komsomol organizations have the right of wide initiative in discussing and raising before appropriate party organizations all questions about the work of enterprises, kolkhozes, sovkhozes and institutions, with the aim of the elimination of shortcomings in their activities and giving them the necessary assistance in the improvement of their work, in the organization of socialist competition, in the conduct of mass campaigns, etc.

X   Party organizations in the Soviet Army, Navy and in transport

*   64.   Leadership of party work in the *Soviet Army and Navy* is carried out by *the Chief Political Administrations of the Soviet Army and Navy of the USSR, and in transport by the Political Administrations of the Ministries of Communications of the USSR, Maritime Transport of the USSR and River Transport of the USSR*, which exercise the authority of departments of the CC of the *Communist Party of the Soviet Union*.[12]

Party organizations in the *Soviet* Army, Navy and in transport work on the basis of special instructions confirmed by the Central Committee.

*   65.   Heads of political administrations of areas, fleets and armies and heads of political departments of the railways must be of 5 years' party standing, and heads of political departments of divisions and brigades of 3 years' party standing.

*   66.   Political organs must maintain close links with local party committees through the constant participation in local party committees of the leaders of political organs, and also the systematic hearing in party committees of reports of the heads of political organs on political work in military units and political departments in transport.

XI   Party groups in non-party organizations

*   67.   In all congresses, meetings and in elected organs of soviet, trade union, co-operative and other mass organizations where there are no less than 3 party members party groups are organized, the task of which is the all-round strengthening of the influence of the party and the execution of its policy among non-party people, the strengthening of party and state discipline, the struggle with bureaucratism and the verification of the implementation of party and soviet directives. The group elects a secretary for current work.

68.   Party groups are subordinate to the appropriate party *organizations* (CC of the *Communist Party of the Soviet Union*, CC of the communist party of a union republic, territory committee, regional committee, area committee, city committee and district committee).

On all questions groups must strictly and without deviation be guided by the decisions of leading party organs.

XII   Finances of the party

69.   The finances of the party and its organizations come from membership dues, income from party enterprises and other receipts.

70.   Monthly membership dues for party members and candidates are established in the following scale *(in percentage of earnings)*:

Monthly earnings	
not more than 500 roubles	*0.5 per cent*
more than 500r but	
not more than 1000r	*1.0 per cent*
from 1001 to 1500r	*1.5 per cent*
from 1501 to 2000r	*2.0 per cent*
more than 2000r	*3.0 per cent*

71.   Entry dues of 2 per cent of *monthly* earnings are collected upon entry to candidature.

AMENDMENTS TO THE 1952 RULES ADOPTED AT THE XX CONGRESS OF THE CPSU, 14–25 FEBRUARY 1956

1. This paragraph was omitted in 1956.
2. An amendment made the period between regular conferences two years,

except for union republics which had regional divisions which could allow four years to elapse between congresses. This was carried into the 1961 Rules.

3. The congress decided that it was inadvisable to specify in the Rules the number of secretaries party committees should have. Henceforth this figure should be set by the CC.
4. This was changed to four months, a frequency carried into 1961.
5. This was changed to two years, a frequency retained in 1961.
6. This was changed to three months and continued thus into 1961. See also note 3.
7. This was changed to once every two years, and was carried into 1961.
8. See note 3.
9. This was changed to once every three months and continued thus into 1961.
10. The number of members and candidates in paragraphs 55 and 56 was changed to 50. This was continued into 1961.
11. An amendment replaced the CC by regional committees, territory committees or the CCs of the communist parties of the union republics. This was retained in 1961.
12. Political departments in transport were omitted.

Rules of the Communist Party of the Soviet Union

Adopted at the XXII Congress of the CPSU, October 1961

The Communist Party of the Soviet Union is the *militant, tried-and-tested vanguard of the Soviet people, which unites on a voluntary basis the most advanced, conscious part of the* working class, the *kolkhoz* peasantry and the intelligentsia of the USSR.

* *Founded by V. I. Lenin as the advanced detachment of the working class, the Communist Party has travelled a glorious path of struggle, and brought the working class and the toiling peasantry to the victory* of the Great October Socialist Revolution, the establishment of the dictatorship of the proletariat in the USSR. *Under the leadership of the Communist Party, the exploiter classes have been liquidated in the Soviet Union and the moral and political unity of Soviet society has taken shape and grown in strength. Socialism has been victorious completely and finally. The Communist Party, the party of the working class, has now become the party of all the Soviet people.*

* *The party exists for and serves the people. It is the highest form of social–political organization, the leading and directing force of Soviet society. The party leads the great creative activity of the Soviet people, imparts an organized, planned, scientifically-based character to its struggle for the achievement of the ultimate goal, the victory of communism.*

* *The CPSU bases its work on unswerving observance of Leninist norms of party life, the principle of the collectivity of leadership, the all-round development of intra-party democracy, the activity and initiative of communists, criticism and self-criticism.*

Ideological and organizational unity, monolithic cohesion of its ranks and a high level of conscious discipline of all communists are an inviolable law of the CPSU. All manifestations of fractionalism and group activity are incompatible with Marxist–Leninist party principles and with party membership.[1]

** *In all its activities the CPSU is guided by the teaching of Marxism–Leninism and by the Programme based on it, in which* *is defined the basic tasks of the party in the period of the construction of communist society.*

In creatively developing Marxism–Leninism, the CPSU decisively struggles against all manifestations of revisionism and dogmatism, which are deeply alien to revolutionary theory.

* *The Communist Party of the Soviet Union is an integral part of the international communist and workers' movement. It firmly adheres to the tried-and-tested Marxist–Leninist principles of proletarian internationalism, actively promotes the strengthening of the unity of the whole international communist and workers' movement and fraternal ties with the great army of communists of all countries.*

I Members of the party, their responsibilities and rights

1. Any citizen of the Soviet Union who accepts the Programme and Rules of the party, *who actively participates in the construction of communism*, who works in one of the party organizations, who carries out the decisions of the party and pays membership dues may be a member of the CPSU.

2. A party member must:

* (a) *struggle for the creation of the material–technical basis of communism, serve as an example of the communist attitude to labour, raise labour productivity, display leadership in all that is new and progressive, support and propagate advanced methods,* master techniques, *perfect* his skills, and *perfect and increase* public, socialist property, the basis of the power and prosperity of the Soviet *Motherland*;

* (b) *firmly and without deviation put party decisions into effect, explain party policy to the masses, assist the strengthening and widening of the party's links with the people, be considerate and attentive to people,* and respond promptly to the enquiries and needs of the workers;

* (c) *actively participate in the political life of the country, in the management of state affairs, in economic and cultural construction, provide an example of the fulfilment of public duty, help the development and strengthening of communist social relations*;

* (d) master Marxist–Leninist *theory, raise one's own ideological level, help in the formation and education of man* *in communist society. Lead a decisive struggle against all manifestations of bourgeois ideology, against remnants of private property psychology, religious prejudices and other survivals from the past, observe the principles of communist ethics*, and place public interests above personal interests;

* (e) *be an active champion of the idea of socialist internationalism and Soviet patriotism among the masses of workers, lead the struggle against the remnants of nationalism and chauvinism, by word and deed assist the strengthening of the friendship of the peoples of the USSR, fraternal links of the Soviet people with the peoples of the countries of the socialist camp, with the proletariats and workers of all countries;*

* (f) in all ways strengthen the *ideological and organizational* unity of the party, *defend the party from penetration of its ranks by people unworthy of the lofty title communist*, be truthful and honest before the party and people, show vigilance and protect party and state secrets;

* (g) develop criticism and self-criticism, *boldly* expose shortcomings and *strive to eliminate them, struggle against ostentation, conceit, complacency and localism, give a decisive rebuff to all attempts at* the suppression of criticism, *resist all actions causing damage to the party and state, and report them to party organs up to the CC CPSU*;

* (h) without deviation carry out the party *line* in the selection of cadres on the basis of their potential and practical qualities. *Be uncompromising in all cases of infringements of Leninist principles in the selection and education of cadres*;

(i) observe party and state discipline, which are equally binding for all members of the party. The party has one discipline, one law for all communists regardless of service and the positions they occupy;

(j) *in every possible way help strengthen the defence might of the USSR, lead a tireless struggle for peace and for friendship between peoples.*

3. A party member has the right:

(a) to vote in elections and be elected to party organs;

(b) *freely to discuss in party meetings, conferences, congresses, at sessions of party committees and in the party press questions of the policy and practical activities of the party, to introduce proposals, openly to discuss and maintain his opinion until the adoption of a decision by the organization;*

(c) to criticize *at party meetings, conferences, congresses and plena of committees* any communist, *regardless of the position he holds. Persons guilty of suppressing criticism and persecuting critics must be called to strict account by the party, right up to expulsion from the CPSU;*

(d) personally to participate *in party meetings, sessions of bureaux and committees when the question* of his activities or behaviour is being discussed;

(e) to address question*s*, statement*s and proposals* to any party instance, up to the CC CPSU, *and to demand an answer to the substance of his address.*

4.   Admission to party membership is made exclusively on an individual basis. Workers, peasants and *representatives of* the intelligentsia who are conscious, active and devoted to the cause of communism are admitted as members of the party. New members are admitted from among the candidates who have completed the established candidate stage.

Persons who have reached 18 years are admitted to the party. Youth up to and including 20 years of age[2] enter the party only through the VLKSM.

The procedure for the admission of candidates as members of the party is as follows:

(a) those entering the party present recommendations of three members of the *CPSU*, of no less than three years' party standing[3] and who have *known them through common productive and public work* for no less than one year.

FIRST NOTE   During admission to the party of members of the VLKSM,[4] the recommendation of a district *or city committee* of the VLKSM is equivalent to the recommendation of one party member.

SECOND NOTE   Members and candidate members of the CC CPSU refrain from giving recommendations.

(b) the question of admission to the party is discussed and decided by the general meeting of the primary party organization;[5] its decision comes into force after confirmation by the district committee, and in cities where there is no district division, by the city party committee.

** During discussion of the question of admission to the party, the participation of those who gave the recommendation is optional.

(c) *citizens of the USSR who are former members of communist and workers' parties of other countries are admitted to the Communist Party of the Soviet Union on the basis of rules established by the CC CPSU.*

** Former members of other parties are admitted to the *CPSU in the normal way, but only with the confirmation of regional committee, territory committee or CC of the communist party of the union republic.*

* 5.   Those who give recommendations bear responsibility *before party organizations for the objectivity of the evaluation of the political, practical and moral qualities of those they recommend.*

6.   Seniority of party membership of those entering the party is counted from the day on which the decision is made by the general meeting of the primary party organization *on the acceptance* of the given candidate into party membership.

7.   *The procedure for the registration of members and candidate members of the party and their transfer from one organization to another is determined by the appropriate instructions of the CC CPSU.*

8.   *The question* of a member or candidate member of the party who has not paid membership dues for three months without valid reasons *is discussed in the primary party organization. If it becomes clear during this that the given member or candidate member of the party has, in fact, lost contact with the party organization, then* he is considered to have left the party, which decision is taken by the primary party organization and submitted for confirmation to the district committee or city committee of the party.

9.   *A member or candidate member of the party who fails to fulfil his duties as laid down in the Rules or commits other misdemeanours shall be called to account and may be subjected to a penalty: admonition, reproof (strict reproof), reproof (strict reproof) with entry on the registration card. The highest party penalty is expulsion from the party.*

Should the necessity arise, as a measure of party punishment a party organization may transfer a party member to candidate status for a period of not more than one year. The decision of a primary party organization on the transfer of a party member to candidate status *is confirmed* by the district committee or the city committee of the party. Upon expiration of the established period, the person transferred to candidate status is admitted to membership in accordance with the regular procedure, and he retains his former party seniority.[6]

For *insignificant* misdemeanours measures of party education and influence *in the form of comradely criticism, party reproach, warning or instruction* must be employed.

* During decision of a question of expulsion from the party, maximum *attention and* thorough investigation of the validity of the charges laid against the communist must be ensured.

10.   The question of the expulsion of a communist from the party is decided by a general meeting of the primary party organization. *The decision of the primary party organization on expulsion from the party is considered adopted if not less than two-thirds of the party members attending the meeting have voted for it, and it* is confirmed by the district committee or city committee of the party. A decision of a district committee or a city committee about expulsion from the party takes effect *after confirmation of it* by the regional or territory committee or the CC of the communist party of the union republic.[7]

Prior to the confirmation by a regional or territory committee or CC of the communist party of a union republic of a decision on expulsion from the *CPSU*,[8] the party card *or candidate member card* remains in the hands of the *communist*, and he has the right to attend closed party meetings.

After expulsion from the party, he retains the right to appeal to higher party organs, up to the CC CPSU, for a two-month period.

11.   *The question of calling to account before the party members and candidate members of the CC of the communist party of a union republic, a territory committee, a regional committee, an area committee, a city committee, a district committee of the party and also members of auditing commissions is discussed in primary party organizations.*

* *Decisions of party organizations imposing penalties on members and candidate members of these party committees and members of auditing commissions are taken in the ordinary way.*

Proposals by party organizations on expulsions from the

CPSU are reported to the party committee of which the given communist is a member. Decisions on expulsion from the party of members and candidate members of the CC of a communist party of a union republic, a territory committee, regional committee, area committee, city committee or district committee of the party and members of auditing commissions are taken at the plenum of the corresponding committee by a two-thirds majority vote of its members.

The question of expulsion from the party of a member or candidate member of the Central Committee of the CPSU or a member of the Central Auditing Commission is decided by the party congress, and in the intervals between congresses, by the plenum of the CC by a two-thirds majority of the Central Committee.

* 12. If a party member has committed a misdemeanour punishable by the criminal code, he is expelled from the party and prosecuted in accordance with the law.

13. Appeals of those expelled from the party or who have been punished, and also decisions of party organizations on expulsion from the party are examined by the appropriate party organs not later than one month from the day of their receipt.

II Candidate members of the party

14. Those entering the party pass through a candidate stage, which is necessary to acquaint the candidate thoroughly with the Programme and Rules of the CPSU and to prepare for entry to party membership. The party organization must help the candidate prepare for entry to membership of the CPSU and verify his personal qualities.

The candidate stage is fixed at one year.

15. The procedure for admission to candidate membership (individual admission, presentation of recommendations, decision of the primary organization on admission and its confirmation) is identical to that for admission to party membership.

16. On the expiry of the candidate stage the primary party organization examines and decides the question of the admission of the candidate to party membership. If during the candidate stage the candidate has not proved his worth and because of his personal qualities cannot be admitted to membership of the

CPSU, the party organization *adopts a decision refusing him party membership, and after confirmation of the given decision by the district or city committee of the party, he is considered to have ceased to be a candidate member of the CPSU.*

17.   Candidate members of the party take part *in all the activities of the party organization* and enjoy the right of a consultative vote in party meetings. *Candidate members of the party may not be elected to leading party organs or as delegates to party conferences and congresses.*

18.   Candidate members of the CPSU pay membership dues *at the same rate as party members.*

III   Organizational structure of the party. Intra-party democracy

19.   The guiding principle of the organizational structure of the party is democratic centralism, which means:

(a) the election of all leading organs of the party from the bottom to the top;

(b) the periodic report of party organs to their party organizations *and to higher organs*;

(c) strict party discipline and the subordination of the minority to the majority;

(d) the unconditionally binding character of decisions of higher organs for lower.

*   20.   The party is built along territorial–production lines: *primary organizations are formed in places of work of communists and are united into district, city, etc. organizations on a territorial basis.* An organization serving a given *territory* is higher than all party organizations serving its parts.

21.   All party organizations are autonomous in deciding local questions, *if* these decisions do not contradict *party policy.*

22.   The highest leading organ of the party organization is: the general meeting (for primary organizations); the conference (for district, *city*, *area*, regional *and territory* organizations); and the congress (for communist parties of the union republics and for the Communist Party of the Soviet Union).

23.   The general meeting, conference or congress elects a bureau or committee, which *are* executive organs and lead all the current work of the *party* organization.

24.   Elections *for party organs* are carried out by closed (secret) ballot. During elections all party members have the unlimited

right to challenge candidates and to criticize them. Voting must take place on each candidate separately. *The candidates for whom more than half the participants of the meeting, conference or congress voted are considered elected.*

25. *During elections for party organs the principle of the systematic renewal of their composition and continuity of leadership is observed.*[9]

At all regular elections the composition of the Central Committee of the CPSU and its Presidium is renewed by not less than one quarter of its composition. Members of the Presidium are elected, as a rule, for no more than three successive terms. Some party activists, by virtue of their acknowledged authority, and high political, organizational and other qualities may be elected to leading organs for a longer period. In such a case the corresponding candidate is considered elected on condition that he receives in closed (secret) ballot no less than three-quarters of the votes.

The composition of the CCs of the communist parties of the union republics, territory committees and regional committees is renewed by not less than one-third at each regular election; the composition of area committees, city committees and district committees of the party and party committees or bureaux of primary party organizations, by one half. In this process members of these leading party organs may be elected for no more than three successive terms. Secretaries of primary party organizations may be elected for no more than two successive terms.

A meeting, conference or congress may, because of political and practical qualities, elect a particular worker to leading organs for a longer period. In such a case no less than three-quarters of the votes of communists participating in the ballot is necessary for election.

Party members who have a leading party organ in connection with the expiry of their term may be re-elected at subsequent elections.

26. *Through all of his activity, a member or candidate member of the CC CPSU must justify the high confidence shown in him by the party. If a member or candidate member of the CC CPSU lets his honour and dignity fall, he may not remain in the Central Committee. The question of the removal of a member or candidate member of the CC from the CC CPSU is decided at a plenum of the Central Committee through closed (secret) ballot. The decision*

is considered adopted if no less than two-thirds of all members of the CC CPSU vote for it.

*   The question of the removal from the party organ of a member or candidate member of a CC of a communist party of a union republic, territory committee, regional committee, area committee, city committee or district committee of the party is decided in the plenum of the appropriate committee. The decision is considered adopted if no less than two-thirds of members *of the given committee vote for it in a closed (secret) ballot.*

* *   *If a member of the Central Auditing Commission does not justify the high confidence shown in him by the party, he must be removed from the Commission. This question is decided in a session of the Central Auditing Commission. The decision is considered adopted if in a closed (secret) ballot no less than two-thirds of votes of members of the Central Auditing Commission are for the removal of the particular members of the Central Auditing Commission from its membership.*

*   *The question of the removal of members of auditing commissions of republican, territory, regional, area, city and district party organizations from those commissions is decided at sessions of the appropriate commissions in the way envisaged for members and candidate members of party committees.*

27.   The free and businesslike discussion of questions of party policy in individual *party* organizations or in the party as a whole is the inalienable right of *a* party member *and an important principle* of intra-party democracy. Only on the basis of intra-party democracy can *criticism and* self-criticism be developed and party discipline, which must be conscious and not mechanical, be strengthened.

Discussion of controversial or insufficiently clear questions is possible within the framework of individual organizations or the party as a whole.

*   *General* party discussion is necessary:

(a) if this necessity is recognized by several party organizations at the regional or republican level;

(b) if there is no sufficiently firm majority in the CC on the most important questions of party policy;

(c) *if the CC CPSU acknowledges the necessity to consult the party as a whole on some questions of policy.*

Wide discussion, especially discussion on an all-union

scale, of questions of party policy, must be *conducted* in such a way *as to ensure the free expression of views of party members and to exclude the possibility of attempts at the formation of* fractional groupings, which destroy the unity of the party, and attempts at schism *in the party*.

*   28.   *The highest principle of party leadership is the collectivity of leadership – the indispensable condition for the normal activities of party organizations, the correct education of cadres, the development of the activity and initiative of communists. The cult of personality and the violations of intra-party democracy linked with it cannot be tolerated in the party, they are incompatible with the Leninist principles of party life.*

The collectivity of leadership does not relieve workers of personal responsibility for matters entrusted to them.

29.   *CCs of the communist parties of the union republics, territory committees, regional committees, area committees, city committees and district committees of the party systematically inform party organizations about their work in the period between congresses and conferences.*

30.   *Meetings of the aktiv of district, city, area, regional and territory party organizations and the communist parties of the union republics are convened for discussion of the most important decisions of the party and for working out measures for their implementation, and also for the examination of questions of local life.*

IV   Higher organs of the party

31.   The supreme organ of the Communist Party of the Soviet Union is the party congress. Regular congresses are convened *by the Central Committee* at least once every four years.[10] The convocation of the party congress and the agenda are announced not less than a month and a half before the congress. *Special* (extraordinary) congresses are convened by the Central Committee of the party on its own initiative or on the demand of not less than one-third of the total number of members represented at the last party congress. Special (extraordinary) congresses are convened within two months. A congress is considered valid if no less than half of all members of the party *are represented at it.*

Norms of representation at the party congress are set by the Central Committee.

32.   If the Central Committee of the party does not convene a *special* (extraordinary) congress as provided for in point 31, the organizations which have demanded the convocation of a *special* (extraordinary) congress have the right to form an organizational committee which enjoys the rights of the Central Committee of the party with respect to the convening of a *special* (extraordinary) congress.

33.   The Congress:

(a) hears and approves the reports of the Central Committee, Central Auditing Commission and other central organizations;

(b) revises, changes *and confirms* the Programme and Rules of the party;

(c) determines the line of the party on questions *of domestic and foreign policy, examines and decides the most important questions of communist construction;*

(d) elects the Central Committee and the Central Auditing Commission.

* 34.   The congress elects the Central Committee and the Central Auditing Commission and determines their sizes. In the event of vacancies occurring in the Central Committee, they are filled from among the candidate members of the CC CPSU elected by the congress.

* 35.   In the intervals between congresses the Central Committee of the Communist Party of the Soviet Union guides all the *activities* of the party, *the local party organs, carries out the selection and assignment of leading cadres, directs the work of central state and public organizations of workers through party groups in them, creates various organs, institutions and enterprises of the party and guides their activities, appoints the editorial boards of the central newspapers and journals working under its supervision, and distributes the funds of the party budget and supervises its use.*

The Central Committee represents the CPSU in dealings with other parties.

** 36.   The CC CPSU regularly informs party organizations about its work.

* 37.   The Central Auditing Commission of the CPSU inspects the speed and correctness of the conduct of business in the central organs of the party, the treasury and enterprises of the Central Committee of the *CPSU*.

38.   The CC CPSU holds no less than one plenary session every six months. Candidate members of the CC participate in plenary sessions of the CC with the right of a consultative vote.

39.   The Central Committee of the Communist Party of the Soviet Union *elects* a Presidium for leadership of the work of the CC between plena, a Secretariat for leadership of current work, chiefly the selection of cadres and organization of the verification of implementation, *and establishes a Bureau of the CC CPSU for the RSFSR.*[11]

40.   The Central Committee of the Communist Party of the Soviet Union organizes a Committee of Party Control attached to the CC.

The Committee of Party Control attached to the CC CPSU:

(a) verifies the observance of party discipline by members and candidate members of the *CPSU*, calls to account communists guilty of violations of the Programme and Rules of the party and of party and state discipline, and also those who infringe party ethics;

(b) examines appeals against decisions of CCs of the communist parties of the union republics and territory and regional committees of the party on expulsions from the party and party punishments.[12]

V   Republican, territory, regional, area, city and district organizations of the party

41.   *Republican, territory, regional, area, city and district party organizations and their committees are guided in their activities by the Programme and Rules of the CPSU, conduct all work for the realization of party policy and organize the implementation of directives of the Central Committee of the CPSU in the republic, territory, region, area, city and district.*

42.   *The basic responsibilities of the republican, territory, regional, area, city and district organizations of the party and their leading organs are:*

(a) *political and organizational work among the masses and mobilization of them for the realization of the tasks of communist construction, the development of industrial and* agricultural production in every possible way, and the fulfilment and over-fulfilment of state plans; care for the steady increase in the material welfare and cultural level of the workers;

(b) *organization of ideological work, propaganda of Marxism–Leninism, increase in the communist consciousness of workers, leadership of the local press, radio and television, supervision over the activities of cultural–educational institutions;*

* (c) *leadership of the soviets, trade unions, komsomol, co-operatives and other public organizations through party groups in them, the wider attraction of workers into the work of these organizations, development of the initiative and activity of the mass as the necessary condition for the gradual transition from a socialist state to communist public self-administration.*

** *Party organizations do not supplant soviet, trade-union, co-operative and other public organizations of workers, do not allow the merging of functions of party and other organs or unnecessary parallelism in work;*

* (d) *selection and assignment of leading cadres, education of them in the spirit of communist ideas, honesty and truthfulness, a high sense of responsibility before the party and people for work entrusted to them;*

(e) *wide attraction of communists into the conduct of party work as non-staff workers, as a form of public work;*

(f) *organization of various institutions and enterprises of the party in their republic, territory, region, area, city or district and leadership of their activities; distribution of party funds within its organization; the provision of systematic information to the higher standing party organ and responsibility before it for their work.*

Leading organs of republican, territory and regional party organizations

43. The highest organ of the regional/territory/republican party organization is the regional/territory party conference or congress of the communist party of the union republic, and in the interval between them, the regional committee/territory committee/CC of the communist party of the union republic.

44. The regular regional/territory conference/congress of the

communist party of the union republic is convened by the regional/territory committee/CC of the communist party of the union republic once every two years, and *special* (extraordinary) *meetings* on decision of the regional/territory committee/CC of the communist party of the union republic or on the demand of one-third of the total membership of organizations in the regional/territory/republican party organization. Congresses of communist parties of union republics having regional divisions (Ukraine, Belorussia, Kazakhstan, Uzbekistan) may be held once every four years.[13]

The norms of representation at the regional/territory conference/congress of the communist party of a union republic are established by the *corresponding party committee.*

The regional/territory conference/congress of the communist party of the union republic hears the reports of the regional/territory committee/CC of the communist party of the union republic and the auditing commission, *at its discretion* discusses *other* questions of party, economic and *cultural construction*, and elects the regional/territory committee/CC of the communist party of the union republic, the auditing commission and delegates to the CPSU congress.[14]

45. Regional/territory committees/CCs of communist parties of the union republics elect *bureaux, which include the secretaries of the committees.* Secretaries must be of no less than five years' party standing. *At the plena of committees the chairmen of party commissions, heads of the departments of these committees and the editors of party newspapers and journals are also confirmed.*

* Secretariats *may be* established in regional/territory committees of the party/CCs of the communist parties of the union republics for the examination of current questions and verification of implementation.

46. The plenum of the regional/territory committee/CC of the communist party of a union republic is convened no less than once every four months.

47. *The regional/territory committee/CC of the communist party of a union republic leads the area, city and district party organizations, checks their activities and systematically hears the reports of the area, city and district committees of the party.*

Party organizations of autonomous republics, and also *autonomous* and other regions in territories and union republics, work under the guidance of territory committees or CCs of the communist parties of the union republics.

Leading organs of area, city and district (rural and urban) party organizations

48. The highest organ of the area/city/district party organization is the area/city/district party conference *or general meeting of communists*, convened by the area/city/district committee at least once every two years,[15] and the extraordinary conference convened on decision of the respective committee or on the demand of one-third of the total membership of the party in the party organization concerned.

The area/city/district conference *(meeting)* hears the reports of the committee and auditing commission, *at its discretion discusses other questions of party, economic and cultural construction*, elects the area/city/district committee, auditing commission and delegates to the regional/territory conference or congress of the communist party of the union republic.

The norms of representation at the area, city and district conference are established by the corresponding party committee.

49. The area/city/district committee elects a bureau, including the secretaries of the committee, *and also confirms the heads of the departments of the committee and editors of newspapers.* Secretaries of the area/city/district committee must be of no less than three years' party standing. Secretaries of committees are confirmed by the regional committee/territory committee/CC of the communist party of the union republic.

* 50. The area/city/district committee organizes and confirms primary party organizations and guides their activities, *systematically hears reports on the work of party organizations, and keeps a record of communists.*

51. The plenum of the area/city/district committee is convened at least once every three months.

* 52. *The area/city/district committee has non-staff instructors, sets up standing or temporary commissions on various questions of party work and uses other means of drawing communists to the activities of the party committee on a public basis.*

VI Primary organizations of the party

53. The basis of the party is the primary organizations.

* Primary party organizations are formed *in places of work of party members* – at plants, factories, in sovkhozes and other enterprises, in kolkhozes, units of the Soviet Army, institutions, educational establishments, etc. where there are no less than three party members. *Territorial primary party organizations may also be established by place of residence of communists in villages and at housing administrations.*[16]

54. In enterprises, kolkhozes and institutions where there are more than 50 members and candidates of the party, party organizations by shop, unit, farm, brigade, department, etc. may be established in the general primary party organization with the permission of the district, city or area committee.

In shop, unit, etc. organizations, and also in primary party organizations numbering less than 50 members and candidates, party groups by brigade and other production sections may be formed.

55. The highest organ of the primary party organization is the party meeting, which is *held* at least once a month.[17]

In large party organizations numbering more than 300 communists the general party meeting is convened when necessary at times fixed by the party committee or on the demand of several shop party organizations.

* 56. For the conduct of current work the primary/*shop* party organization elects a bureau for one year, *the size of which is established by the party meeting.* In primary *and shop* party organizations numbering less than 15 party members, a secretary *and deputy secretary of the party organization are* elected, not a bureau.

Secretaries of primary and shop party organizations must be of no less than one year's party standing.

Primary party organizations numbering less than *150* members of the party, as a rule, *will not have positions filled by party workers freed from production.*

* 57. In large enterprises and institutions numbering more than 300 members and candidates of the party, *and, when necessary, in organizations numbering more than 100 communists with special production conditions and territorial dispersion*, with the permission of the regional committee, territory committee or CC of the communist party of the union republic, party committees may be formed with the shop party organizations in these enterprises and institutions being granted the rights of a primary party organization.

In kolkhoz[18] party organizations where there are 50 communists, party committees may be formed.[19]

The party committee is elected for one year, and its size is determined by the general party meeting or conference.[20]

* 58.   *In its activities the primary party organization is guided by the Programme and Rules of the CPSU. It conducts work directly among the workers, unites them around the Communist Party of the Soviet Union, and organizes the masses for the realization of party policies, for the struggle for the construction of communism.*

The primary party organization:

(a) *admits new members to the CPSU;*

(b) *educates communists in the spirit of devotion to the cause of the party, ideological conviction and communist ethics;*

* (c) *organizes the study by communists of Marxist–Leninist theory in close connection with the practice of communist construction, opposes all attempts at revisionist perversions of Marxism–Leninism and its dogmatic interpretation;*

* (d) *concerns itself with increasing the vanguard role of communists in labour, socio-political and economic life of the enterprise, kolkhoz, institutions, educational establishment, etc.;*

* (e) *acts as an organizer of the workers in the resolution of the regular tasks of communist construction, heads socialist emulation for the realization of state plans and the obligations of the workers, mobilizes the masses for the exposure and best use of the internal reserves of enterprises and kolkhozes, for the wide introduction into production of the achievements of science, technology and the experience of advanced workers, strives for the strengthening of labour discipline, the steady increase in the productivity of labour, improvement in the quality of production, concern for the protection and increase of public wealth in enterprises, sovkhozes, and kolkhozes;*

* (f) *conducts mass-agitation and propaganda work, educates the masses in the spirit of communism, helps workers to acquire proficiency in administration of state and public affairs;*

(g) *on the basis of the wide development of criticism and self-criticism leads the struggle against manifestations of bureaucratism, localism, violations of state discipline, suppresses attempts to deceive the state, takes measures against slackness, extravagance and wastefulness in enterprises, kolkhozes and institutions;*

** (h) *renders assistance to the area committee, city committee and district committee in all of their activities and reports to them on its work.*

** *The party organization must see to it that each communist should observe in his own life and cultivate among workers the moral principles set forth in the Programme of the CPSU, the moral code of the builder of communism:*

- *devotion to the cause of communism, love for the socialist Motherland, for the countries of socialism;*
- *conscientious labour for the good of society; he who does not work does not eat;*
- *concern by everyone for the protection and increase of public property;*
- *high consciousness of public duty, intolerance toward violations of public interests;*
- *collectivism and comradely mutual assistance; one for all and all for one;*
- *humane attitudes and mutual respect between people; man is a friend, comrade and brother to man;*
- *honesty and truthfulness, moral purity, simplicity and modesty in public and personal life;*
- *mutual respect in the family, concern for the education of children;*
- *irreconcilability to injustice, parasitism, dishonesty, careerism and money-grubbing;*
- *friendship and brotherhood of all peoples of the USSR, intolerance of national and racial hostility;*
- *irreconcilability to enemies of communism, the cause of peace and the freedom of peoples;*
- *fraternal solidarity with the workers of all countries, with all peoples.*

59. Primary party organizations in productive and trading enterprises, sovkhozes, kolkhozes and also *design organizations, construction bureaux and scientific–research institutions directly*

linked with production enjoy the right of supervision over the activities of the administration.[21]

Party organizations in ministries, *state committees, sovnarkhozes*[22] *and other central and local soviet and economic institutions and departments* which do not exercise supervision functions over *the activities of the administration,*[23] *must actively promote the perfection of the work of the apparatus, educate the employees in the spirit of a high level of responsibility for the work entrusted to them, take measures for strengthening state discipline and the improvement of services to the population, lead a decisive struggle against bureaucratism and red tape, promptly inform appropriate party organs about shortcomings in the work of institutions and also individual workers, regardless of the posts they occupy.*

VII   Party and Komsomol

* 60.   *The All-Union Leninist Communist Youth League is an independent public organization of youth, the active assistant and reserve of the party. The Komsomol helps the party to educate youth in the spirit of communism, to draw it into the practical construction of the new society, to prepare a generation of thoroughly developed people who will live, work and administer public affairs under communism.*

* 61.   Komsomol organizations *enjoy* the right of wide initiative in discussing and raising before the appropriate party organizations questions about the work of enterprises, kolkhozes and institutions. They must be in deed the active champions of party directives in all spheres of communist construction, especially where there are no primary party organizations.

62.   The VLKSM works *under* the leadership of the Communist Party of the Soviet Union. The work of local organizations of the VLKSM is directed and supervised by the corresponding republican, territory, regional, *area*, city and district party organizations.

* *Local party organs and primary party organizations rely upon Komsomol organizations in work for the communist education of youth, and support and publicize their useful undertakings.*

* 63. Members of the VLKSM *who have been admitted* to the CPSU leave the Komsomol at the moment of their entry to the party if they do not occupy leading posts in Komsomol organizations.

VIII Party organizations in the Soviet Army

64. *In their activities party organizations in the Soviet Army are guided by the Programme and Rules of the CPSU and work on the basis of instructions confirmed by the Central Committee.*

Party organizations in the Soviet Army ensure the realization of party policy in the Armed Forces, unite their personnel around the Communist Party, educate soldiers in the spirit of the ideas of Marxism–Leninism and selfless devotion to the socialist Motherland, actively assist the strengthening of the unity of army and people, are concerned about strengthening military discipline, mobilize personnel for the implementation of the tasks of military and political training, the mastering of new techniques and weapons, the irreproachable implementation of their military duty and the orders and instructions of the command.

65. Leadership of party work in the *Armed Forces* is carried out by the *Central Committee of the CPSU through the Chief Political Administration of the Soviet Army and Navy*, which exercises the authority of a department of the CC CPSU.

* Heads of political administrations of areas and fleets and heads of political departments of *armies* must be of five years' party standing, and heads of political departments of *formations* – three years' party standing.

66. *Party organizations and* political organs *of the Soviet Army* maintain close links with local party committees, *and systematically inform them about political work in military units. Secretaries of military party organizations and leaders of political organs participate in the work of local party committees.*

XI Party groups in non-party organizations

* 67. Party groups are organized in congresses, *conferences* and meetings *convened by* soviet, trade union, co-operative and other mass organizations of *workers*, and also in the elected

organs of these organizations, where there are no less than three party members.

The task of these groups is the all-round strengthening of the influence of the party and the execution of its policy among non-party people, the strengthening of party and state discipline, the struggle with bureaucratism and the verification of the implementation of party and soviet directives.

68.   Party groups are subordinate to the appropriate party organs: to the Central Committee of the Communist Party of the Soviet Union, CC of the communist party of a union republic, territory committee, regional committee, area committee, city committee, and district committee of the party.

On all questions *party* groups must strictly and without deviation be guided by the decisions of leading party organs.

XII   Finances of the party

69.   The finances of the party and its organizations come from membership dues, income from party enterprises and other receipts.

70.   Monthly membership dues for party members and candidates are established in the following scale:

Monthly earnings	
up to 50 roubles	*10 kopecks*
51–100r	*0.5 per cent of monthly earnings*
101–150r	*1.0 per cent of monthly earnings*
151–200r	*1.5 per cent of monthly earnings*
201–250r	*2.0 per cent of monthly earnings*
251–300r	*2.5 per cent of monthly earnings*
above 300r	*3.0 per cent of monthly earnings*

71.   Entry dues of 2 per cent of monthly earnings are collected upon entry to *party* candidature.

AMENDMENTS TO THE 1961 RULES ADOPTED AT THE XXIII CONGRESS OF THE CPSU, 29 MARCH–8 APRIL 1966 AND THE XXIV CONGRESS OF THE CPSU, 30 MARCH–9 APRIL 1971

1.   The following sentence was added in 1966: 'The party rids itself of persons

who infringe the Programme and Rules of the CPSU and who, by their conduct, compromise the lofty title of communist.'

2. Twenty-three from 1966.
3. Five years' standing from 1966.
4. In 1966 this was amended to: 'Members of the VLKSM who join the party present the recommendation of a district or city committee of the VLKSM, which is equivalent to the recommendation of one party member.'
5. In 1966 the following was inserted at this point: 'its decision is considered adopted if no less than two-thirds of the party members present at the meeting vote for it'.
6. This paragraph was omitted in 1966.
7. The final sentence was omitted in 1966.
8. In 1966 confirmation by a regional or territory committee or the CC of the communist party of a union republic was replaced by confirmation by a district or city committee.
9. In 1966 this sentence was added to #24 in amended form: 'During elections for all party organs – from primary organizations up to the Central Committee of the CPSU – the principle of the systematic renewal of their composition and continuity of leadership is observed.' The remainder of #25 was omitted and subsequent articles up to #40 moved up in their numerical sequence.
10. This was changed to once every five years in 1971.
11. In 1966 this article was changed to the following: 'The Central Committee of the Communist Party of the Soviet Union elects a Politburo for leadership of the work of the party between plena of the CC, and a Secretariat for leadership of current work, chiefly the selection of cadres and the organization of the verification of implementation. The Central Committee elects the General Secretary of the CC CPSU.'
12. A new article was added in 1966: 'In the period between congresses of the party, the Central Committee of the CPSU may as necessary convene an All-Union party conference for discussion of urgent questions of party policy. The procedure for the conduct of an All-Union party conference is determined by the CC CPSU.'
13. In 1966 this paragraph was replaced by the following: 'The regular regional/territory conference is convened by the regional/territory committee once every two years. The regular congress of a communist party of a union republic is convened by the CC of the communist party at least once every four years. Special (extraordinary) conferences and congresses are convened on decision of the regional/territory committee/ CC of the communist party of the union republic or on the demand of one-third of the total membership of organizations in the regional/ territory/republican party organization.' In 1971 the regularity of regional/ territory conferences became two–three years and of the union republican congress five years.
14. In 1966 the following paragraph was added: 'In the period between congresses of the communist parties of the union republics, when necessary the CC of the communist party can convene republican party conferences for discussion of the most important questions of the activities

of party organizations. The procedure for the conduct of republican party conferences is determined by the CCs of the communist parties of the union republics.'

15. Changed in 1971 to every two–three years.
16. The following paragraph was added in 1971: 'In individual cases, with the permission of the regional/territory committee/CC of the communist party of a union republic, primary party organizations may be established in the framework of several enterprises in the one production combine and, as a rule, extend over the territory of one or several districts of a single city.'
17. In 1966 the following sentence was added: 'In party organizations which have shop organizations, a general party meeting is held at least once every two months.'
18. The words 'and sovkhoz' were added in 1966.
19. The following paragraph was added in 1966: 'In party organizations numbering more than 500 communists, in individual cases with the approval of the regional/territory committee/CC of the communist party of the union republic, party committees may be established in large factory shops, and the party organizations of the production divisions are granted the rights of a primary party organization.'
20. In 1971 this sentence was changed to: 'Party committees are elected for two–three years, and their size is determined by the general party meeting or conference.'

    In 1966 a new article was inserted at this point: 'Party committees of primary organizations numbering more than 1000 communists, with the approval of the CC of the communist party of the union republic may be granted the rights of a district party committee on questions of admission to the CPSU, registration of party members and candidates and examination of the personal affairs of communists. Inside these organizations, if necessary, party committees may be organized in shops, while party organizations in production sections are granted the rights of primary party organizations. Party committees which have been granted the rights of district committees of the party are elected for a two-year period.' Although the congress adopted this amendment, the final two sentences have not been included in the published versions of the Rules available since 1966.
21. In 1971 this paragraph was replaced by the following: 'Primary party organizations of enterprises in industry, transport, communications, construction, material–technical supply, trade, food service, communal–cultural services, kolkhozes, sovkhozes and other agricultural enterprises, design organizations, construction bureaux, scientific research institutes, educational establishments, cultural–educational and health institutions enjoy the right of supervision over the activities of the administration.'
22. The sovnarkhoz was omitted in 1966.
23. In 1971 the first part of this paragraph was replaced by the following: 'Party organizations in ministries, state committees and other central and local soviet and economic institutions and departments exercise supervision over the work of the apparatus in the implementation of directives of party and government, the observance of Soviet laws. They must actively promote . . .'

Rules of the Communist Party of the Soviet Union

Adopted at the XXVII Congress of the CPSU, February–March 1986

The Communist Party of the Soviet Union is the militant, tried-and-tested vanguard of the Soviet people, which unites on a voluntary basis the most advanced, conscious part of the working class, the kolkhoz peasantry and the intelligentsia of the USSR.

Founded by V. I. Lenin as the advanced detachment of the working class, the Communist Party has travelled a glorious path of struggle, and brought the working class and the toiling peasantry to the victory of the Great October Socialist Revolution, the establishment of the dictatorship of the proletariat in *our country*. Under the leadership of the Communist Party, the exploiter classes have been liquidated in the Soviet Union, *and the socio-political and ideological unity of the multinational Soviet society has taken shape and is constantly growing in strength.* Socialism has been victorious completely and finally. *The proleterian state has grown into the state of the entire people. The country has entered the stage of developed socialism.*[1]

The CPSU, *remaining in its class essence and ideology the party of the working class,* has become the party of all the people.

The party exists for and serves the people. It is the highest form of social-political organization, *the nucleus of the political system*, the leading and directing force of Soviet society. *The party determines the general perspective of the development of the country, ensures the scientific leadership* of the creative activity of the people, imparts an organized, planned and *single-minded* character to its struggle for the achievement of the ultimate goal, the victory of communism.

The CPSU bases its work on unswerving observance of Leninist norms of party life, *the principles of democratic centralism and* the collectivity of leadership, the all-round development of intra-party democracy, the *creative* activity of communists, criticism and self-criticism, *and wide publicity*.

Ideological and organizational unity, monolithic cohesion of its ranks and a high level of conscious discipline of all communists are an inviolable law of the CPSU. All manifestations of fractionalism and group activity are incompatible with Marxist–Leninist party principles and with party membership. The party rids itself of persons who infringe the Programme and Rules of the CPSU and who, by their conduct, compromise the lofty title of communist.[2]

In creatively developing Marxism–Leninism, the CPSU decisively struggles against all manifestations of revisionism and dogmatism, which are deeply alien to revolutionary theory.

The Communist Party of the Soviet Union is a constituent part of the international communist movement. It firmly adheres to the tried-and-tested Marxist–Leninist principles of proletarian, *socialist* internationalism, actively assists the strengthening of *the co-operation and cohesion of fraternal socialist countries, of the world system of socialism and* the international communist and workers' movement, *and displays solidarity with the peoples struggling for national and social liberation, against imperialism, and for the preservation of peace.*

I Members of the party, their responsibilities and rights

1. Any citizen of the Soviet Union who accepts the Programme and Rules of the party, who actively participates in the construction of communism, who works in one of the party organizations, who carries out the decisions of the party and pays membership dues may be a member of the CPSU.

2. A party member must:

(a) firmly and without deviation put *the general line and directives* of the party into effect, explain the *domestic and foreign* policy of the *CPSU* to the masses, *organize the working people for its implementation*, and assist the strengthening and widening of the party's links with the people:

(b) *be an example in labour, protect and increase socialist property, persistently achieve an increase in the effectiveness of production, the steady growth in the productivity of labour, improvement in the quality of production, the introduction into the national economy of the achievements of contemporary science and technology; perfect his own qualifications, come forward as an active advocate of all that is new and progressive, and make a maximum contribution to the acceleration of the socio-economic development of the country;*[3]

(c) actively participate in the political life of the country, in the management of state *and public* affairs, *serve as* an example *in the* fulfilment of *civic* duty, *actively promote the ever fuller implementation of the socialist self-administration of the people*;

(d) master Marxist–Leninist theory, *expand his own political and cultural horizon, assist in all ways the increase in the consciousness and ideological–moral growth of the Soviet people.* Lead a decisive struggle against all manifestations of bourgeois ideology, private ownership psychology, religious prejudices *and other views and morals alien to the socialist way of life*;

(e) *strictly observe the norms of communist morality, assert the principle of social justice which is inherent to socialism,* put public above personal interests, *display modesty and decency, sensitivity and attention to people,* respond promptly to working people's *requirements* and needs, be truthful and honest before the party and the people;

(f) *consistently propagate* the idea of socialist internationalism and Soviet patriotism among the masses of workers, lead the struggle against *manifestations* of nationalism and chauvinism, *actively* assist the strengthening of the friendship of the peoples of the USSR, fraternal links *with the countries of socialism,* with the proletariats and workers of the *whole world*;

(g) in every possible way help strengthen the defence might of the USSR, lead a tireless struggle for peace and for friendship between peoples.

(h) strengthen the ideological and organizational unity of the party, defend the party from penetration of its ranks by people unworthy of the lofty title of communist, show vigilance and protect party and state secrets;

(i) develop criticism and self-criticism, boldly expose shortcomings and strive to eliminate them, struggle against ostentation, conceit, complacency *and eyewash*, give a decisive rebuff to all attempts at the suppression of criticism, resist *bureaucratism*, localism, *departmentalism* and all actions causing damage to the party and state, and report them to party organs up to the CC CPSU;

(j) without deviation carry out the party line in the selection of cadres on the basis of their political, practical and *moral* qualities. Be uncompromising in all cases of infringements of Leninist principles in the selection and education of cadres;

(k) observe party and state discipline, which are equally binding for all members of the party. The party has one discipline, one law for all communists regardless of service and the positions they occupy.

3. A party member has the right:

(a) to vote in elections and be elected to party organs;

(b) freely to discuss in party meetings, conferences, congresses, at sessions of party committees and in the party press questions of the policy and practical activities of the party, to introduce proposals, openly to discuss and maintain his opinion until the adoption of a decision by the organization;

(c) to criticize at party meetings, conferences, congresses and plena of the committees *of any party organ* any communist, regardless of the position he holds. Persons guilty of suppressing criticism and persecuting critics must be called to strict account by the party, right up to expulsion from the CPSU;

(d) personally to participate in party meetings, sessions of bureaux and committees when the question of his activities or behaviour is being discussed;

(e) to address questions, statements and proposals to any party instance, up to the CC CPSU, and to demand an answer to the substance of his address.

4. Admission to party membership is made exclusively on an individual basis. *Citizens from among* the workers, peasants and intelligentsia who are conscious, active and devoted to the cause of communism are admitted as members of the party. New members are admitted from among the candidates who have completed the established candidate stage.

Persons who have reached 18 years are admitted to the party. Youth up to and including 25 years of age enter the party only through the VLKSM.

The procedure for the admission of candidates as members of the party is as follows:

(a) those entering the party present recommendations of

three members of the CPSU, of no less than five years' party standing and who have known them through common productive and public work for no less than one year.

FIRST NOTE Members of the VLKSM who join the party present the recommendation of a district or city committee of the VLKSM, which is equivalent to the recommendation of one party member.

SECOND NOTE Members and candidate members of the CC CPSU refrain from giving recommendations;

(b) the question of admission to the party is discussed and decided by the general meeting of the primary party organization; its decision is considered adopted if no less than two-thirds of the party members present at the meeting vote for it and it comes into force after confirmation by the district committee, and in cities where there is no district division, by the city party committee.

The question of entry to the party may be discussed without the participation of those giving recommendations. Admission to the party takes place, as a rule, at open party meetings;

(c) citizens of the USSR who are former members of communist and workers' parties of other countries are admitted to the Communist Party of the Soviet Union on the basis of rules established by the CC CPSU.

5.   Those who give recommendations bear responsibility before party organizations for the objectivity of the evaluation of the political, practical and moral qualities of those they recommend, *and render them assistance in their ideological–political growth.*

6.   Seniority of party membership of those entering the party is counted from the day on which the decision is made by the general meeting of the primary party organization on the acceptance of the given candidate into party membership.

7.   The procedure for the registration of members and candidate members of the party and their transfer from one organization to another is determined by the appropriate instructions of the CC CPSU.

8.   The question of a member or candidate member of the party who has not paid membership dues for three months without valid reasons is discussed in the primary party organization. If it becomes clear during this that the given

member or candidate member of the party has in fact lost contact with the party organization, then he is considered to have left the party, which decision is taken by the primary party organization and submitted for confirmation to the district committee or city committee of the party.

9. A member or candidate member of the party who fails to fulfil his duties as laid down in the Rules or commits other misdemeanours shall be called to account and may be subjected to a penalty: admonition, reproof (strict reproof), reproof (strict reproof) with entry on the registration card. The highest party penalty is expulsion from the party.

For insignificant misdemeanours measures of party education and influence in the form of comradely criticism, party reproach, warning or instruction must be employed.

A communist who has committed an offence must answer for it, above all, to the primary party organization. In the case of a communist being called to account before the party by a higher standing organ, the primary party organization is informed of this.

During the review of the question of calling a communist to account before the party, maximum attention and thorough investigation of the validity of the charges laid against the communist must be ensured.

No later than a year after a penalty has been imposed on a party member, the party organization hears from him how he is rectifying his shortcomings.

10. The question of the expulsion of a communist from the party is decided by a general meeting of the primary party organization. The decision of the primary party organization on expulsion from the party is considered adopted if not less than two-thirds of the party members attending the party meeting have voted for it, and it is confirmed by the district committee or city committee of the party.

Prior to the confirmation by a district committee or city committee of the party of a decision on expulsion from the CPSU, the party card or candidate member card remains in the hands of the communist, and he has the right to attend closed party meetings.

After expulsion from the party, he retains the right to appeal to higher party organs, up to the CC CPSU, for a two-month period.

11.   The question of calling to account before the party members and candidate members of the CC of the communist party of a union republic, a territory committee, a regional committee, an area committee, a city committee, a district committee of the party and also members of auditing commissions is discussed in primary party organizations and decisions imposing penalties on *them* are taken in the ordinary way.

Proposals by party organizations on expulsion from the CPSU are reported to the party committee of which the given communist is a member. Decisions on expulsion from the party of members and candidate members of the CC of a communist party of a union republic, a territory committee, regional committee, area committee, city committee or district committee of the party and members of auditing commissions are taken at the plenum of the corresponding committee by a two-thirds majority vote of its members.

The question of expulsion from the party of a member or candidate member of the Central Committee of the CPSU or a member of the Central Auditing Commission *of the CPSU* is decided by the party congress, and in the *periods* between congresses, by the plenum of the CC by a two-thirds majority of the *CC CPSU*.

12.   *For the infringement of Soviet laws, the party member bears a dual responsibility – before the state and before the party. A person* who has committed a misdemeanour punishable by the criminal code, *is excluded from the ranks of the CPSU.*

13.   Appeals of those expelled from the party or who have been punished, and also decisions of party organizations on expulsion from the party are examined by the appropriate party organs not later than *two months* from the day of their receipt.

II   Candidate members of the party

14.   Those entering the party pass through a candidate stage, which is necessary to acquaint the candidate thoroughly with the Programme and Rules of the CPSU and to prepare for entry to party membership. The party organizations must help the candidate prepare for entry to membership of the CPSU and verify his personal qualities *in practical deeds, in the implementation of party and public assignments.*

The candidate stage is fixed at one year.

15.   The procedure for admission to candidate membership (individual admission, presentation of recommendations, decision of the primary organization on admission and its confirmation) is identical to that for admission to party membership.

16.   On the expiry of the candidate stage the primary party organization examines and decides the question of the admission of the candidate to party membership. If during the candidate stage the candidate has not proved his worth and because of his personal qualities cannot be admitted to membership of the CPSU, the party organization adopts a decision refusing him party membership, and after confirmation of the given decision by the district or city committee of the party, he is considered to have ceased to be a candidate member of the CPSU.

17.   Candidate members of the party take part in all the activities of the party organizations and enjoy the right of a consultative vote in party meetings. Candidate members of the party may not be elected to leading party organs or as delegates to party conferences and congresses.

18.   Candidate members of the CPSU pay membership dues at the same rate as party members.

III   Organizational structure of the party. Intra-party democracy

19.   The guiding principle of the organizational structure, *of the life and activities* of the party, is democratic centralism, which means:

(a) the election of all leading organs of the party from the bottom to the top;

(b) the periodic report of party organs to their party organizations and to higher organs;

(c) strict party discipline and the subordination of the minority to the majority;

(d) the unconditionally binding character of decisions of higher organs for lower;

(e) *collectivity in the work of all organizations and leading organs of the party and the personal responsibility of every communist for the implementation of his duties and party commissions.*[4]

20.   The party is built along territorial–production lines:

primary organizations are formed in places of work of communists and are united into district, city, *and other* organizations on a territorial basis. An organization *which unites the communists of a given area is higher than all of the component party organizations of that area.*

21.   All party organizations are autonomous in deciding local questions, if these decisions do not contradict party policy.

22.   The highest leading organ of the party organization is the general meeting, *conference* (for primary organizations), the conference (for district, city, area, regional and territory organizations), and the congress (for communist parties of the union republics and for the Communist Party of the Soviet Union). *A meeting, conference or congress is considered competent if participating in it is more than half the members of the party organization or of the elected delegates.*

23.   The general meeting, conference or congress elects a bureau or committee, which are executive organs and lead all the current work of the party organization.

An apparatus is established in the CC CPSU, CCs of the communist parties of the union republics, territory committees, regional committees, area committees, city committees and district committees of the party for the conduct of current work of an organizational nature, verification of the implementation of party decisions, and for rendering assistance to lower organizations in their activities.

The structure and staff of the party apparatus is defined by the Central Committee of the CPSU.

24.   Elections for party organs are carried out by closed (secret) ballot.

At meetings of primary and shop organizations numbering less than 15 party members and of party groups, the election of the secretary and deputy secretary of the party organization and the party group organizers may, with the agreement of the communists, be conducted by open ballot. In these primary organizations elections for delegates to district and city party conferences are conducted in the same way.[5]

During elections all party members have the unlimited right to challenge candidates and to criticize them. Voting must take place on each candidate separately. The candidates for whom more than half the participants of the meeting, conference or congress voted are considered elected.

During elections for all party organs – from primary

organizations to the Central Committee of the CPSU – the principle of the systematic renewal of their composition and continuity of leadership is observed.

25.   Through all of *their* activity, member*s* and candidate member*s* of the CC CPSU, *a CC of a communist party of a union republic, a territory committee, a regional committee, an area committee, a city committee and a district committee* must justify the high confidence shown in *them*. If a member or candidate member of a party committee lets his honour and dignity fall, he may not remain in the *committee*.

The question of the removal of a member or candidate member of a *party committee* from that body is decided at the plenum of the *given* committee. The decision is considered adopted if no less than two-thirds of members of the given committee vote for it in a closed (secret) ballot.

The question of the removal of members of the Central Auditing Commission of the CPSU and of the auditing commissions of local party organizations from these commissions is decided at sessions *of them* in the way envisaged for members and candidate members of party committees.

26.   The free and businesslike discussion of questions of party policy in *the party and in all of its organizations* is an important principle of intra-party democracy.[6] Only on the basis of intra-party democracy *is it possible to ensure the high creative activity of communists, open* criticism and self-criticism and *strong* party discipline, which must be conscious and not mechanical.

Discussion of controversial or insufficiently clear questions is possible within the framework of individual organizations or by the party as a whole. General party discussion *takes place*:

(a) *on the initiative of the CC CPSU if it acknowledges the necessity to consult the party as a whole on some questions of policy*;

(b) *on the proposal of several party organizations at the republican, territory or regional level.*[7]

Wide discussion, especially on an all-union scale, of questions of party policy, must be conducted in such a way as to ensure the free expression of views of party members and to exclude the possibility of attempts at the formation of fractional groupings and attempts at schism in the party.[8]

27.   The highest principle of party leadership is the collectivity of leadership – the indispensable condition for the normal

activities of party organizations, the correct education of cadres, the development of the activity and initiative of communists, and a *reliable guarantee against the adoption of volitional, subjective decisions, manifestations of the cult of personality, and the infringement of Leninist norms of party life.*

The collectivity of leadership *assumes personal responsibility for matters entrusted to people, constant supervision over the activities of every party organization, of every worker.*[9]

28. *The CC CPSU*, CCs of the communist parties of the union republics, territory committees, regional committees, area committees, city committees and district committees of the party systematically inform party organizations about their work in the period between congresses and conferences, *about the realization of critical remarks and proposals of communists.*[10]

An irrevocable principle for party committees and primary party organizations is also the objective and timely informing of higher standing party organs about their activities and the situation in the localities.[11]

29. Meetings of the aktiv of district, city, area, regional and territory party organizations and the communist parties of the union republics are convened for discussion of the most important decisions of the party and for working out measures for their implementation, and also for the examination of questions of local life.

30. Standing or temporary commissions *and workers' groups* on various questions of party work can be established in party committees, and other means *can also be used* to draw communists to the activities of the party organs on a public basis.

IV Higher organs of the party

31. The supreme organ of the Communist Party of the Soviet Union is the party congress. Regular congresses are convened by the Central Committee at least once every five years. The convocation of the party congress and the agenda are announced not less than a month and a half before the congress. Special (extraordinary) congresses are convened by the Central Committee of the party on its own initiative or on the demand of not less than one-third of the total number of members

represented at the last party congress. Special (extraordinary) congresses are convened within two months. A congress is considered valid if no less than half of all members of the party are represented at it.

Norms of representation at the party congress are set by the Central Committee.

32.   If the Central Committee of the party does not convene a special (extraordinary) congress as provided for in *paragraph* 31, the organizations which have demanded the convocation of a special (extraordinary) congress have the right to form an organizational committee which enjoys the rights of the Central Committee of the party with respect to the convening of a special (extraordinary) congress.

33.   The Congress:

(a) hears and approves the reports of the Central Committee, Central Auditing Commission and other central organizations;

(b) revises, changes and confirms the Programme and Rules of the party;

(c) determines the line of the party on questions of domestic and foreign policy, examines and decides the most important questions *of party and state life*, of communist construction;

(d) elects the Central Committee and the Central Auditing Commission.

34.   The congress elects the Central Committee and the Central Auditing Commission and determines their sizes. In the event of vacancies occurring in the Central Committee, they are filled from among the candidate members of the CC CPSU.

35.   In the *periods* between congresses the Central Committee of the Communist Party of the Soviet Union guides all the activities of the party, the local party organs, carries out the selection and assignment of leading cadres, directs the work of central state and public organizations of workers, creates various organs, institutions and enterprises of the party and guides their activities, appoints the editorial boards of the central newspapers and journals working under its supervision, and distributes the funds of the party budget and supervises its use.

The Central Committee represents the CPSU in dealings with other parties.

36.   The Central Auditing Commission of the CPSU inspects

observance of the established procedure for handling business, work done in considering letters, applications and complaints from workers in the central organs of the party, the correctness of the use of the party budget, including the payment, collection and accounting of party membership dues, and also the financial–economic activities of enterprises and institutions of the Central Committee of the CPSU.

37.   The CC CPSU holds no less than one plenary session every six months. Candidate members of the CC participate in plenary sessions of the CC with the right of a consultative vote.

38.   The Central Committee of the Communist Party of the Soviet Union elects a Politburo for leadership of the work of the party between plena of the CC, and a Secretariat for leadership of current work, chiefly the selection of cadres and organization of the verification of implementation. The Central Committee elects the General Secretary of the CC CPSU.

39.   The Central Committee of the Communist Party of the Soviet Union organizes a Committee of Party Control attached to the CC.

The Committee of Party Control attached to the CC CPSU:

(a) verifies the observance of party discipline by members and candidate members of the CPSU, calls to account communists guilty of violations of the Programme and Rules of the party and of party and state discipline, and also those who infringe party ethics;

(b) examines appeals against decisions of CCs of the communist parties of the union republics and territory and regional committees of the party on expulsions from the party and party punishments.

40.   In the period between congresses of the party, the Central Committee of the CPSU may as necessary convene an All-Union party conference for discussion of urgent questions of party policy. The procedure for the conduct of an All-Union party conference is determined by the CC CPSU.

V   Republican, territory, regional, area, city and district organizations of the party

41.   Republican, territory, regional, area, city and district party organizations and their committees are guided in their activities by the Programme and Rules of the CPSU, conduct all work for

the realization of party policy and organize the implementation of directives of the Central Committee of the CPSU in the republic, territory, region, area, city and district.

42. The basic responsibilities of the republican, territory, regional, area, city and district party organizations and their leading organs are:

(a) political and organizational work among the masses and mobilization of communists and all workers for the realization of the tasks of communist construction, *the acceleration of socio-economic development on the basis of scientific–technical progress, an increase in the effectiveness of social production and labour productivity, an improvement in the quality of production, the fulfilment of state plans and socialist responsibilities, and ensuring steady growth* in the material welfare and cultural level of the workers;[12]

(b) organization of ideological work, propaganda of Marxism–Leninism, increase in the communist consciousness of workers, leadership of the local press, radio and television, and supervision over the activities of *scientific*, cultural and *national* educational institutions;

(c) leadership of the Soviets *of people's deputies*, trade unions, komsomol, *co-operative*[13] and other public organizations through *communists working in them*, the wider attraction of workers into the work of these organizations, development of the initiative and activity of the mass as the necessary condition *for the further deepening of socialist democracy*;

(d) *strict observance of Leninist principles and methods of leadership, consolidation of the Leninist style in party work, in all spheres of state and economic administration, ensuring the unity of ideological, organizational and economic activities, the strengthening of socialist legality*,[14] *state and labour discipline, order and organization in all sectors*;

(e) *conduct of cadre policy*, education of cadres in the spirit of communist ideas, *moral purity*, a high sense of responsibility before the party and people for work entrusted to them;

(f) organization of various institutions and enterprises of the party in their republic, territory, region, area, city or district and leadership of their activities; distribution of party funds within its organization; *the systematic informing* of the higher standing party organ and responsibility before it for their work.

Leading organs of republican, territory and regional party organizations

43.   The highest organ of the republican/territory/regional party organization is the congress of the communist party of the union republic/territory/regional party conference, and in the *period* between them, the CC of the communist party of the union republic/territory committee/regional committee.

44.   The regular congress of a communist party of a union republic is convened by the CC of the communist party at least once every five years. The regular territory/regional conference is convened by the territory/regional committee once every two–three years. Special (extraordinary) congresses and conferences are convened on decision of the CC of the communist party of the union republic/territory/regional committee or on the demand of one-third of the total membership of organizations in the republic/territory/regional organization.

The norms of representation at the congress of the communist party of a union republic/territory/regional conference are established by the corresponding party committee.

The congress of the communist party of the union republic/ territory/regional conference hears the reports of the CC of the communist party of the union republic/territory/regional committee and the auditing commission, at its discretion discusses other questions of party, economic and cultural construction, and elects the CC of the communist party of the union republic/territory/regional committee, the auditing commission and delegates to the CPSU congress.

In the period between congresses of the communist parties of the union republics, when necessary the CC of the communist party can convene republican party conferences for discussion of the most important questions of the activities of party organizations. The procedure for the conduct of *them* is determined by the CCs of the communist parties of the union republics.

45.   CCs of communist parties of the union republics/territory/

regional committees elect bureaux, which include the secretaries of the committees. Secretaries must be of no less than five years' party standing. At the plena of committees, heads of the departments of these committees, the chairmen of party *control* commissions and the editors of party newspapers and journals are confirmed.

Secretariats *are* established in CCs of the communist parties of the union republics/territory/regional committees of the party for the examination of current questions and verification of implementation.

46.   The plenum of the CC of the communist party of a union republic/territory/regional committee is convened no less than once every four months.

47.   The CC of the communist party of a union republic/ territory/regional committee leads the area, city and district party organizations, checks their activities and systematically hears the reports of the corresponding party committees.

Party organizations of autonomous republics, and also autonomous and other regions in union republics and territories, work under the guidance of CCs of the communist parties of the union republics or territory committees.

Leading organs of area, city and district (rural and urban) party organizations

48.   The highest organ of the area/city/district party organization is the area/city/district party conference or general meeting of communists, convened by the area/city/district committee at least once every two–three years, and the extraordinary conference convened on decision of the respective committee or on the demand of one-third of the total membership of the party in the party organization concerned.

The area/city/district conference (meeting) hears the reports of the committee and auditing commission, at its discretion discusses other questions of party, economic and cultural construction, elects the area/city/district committee, auditing commission and delegates to the regional/territory conference or congress of the communist party of the union republic.

The norms of representation at the area, city and district conference are established by the corresponding party committee.

49.   The area/city/district committee elects a bureau, including the secretaries of the committee, and also confirms the heads of the departments of the committee, *the chairman of the party commission* and editors of newspapers. Secretaries of the area/city/district committee must be of no less than *five* years' party standing. Secretaries of committees are confirmed by the regional committee/territory committee/CC of the communist party of the union republic.

50.   The area/city/district committee *establishes* primary party organizations and guides their activities, systematically hears reports on the work of party organizations, and keeps a record of communists.

51.   The plenum of the area/city/district committee is convened at least once every three months.

VI   Primary organizations of the party

52.   The basis of the party is the primary organizations.

Primary party organizations are formed in places of work of party members – at plants, factories, in sovkhozes and other enterprises, in kolkhozes, units of the *Armed Forces*, institutions, educational establishments, etc. where there are not less than three party members. *Should the necessity arise* territorial primary party organizations may also be established by place of residence of communists.

In individual cases, with the permission of the regional/ territory committee/CC of the communist party of a union republic, party organizations may be established in the framework of several enterprises in the one production combine and, as a rule, extend over the territory of one or several districts of a single city.

53.   In enterprises, kolkhozes and institutions where there are more than 50 members and candidate *members of the CPSU*, party organizations by shop, unit, farm, brigade, department, etc. may be established in the general primary party organization with the permission of the district, city or area committee.

In shop, unit and similar organizations, and also in primary party organizations numbering less than 50 members and candidates, party groups by brigade and other production sections may be formed.

54.   The highest organ of the primary party organization is the

party meeting, which is held at least once a month. In party organizations which have shop organizations, *both* general *and shop* meetings are convened at least once every two months.

In large party organizations numbering more than 300 communists the general party meeting is convened when necessary at times fixed by the party committee or on the demand of several shop party organizations.

55.   For the conduct of current work the primary/shop party organization elects a bureau for *two–three* years, the size of which is established by the party meeting. In primary and shop organizations numbering less than 15 party members, a secretary and deputy secretary of the party organization are elected, not a bureau. *Elections in these organizations are held annually.*[15]

Secretaries of primary and shop organizations must be of no less than one year's party standing.

Primary party organizations numbering less than 150 members of the party, as a rule, will not have positions filled by party workers freed from production.

56.   In large enterprises and institutions numbering more than 300 members and candidate *members* of the party, and, when necessary, in organizations numbering more than 100 communists with special production conditions and territorial separation, with the permission of the regional committee, territory committee or CC of the communist party of the union republic, party committees may be formed with the shop party organizations being granted the rights of primary party organizations.

Party committees may be formed in party organizations of kolkhozes, sovkhozes *and other enterprises in the agricultural economy* where there are 50 communists.

In party organizations numbering more than 500 communists, in individual cases with the approval of the regional/territory committee/CC of the communist party of the union republic, party committees may be established in large factory shops, and the party organizations of the production divisions are granted the rights of a primary party organization.

Party committees are elected for two–three years, and their size is determined by the general party meeting or conference.

Party committees, party bureaux and secretaries of primary and shop party organizations systematically inform communists at party meetings about their work.

57.   Party committees of primary organizations numbering more than 1000 communists, with the approval of the CC of the communist party of the union republic may be granted the rights of a district party committee on questions of admission to the CPSU, registration of members and candidate *members* of the party and examination of the personal affairs of communists.

These organizations may elect enlarged party committees within which bureaux are formed for leadership of current work.

58.   In its activities the primary party organization is guided by the Programme and Rules of the CPSU. *It is the political nucleus of the labour collective*, conducts work directly among the workers, unites them around the *party, organizes them for the implementation of the tasks of communist construction, and actively takes part in the conduct of the party's cadre policy.*

The primary party organization:

(a) admits new members to the CPSU;

(b) educate communists in the spirit of devotion to the cause of the party, ideological conviction and communist ethics;

(c) organizes the study by communists of Marxist–Leninist theory in close connection with the practice of communist construction, *struggles* against *any manifestations of bourgeois ideology, revisionism and dogmatism, backward views and moods;*[16]

(d) concerns itself with the increase of the vanguard role of communists in labour and socio-political life, *with their exemplary conduct in private life, hears the reports of members and candidate members of the CPSU on their implementation of their responsibilities under the rules and party assignments;*[17]

(e) acts as an organizer of the workers in the resolution of the tasks of *economic and social development*, heads socialist emulation for the realization of state plans and obligations,[18] *the intensification of production*, the increase of labour productivity and the quality of production, the wide introduction into production of the achievements of science and technology, of advanced experience, mobilizes the *workers* for the *procurement* of internal reserves, *achieves a rational, economic use of material, labour and financial resources,* concern for the protection and increase of public wealth, *for the improvement of conditions of people's work and daily life;*

(f) conducts mass agitation and propaganda work, educates the *workers in the spirit of devotion to the ideas of communism, Soviet patriotism, the friendship of peoples,* helps them to cultivate a high level of political culture, increases their social activity and responsibility;[19]

(g) *assists the development among communists and all workers of the habits of participation in socialist self-administration, ensures an increase in the role of the labour collective in the administration of the enterprise and institution, and directs the work of trade union, komsomol and other public organizations;*[20]

(h) on the basis of the wide development of criticism and self-criticism, leads the struggle against manifestations of bureaucratism, localism, *departmentalism,* violations of state, *labour and production* discipline, suppresses attempts to deceive the state, takes measures against slackness, extravagance and wastefulness, *and achieves the consolidation of a sensible form of life.*[21]

59. Primary party organizations of enterprises in industry, transport, communications, material–technical supply, trade, food service, communal–cultural services, kolkhozes, sovkhozes and other agricultural enterprises, design organizations, construction bureaux, scientific research institutes, educational establishments, cultural–educational and health institutions enjoy the right of supervision over the activities of the administration.

Party organizations in ministries, state committees and other central and local soviet and economic institutions and departments exercise supervision over the work of the apparatus in the implementation of directives of party and government, the observance of Soviet laws. They must actively promote the perfection of the work of the apparatus, *the selection, placement*[22] *and education of their employees, increase their* responsibility for the work entrusted to them, *the development of branches of service of the population,*[23] take measures for improving state discipline, lead a decisive struggle against bureaucratism and red-tape, promptly inform appropriate party organs about shortcomings in the work of institutions and also individual workers, regardless of the posts they occupy.

NOTE *Commissions may be set up in primary party organizations for the exercise of the right of control over the activities of the administration and for the work of the apparatus in individual areas of production activity.*

VII   The party and state and public organizations

60.   *The CPSU, acting within the framework of the Constitution of the USSR, exercises political leadership over state and public organizations and directs and co-ordinates their activities.*[24]

Party organizations and communists working in state and public organizations ensure that these organizations in full measure have exercised their constitutional powers, rights and duties under the rules and have widely drawn workers into administration and the resolution of political, economic and social questions.[25] *Party organizations do not substitute themselves for soviet, trade union, co-operative and other public organizations, and they do not allow the merging of functions of party and other organs.*[26]

61.   Party groups are organized at congresses, conferences and meetings convened by state and public organizations, as well as in the elected organs of these organizations where there are no less than three members of the party. The tasks of these groups *are the execution of party policy*[27] *in the corresponding non-party organizations, the strengthening of the influence of communists on the state of affairs in these organizations, the development of democratic norms in their activities*, the strengthening of party and state discipline, struggle with bureaucratism, and verification of the implementation of party and soviet directives.

62.   The work of party groups in non-party organizations is guided by the appropriate party organ: CC CPSU, CC of the communist party of a union republic, territory committee, regional committee, area committee, city committee or district committee of the party.

VIII   Party and komsomol

63.   The All-Union Leninist Communist Youth League is an independent public–*political* organization of youth, the active

assistant and reserve of the party. The komsomol helps the party to educate youth in the spirit of communism, to draw it into the practical construction of the new society, *into the management of state and public affairs, to form* a generation of thoroughly developed people, *prepared for labour and the defence of the Soviet Motherland.*

64. *Komsomol organizations must be* active conductors of the party *line in all spheres of productive and public life. They* enjoy the right of wide initiative in discussing and raising before the appropriate party organizations questions about the work of enterprises, kolkhozes, institutions and *educational establishments, and they take a direct part in resolving these questions, especially if they concern the work, everyday life, teaching and upbringing of the youth.*

65. The VLKSM works under the leadership of the Communist Party of the Soviet Union. The work of local organizations of the VLKSM is directed and supervised by the corresponding republican, territory, regional, area, city and district party organizations.

Local party organs and primary party organizations rely upon komsomol organizations in the work for the communist education of youth *and the mobilization of them for the resolution of concrete tasks of productive and social life,*[28] support their useful undertakings, *and render all-round assistance to them in their activity.*

66. Members of the VLKSM who have been admitted to the CPSU leave the komsomol at the moment of their entry to the party if they *are not members of elected Komsomol organs and are not engaged in komsomol work.*

IX Party organizations in the Armed Forces

67. In their activities party organizations in the *Armed Forces* are guided by the Programme and Rules of the CPSU and work on the basis of instructions confirmed by the Central Committee. They ensure the realization of party policy in the Armed Forces, unite their personnel around the Communist Party, educate soldiers in the spirit of the ideas of Marxism–Leninism and selfless devotion to the socialist Motherland, actively assist the strengthening of the unity of army and people, and they are concerned to *increase the military preparedness of the forces,*

strengthen military discipline, mobilize personnel for the implementation of the tasks of military and political training, the mastering of new techniques and weapons, the irreproachable implementation of their military duty and the orders and instructions of the command.

68.   Leadership of party work in the Armed Forces is carried out by the Central Committee of the CPSU through *political organs*.[29] The Chief Political Administration of the Soviet Army and Navy exercises the authority of a department of the CC CPSU.

Heads of political administrations of areas and fleets and heads of political departments of armies, *flotillas and formations* must be of five years' party standing.

69.   Party organizations and political organs of the *Armed Forces* maintain close links with local party committees, and systematically inform them about political work in military units. Secretaries of military party organizations and leaders of political organs participate in the work of local party committees.

X   Finances of the party

70.   The finances of the party and its organizations come from membership dues, income from party enterprises and other receipts.

The manner in which party funds are used is determined by the Central Committee of the CPSU.

71.   Monthly membership dues for members and candidate members of the CPSU are established in the following scale:

Monthly earnings	
up to 70 roubles	*10 kopecks*
71–100r	*20 kopecks*
101–150r	*1.0 per cent of monthly earnings*
151–200r	*1.5 per cent of monthly earnings*
201–250r	*2.0 per cent of monthly earnings*
251–300r	*2.5 per cent of monthly earnings*
above 300r	*3.0 per cent of monthly earnings*

72.   Entry dues of 2 per cent of monthly earnings are *paid* upon entry to party candidature.

NOTES

1. The final sentence was not included in the draft Rules published in *Pravda* on 2 November 1985.
2. In the draft Rules, the following paragraph was included at this point: 'In all its activities the CPSU is guided by the teaching of Marxism–Leninism and by its Programme, in which is defined the tasks of the planned and all-round perfection of socialism, of the further advance of Soviet society to communism on the basis of the acceleration of the socio-economic development of the country.'
3. In the draft Rules, this paragraph read as follows: '(b) be an example of a conscientious, creative attitude to labour, of a high sense of organization and discipline, protect and increase socialist property – the economic basis of the Soviet economic structure. Persistently to achieve an increase in the effectiveness of production, the steady growth in the productivity of labour, the introduction into the national economy of the achievements of contemporary science and technology; to perfect his own qualifications, to support and spread advanced knowhow, to come forward as an active advocate of all that is new and progressive;'.
4. Point (e) was not included in the draft Rules.
5. The final sentence was not included in the draft Rules.
6. In the draft Rules, this was also declared to be 'the inalienable right of a party member'.
7. In the draft Rules, this section was as it had been in 1961.
8. In the draft Rules, this sentence was as it had been in 1961.
9. In the draft Rules, this sentence was as it had been in 1961.
10. The words beginning 'about the realization. . .' were not found in the draft Rules.
11. This paragraph was not found in the draft Rules.
12. In the draft Rules, this paragraph was as follows: 'political and organizational work among the masses and mobilization of them for the realization of the tasks of communist construction, the development and increase in the effectiveness of industrial and agricultural production in every possible way, the fulfilment and over-fulfilment of state plans, and for ensuring steady growth in the material welfare and cultural level of the workers;'.
13. Co-operatives were not included in the draft Rules.
14. Socialist legality was not included in the draft Rules.
15. The final sentence was not included in the draft Rules.
16. In the draft Rules, this paragraph read as follows: 'organizes study by communists of Marxist–Leninist theory in close connection with the practice of communist construction, struggles against all attempts at revisionist perversions of Marxism–Leninism and its dogmatic interpretation, against any manifestations of bourgeois ideology, of backward views and moods:'.
17. In the draft Rules, this was as follows: 'concerns itself with increasing the vanguard role of communists in labour and the socio-political and economic life of the enterprise, kolkhoz, institution, educational establishment etc.;'.

18. In the draft Rules, the latter were referred to as 'the obligations of the workers'.
19. In the draft Rules, this was as follows: 'conducts mass agitation and propaganda work, educates the workers in the spirit of devotion to the ideas of communism, Soviet patriotism and the friendship of peoples, helps them to cultivate a high level of political culture, in accordance with the law ensures an increase in the role of the labour collective in the administration of enterprises and institutions, and promotes the development of the activity of trade union, komsomol and other public organizations;'.
20. This was not included in the draft Rules in this form. See note 19.
21. In the draft Rules, the section 'and achieves the consolidation of a sensible form of life' was not to be found. In its place was 'in enterprises, kolkhozes and institutions'. There was also a further point, which read 'renders assitance to the area committee, city committee and district committee in all their activities and reports to them on its work'.
22. Selection and placement were not included in the draft Rules.
23. In the draft Rules this was referred to in terms of 'the improvement of services to the population'.
24. In the draft Rules, this sentence read: 'The CPSU exercises leadership over state and public organizations through the communists working in them.'
25. In the draft Rules, the section following the word 'rules' read 'to promote the wide drawing in of workers to their work'.
26. Nor, according to the draft Rules, 'unnecessary parallelism in work'.
27. In the draft Rules, the tasks were 'the all-round strengthening of the influence of the party and the execution of its policy in the corresponding non-party organizations, the development of the activity and increase in the responsibility of communists for the state of affairs in these organizations, strict observance of democratic norms. . .'
28. The words beginning 'and the mobilization. . .' were not in the draft Rules.
29. In the draft Rules, leadership was said to be carried out directly through the Chief Political Administration.

Index